TEACHING LANGUAGES IN THE PRIMARY SCHOOL

Philip Hood and Kristina Tobutt

Second Edition

Teaching Languages in the Primary School

Los Angeles | London | New Delhi
Singapore | Washington DC

Los Angeles | London | New Delhi
Singapore | Washington DC

SAGE Publications Ltd
1 Oliver's Yard
55 City Road
London EC1Y 1SP

SAGE Publications Inc.
2455 Teller Road
Thousand Oaks, California 91320

SAGE Publications India Pvt Ltd
B 1/I 1 Mohan Cooperative Industrial Area
Mathura Road
New Delhi 110 044

SAGE Publications Asia-Pacific Pte Ltd
3 Church Street
#10-04 Samsung Hub
Singapore 049483

Editor: James Clark
Assistant editor: Rachael Plant
Production editor: Tom Bedford
Copyeditor: Michelle Clarke
Proofreader: Jill Birch
Indexer: Martin Hargreaves
Marketing manager: Dilhara Attygalle
Cover design: Naomi Robinson
Typeset by: C&M Digitals (P) Ltd, Chennai, India
Printed in India at Replika Press Pvt Ltd

Library of Congress Control Number: 2014940522

British Library Cataloguing in Publication data

A catalogue record for this book is available from
the British Library

ISBN 978-1-4462-9512-0
ISBN 978-1-4462-9513-7 (pbk)

At SAGE we take sustainability seriously. Most of our products are printed in the UK using FSC papers and boards.
When we print overseas we ensure sustainable papers are used as measured by the Egmont grading system.
We undertake an annual audit to monitor our sustainability.

CONTENTS

ABOUT THE AUTHORS

Philip Hood has managed primary (Initial Teacher Education, or, ITE) provision and has researched primary languages and early years learning for 20 years at the University of Nottingham.

Kristina Tobutt is a Foundation Stage Leader in a Nottingham primary school, has coordinated primary languages and acted as associate consultant for primary languages since 2005.

PREFACE

Who is this new edition of the book for?

This book is written for a range of audiences. It has been fully updated to take into account all of the changes introduced by the coalition government of 2010–2015, including the new National Curriculum. We aim to offer a full introduction to the planning, teaching and assessment of modern language (ML) teaching in the primary sector. In addition to that, we also intend to open up the wider theme of how languages can play a full part in the whole curriculum. Other writers have included this in discussion but have concluded that it is very difficult to attain (Driscoll and Frost, 1999; Martin, 2000; Muijs et al., 2005).

The book is certainly written for teachers in training (following QTS, PGCE or BEd routes) and not just for those who are specialising in ML. An understanding of how to teach a language effectively will increasingly be part of a competent primary teacher's repertoire as, from 2014, the subject finally becomes part of the new National Curriculum. To help with this, the book contains references to the *Teachers' Standards* and provides links, where relevant, to DfE documentation, as well as to useful archived items that remain available.

We hope, too, that the book will be used by teacher-educators as a support for their sessions with ML specialists and as a way of showing that ML shares many attributes with other subjects and can contribute to children's broader language development. In the new school-based Initial Teacher Education (ITE) courses there may be more need for independent study materials and we hope that the book works as a coherent package for such beginner teachers. We have also linked theory to practice and have provided some authentic examples of different approaches. In addition, the more theoretical Chapter 9 draws together material about communicative teaching, task-based learning and content and language integrated learning (CLIL) written with primary languages in mind.

We also intend the book for experienced teachers who have an ML teaching or coordination role and want to enter into a dialogue about approaches, materials and objectives. This will include experienced primary teachers who know how to teach primary age children but who are perhaps less confident with language teaching approaches. It will also include secondary teachers with an outreach role who realise that secondary methodology does not transfer particularly well to primary schools. An important aspect of the book is that we outline language teaching approaches centred firmly on the needs of primary age children. As part of this, we intend that the book can be used for whole-staff INSET, with suggestions for activities and reflection tasks offered to busy CPD coordinators.

We intend this book to be user-friendly throughout, so it offers a range of different resources to a range of different audiences.

If you have come to it seeking an introduction to the background to teaching languages at primary level – ' Why and why now?' from both a policy and a child-centred perspective – you should start with Chapter 1.

If you have come to it seeking a practical but also a global, more philosophical overview of what language learning can offer your school, then you should look at Chapter 2.

If you wish to gain an overview of how language learning might look in the Early Years Foundation Stage, then you should look at Chapter 3.

Chapter 4 looks specifically at how you might launch language learning in a school, and considers Year 1 and Year 3 starting points. You will find that Chapters 5 and 6 follow logically from that, dealing with progression in different ways.

If you have come to the book specifically to consider the role of the new National Curriculum and its implications for planning for progression, then Chapter 7 deals with those issues.

If your focus is on how to assess language learning and how to structure coherent transition to KS3, then Chapter 8 has been updated to address this.

If you are interested in the theory that underpins communicative, task- and content-based, cross-curricular approaches, such as content and language integrated learning (CLIL), then you should turn to Chapter 9.

How the book is organised

To serve our various aims and purposes, we have included a range of features to increase its interactivity and set up the dialogue we referred to earlier.

- Each chapter begins with an Introductory vignette, drawn from policy or practice, that acts as an initial thinking point.
- Each chapter has clear objectives, again as an advance organiser for the reader. Relevant 'Teachers' standards' (DfE, 2013a) are given at this point.
- Each chapter finishes with a summary of main messages and some key further reading, consisting of references to websites or documents.
- Each chapter has embedded in it reflection points, which are intended to support conceptualisation of the language teaching and learning process.
- Many chapters contain suggestions for pedagogical tasks to try in the classroom, together with associated reflection points.

ACKNOWLEDGEMENTS

Thanks go to the hundreds of primary age pupils the authors have taught in the last ten years whose approaches to learning have shaped our practice.

SAGE would like to thank the following people whose comments helped to shape the new edition:

Nicole Cherry, Newman University
Elizabeth Freedman, University of Greenwich
Marnie Seymour, University of Winchester
Christina Skarbek, Oxford Brookes University
Lucy Woodley, University of Roehampton

CHAPTER 1

WHAT IS THE BACKGROUND TO PRIMARY LANGUAGE LEARNING?

Chapter objectives

- To offer a philosophical view of the need for early language learning.
- To detail and interpret the rationale for the implementation of compulsory primary language learning in 2014.
- To explore aspects of motivation and self-esteem in younger learners.
- To explain the intentions of the different elements in the book.

Teachers' standards		
A teacher must:		
3		Demonstrate good subject and curriculum knowledge
	b	demonstrate a critical understanding of developments in the subject and curriculum areas, and promote the value of scholarship

Source: DfE, 2013a

Introductory vignette

The European Year of Languages 2001 highlighted the many ways of promoting language learning and linguistic diversity. The European Council in Barcelona in March 2002 recognised the need for European Union and Member State action to improve language learning; they called for *'further action ... to improve the mastery of basic skills, in particular by teaching at least two foreign languages to all from a very early age'* (Commission of the European Communities, 2003: 7, emphasis added).

 ## Initial reflection point

How far do you consider that the UK, and specifically England, has gone in responding to this call? Remember that the UK did sign the Barcelona Agreement in 2002.

Response

It is interesting to compare the Barcelona Agreement statement above with one made by the Department for Education and Skills (DfES), who, in '14–19: Opportunity and excellence' (DfES, 2003), ended the status of modern languages as a core subject up to age 16. The paper also set out the then Labour government's intention to introduce languages from the age of seven (DfES, 2003: 22, emphasis added):

> **3.2** We announced our conclusions on modern foreign languages in our Language Strategy in December. We are committed to supporting language learning, because of its vital contribution to cultural understanding and economic competitiveness. *However, we do not believe that requiring schools to teach languages to every young person beyond the age of 14 is the best way to achieve this objective, particularly where students struggle with a subject in which they have little interest or aptitude.* Every young person at this stage will be entitled to study a language if they wish, and we shall require schools to provide this entitlement to every young person that wants it. Our National Languages Strategy set out our plans to deliver an entitlement to language learning for pupils from the age of seven by 2010. Individual schools may continue to require pupils to study languages as part of their school policy.

Eight years later, we see the following from the coalition government, also addressing the subject of languages in KS4. 'The Minister of State for Schools, Nick Gibb MP, told us that the EBac was a conscious method of improving take-up:

In 2002, something like three quarters of the whole cohort took a modern foreign language to GCSE. Last year, that figure was 43%, and if you strip out the independent sector it is just above a third. That is a concern. Geography has fallen from 45% of students taking it in 1995 to 26% of students taking it in 2010. History is down from 39% to 31%. So we are trying to address some very real concerns.

'The Minister also explained that some schools appear to have dismissed these subjects completely:

These subjects are entitlement subjects ... Most of them are actually compulsory and must be studied to the age of 16. And yet there are 175 secondary schools where no pupils were entered for all the English Bac subjects; there were 169 schools where there were no French entries, and there were 137 schools where no pupils were entered for geography.' (www.publications.parliament.uk/pa/cm201012/cmselect/cmeduc/851/85107.htm)

There are continuing implications of the removal of compulsory language learning post-14. The 2013 statement clearly promotes language learning in KS4, but there has been no discussion of restoring it to compulsory status. The commitment to primary language learning was made in 2003 and is finally being fulfilled in 2014 with its inclusion in the compulsory KS2 curriculum. The UK, and especially England, stands apart from all other EU countries in the lack of priority given to language learning throughout school-level education, as we show over the next few pages. We should say at this point that both Wales and Scotland have their own policies with regard to language learning and that some of what we discuss here does not apply to those parts of the UK.

Language teaching in England: some current issues

 Reflection point

Do you know the status of modern languages at the different points from Foundation Stage to KS5? Do you know how this compares with other EU countries? How much do you know about why and how this pattern has emerged? (See Table 1.1 for a response.)

Before we turn to the recent initiatives and policy documents that have brought about the introduction of compulsory primary languages in 2014, we will offer a statement of our philosophy on early language learning to offer a further insight into the nature of this book.

We believe passionately that the introduction of modern languages (ML) into the primary curriculum is a vital step towards restoring some credibility in this very important area to England (as the other countries in the UK have their own policies with regard to language learning). As a developed nation that is itself pluricultural and plurilingual, the UK has a responsibility to play a role in a modern world that seeks to work towards global collaboration. Respect for other people's cultures is impossible without respect for their languages. Global English is a reality but not a substitute for communication that also uses other mother tongues. The recent dramatic drop in the numbers of students studying ML at 14–16 and at A level has yet to have an impact on our commercial, industrial and cultural competence internationally.

There was, in the decision to take ML out of the core 14–16 curriculum, an admission that something was not right in the teaching methods being used. This was not addressed with teachers and students in the sector itself, but, instead, a decision was made at government level that disenfranchised dedicated teachers and devalued the subject. When the European Union as an institution, as we showed at the beginning of the chapter, is working towards its young people having competence in *two* other languages, we removed the immediate need for even *one* language at a level that goes beyond basic survival.

The introduction of languages into primary schools was an attempt to 'start again', but without a skilled workforce in sufficient numbers. Paradoxically, at the time when fresh numbers of new primary teachers will be needed to expand the capability of the schools to deliver ML over the next ten years, the supply of those teachers with a language qualification has been and will continue to be dropping.

This makes it even more vital that we offer our primary teachers language enhancement and discuss openly and fully what we need to do to ensure that children's undoubted interest in and enjoyment of language learning is opened up, developed and nourished. We cannot afford to hand children over to secondary colleagues with any generalised disillusion or disaffection in this area.

As we will see later in this chapter, younger learners have certain advantages over later beginners in aspects of learning potential, motivation and the role that the subject can have in promoting their own self-esteem. We owe it to the children to demonstrate the relevance and value of using another language and need to offer them active, engaging and challenging ways of learning, just as we do in all their other subjects.

Some teachers will understandably find the wider agenda for language learning outlined in the book daunting as they feel their own language competence is not at a high enough level. We feel it is important to outline visions of how primary language teaching could and should develop over the next ten years, so all involved are aware of possible directions for their work.

Table 1.1   The status of languages as a curriculum subject in four EU countries (see http://eacea.ec.europa.eu/education/eurydice/documents/key_data_series/143EN_HI.pdf for further details)

Age (KS)	Country/ML status			
	England	**France**	**Germany**	**Spain**
3–5 (EYFS)	Optional	Optional	Optional	Optional
5–7 (KS1)	Optional	Compulsory from age 6	Optional	Compulsory from age 6
7–11 (KS2)	Compulsory from age 7 from 2014	Compulsory	Compulsory from age 8	Compulsory
11–14 (KS3)	Compulsory one language, two languages sometimes offered	Compulsory, including two languages where possible	Compulsory, including two languages for the more able	Compulsory
14–16 (KS4)	Optional. The 2013 take-up of 44% (reduced from a high of 78% in 2001, but this was a significant rise from 2011/2012)	Compulsory, including two languages where possible	Compulsory, including two languages where possible	Compulsory
16–19 (KS5)	Optional and rarely studied	Compulsory to 18 in any education/ training	Compulsory to 18 in any education/ training	Optional, but compulsory for academic study

Table 1.2   Summary of the important stages in the development of primary languages as a compulsory curriculum element

Date/development	Main points/Web address
1999 National Centre for Early Language Learning (NACELL) founded	The main official website for primary language teaching in England www.primarylanguages.org.uk/home/nacell.aspx
1999–2001 Good Practice Projects coordinated by NACELL	18 separate projects – details no longer available
2000 Nuffield enquiry into language learning – *Languages: The next generation*	A major independent enquiry into language learning – *Languages: The next generation* www.nuffieldfoundation.org/sites/default/files/languages_finalreport.pdf
2002 *Languages for All, Languages for Life* published	The government's action plan for language teaching http://webarchive.nationalarchives.gov.uk/20130401151715 www.education.gov.uk/publications/eOrderingDownload/DfESLanguagesStrategy.pdf

(Continued)

Table 1.2   (Continued)

Date/development	Main points/Web address
2003 Pathfinder Projects	The government funded 19 LAs to develop KS2 languages provision. The evaluation report summary can be accessed at: http://webarchive.nationalarchives.gov.uk/20130401151715/www.education.gov.uk/publications/eOrderingDownload/RR692.pdf
2004 *Piece by Piece* published	An initial document for heads and governors about introducing languages to primary schools (no longer available online)
2005 The KS2 Framework introduced	www.primarylanguages.org.uk/policy__research/policy_and_reform/key_stage_2_framework.aspx
2007 The Dearing Review of language learning	The recommendations from an enquiry into language learning and teaching headed by Lord Dearing http://dera.ioe.ac.uk/7613/1/LanguageReview.pdf
2007 Primary Languages Training Zone website launched	The official training website for primary languages in England (note that some parts of the website no longer function properly) www.primarylanguages.org.uk/home.aspx
2007 White Paper	The government announced that primary languages will have compulsory status by 2011 (NB: see next)
2009–2010 *Rose Review of the National Curriculum*	This failed to materialise as the government changed in 2010 and the new Rose Curriculum, which contained compulsory KS2 languages, was cancelled.
2011	Primary Strategy ended – the disappearance of funding meant most local consultants for languages were made redundant
2012	The Government announced that languages will be compulsory from 2014, but there will be no extra funding. At this point there was uncertainty about the curriculum and the status of the KS2 Framework. CILT became an arm of CfBT
2012 *Lessons from Abroad* report (CfBT)	This report provided an evidence base for language learning within various primary curricula across the world. It focuses on international research and developments in early language learning and common challenges and policy responses www.cfbt.com/en-GB/Research/Research-library/2012/r-lessons-from-abroad-2012
2013	The new National Curriculum was published, with a programme of study for KS2 and KS3 languages. Languages are to be compulsory at KS2 from September 2014.

Primary languages – rebirth and transition: a summary

Let us turn to a brief summary of the important stages that have occurred since the mid-1990s. To make the development clearer we have summarised the major documents and initiatives in Table 1.2. Below we will explore each item in a little more detail.

Recognising the need for coherence

From the mid-1990s on, there was a gradual development in awareness that the very disparate range of approaches to primary languages provision, often through clubs rather than on the curriculum, should be given more coherence. Scotland had invested a great deal of money and time at the beginning of the decade in ensuring both language provision and training for primary teachers at the upper end of school. Although the House of Lords (Parliament, 1990) had debated language learning at primary level in England, the government of the day was less inclined to act at that point.

During the 1990s, there were some very good developments in certain areas. For example, one local authority (LA) – Kent – invested a great deal in linking with France and developing materials for learning French. This was fuelled by teachers who saw that they had a resource almost on their doorstep. They were anxious to use children's natural curiosity about and, in many cases, familiarity with an area of France that opened out from Calais and Boulogne and was minutes rather than hours away via fast ferries or the newly opened Channel Tunnel. Materials (eventually published as *Pilote* (Rumney, 1990)) produced by this group were in a fresh format that acknowledged the needs of younger learners and raised the whole agenda for primary languages very successfully.

In an article in the *Curriculum Journal* (Hood, 1994), we argued that the Burstall Report (Burstall et al., 1974) had been very partially interpreted when the decision was made in the mid-1970s to end the primary French initiative that had run since the mid-1960s. It was now important to look forward and avoid the earlier mistakes. These had centred on a lack of information and action at the point of transition to secondary education and a lack of differentiation built into teaching at all levels.

A very positive step was taken when the Centre for Information on Language Teaching and Research (CILT) formed the semi-autonomous branch NACELL (The National Centre for Early Language Learning) in 1999 and a website was launched that became for a while the focal point for early language learning (ELL). A project was set up that investigated existing best practice provision and 18 schemes were drawn together under the banner of the Good Practice Project and summarised on the website.

Some teaching sequences were filmed and what became a very popular series of three videos was begun. The regional network of Comenius Centres that CILT had instigated in 1990 began to address learning at primary level. Key books written at this time (for example, Driscoll and Frost, 1999; Cameron, 2001; Sharp, 2001) set out the agenda for early language learning in general.

After the Nuffield Foundation's report, 'Languages: The next generation' (2000) was published, attention became much more widely fixed on primary languages. This was a positive move, but the initial need was to highlight the problems. The report took a serious critical stance at a number of points. For example (2000: 62):

> The work of the enquiry has highlighted the serious mismatch between what the UK needs in languages capability and what the education system is providing ... The present system is incoherent, fragmented and increasingly ineffective in meeting national needs.

The report gained much respect and the strong views expressed were not ignored. The Labour government also acknowledged the shortfall in our national provision in its own review published two years later (DfES, 2002: 10):

> For too long we have failed to value language skills or recognise the contribution they make to society, to the economy and to raising standards in schools. This has led to a cycle of national underperformance in languages, a shortage of teachers, low take up of languages beyond schooling and a workforce unable to meet the demands of a globalised economy. We need to challenge these attitudes and inspire people of all ages to learn languages throughout life.

Moving towards a solution

The Nuffield enquiry was exhaustive. It produced 15 major recommendations, which themselves contained several smaller objectives. In total there were 121 separate points made. Clearly here is not the place to explore these in detail, but it is important to note that these recommendations covered all stages of language learning and all aspects, from the organisation of the curriculum to the recruitment of teachers and the need for coherent organisation at government level, including the appointment of a National Languages Director. At the same time, the Nuffield Foundation also made research and development grants available to people looking to innovate in the primary languages area. This made the Labour government's task easier as it worked to produce the 2002 strategy and later ordered the Dearing Review (DfES, 2007a). The decision to end the compulsory status of languages in KS4 seems increasingly strange in the light of all this and as time passes. Indeed, within three years of the decision having been implemented, quotas and targets for languages were being announced, with a figure of 50 per cent KS4 languages take-up demanded from schools by education ministers in communications addressed to heads in 2006 and 2007.

The government, in tune with the Nuffield Foundation, also noted the need for a change of approach (DfES, 2002: 7):

> Transforming language competence in this country means first of all transforming language learning in schools – we depend on embedding language learning in primary schools to make our strategy work and then ensuring that opportunity to learn languages has a key place in the transformed secondary school of the future.

In 2005, a new framework for primary language teaching in KS2 was published. This departed from previous ML curriculum specifications such as Qualifications and Curriculum Authority (QCA) Schemes and General Certificate of Secondary Education (GCSE) syllabuses in that it remained resolutely content-free and instead highlighted strands of progression. The earlier KS3 Framework had focused quite heavily on knowledge about language in the way it was structured and through its objectives in an attempt to raise the cognitive nature of language learning at that stage. This framework was based on the view that teachers needed to link their objectives to the National Literacy Strategy (NLS), but, in combining listening and speaking into oracy, reading and writing into literacy and by adding intercultural understanding to create three major strands, it set out a new pathway for visualising language learning.

The Dearing Review was conducted in 2006 and reported in 2007 (DfES, 2007a). It affirmed the need for primary languages to become an entitlement in 2010 and went a stage further, calling for it to be compulsory. This suggestion was accepted by the government in a White Paper, with 2011 set for this step to be implemented. Although this meant there was a ten-year span from Nuffield to entitlement, it represented the culmination of a very definite series of steps that had weighed up the needs at each stage, where decisions seemed to have been made for good reasons, and so this was seen as a permanent sign of progress. The Primary Languages Training Zone website, which went live in March 2007, was further evidence of a large-scale commitment.

A review of the primary National Curriculum in total was planned to build on the newly established Early Years Foundation Stage Framework and both this (the Rose Review, 2009) and the Cambridge Primary Review (Alexander, 2009) recommended that subjects be seen not discretely, but in clusters. This represented a root and branch re-evaluation of compulsory schooling, at least in England and Wales. With this, the role of ML teaching was also reassessed and there were suggestions that it should be integrated into a communication and language 'subject domain'. This intention meant that, for the first time, ML would be considered as a part of a whole set of subjects rather than as an optional add-on, ungoverned by general regulation, but also unnoticed by those who set policy.

Why has this movement for earlier language learning begun so strongly since the millennium? Can we be sure of the potential gains in comparison with the 11-year-old starting point that has persisted for so long?

Is it true that younger learners are at an advantage in language learning?

In fact few L2 [second language] researchers now question the proposition that those learners whose exposure to the L2 begins early in life (and whose exposure is substantial) for the most part eventually attain higher levels of proficiency than those whose exposure begins in adolescence or adulthood. (Singleton, 2003: 3)

There is a small amount of disagreement between different researchers about the advantages and disadvantages of different starting ages.

Different aspects of language proficiency can reach higher levels from both early *and* later starting points, although all researchers seem to agree that pronunciation and intonation generally develop better the younger the start age. Many claim that written grammatical accuracy and knowledge about language is likely to be no better among the early beginners, with some claiming that adolescent beginners achieve higher proficiency. The notion of a critical age for language learning (proposed by Lenneberg, 1967) was discussed fully in Birdsong (1999), but was not resolved.

Depending on the research focus, findings can be contradictory, but we can be clear that stronger motivation is associated with younger learners and this seems to persist into adolescence and adulthood if learning continues consistently. In an environment such as a primary school, where the general motivation for learning is often quite strong (and where, we should emphasise, there is established high-quality teaching, at least of other subjects), then the opportunities for faster progress are clearly greater.

Much of this book will therefore address the need to show children that they *can* progress in language learning and their competence in a variety of skills, both receptive and productive, will grow with each year. Much of it will address the need to engage them as learners with stimulating, challenging and enjoyable activities. Within this high-motivation environment, teachers have an opportunity, specifically in language learning (Hood, 2006), to raise children's self-esteem and underpin their learning across the curriculum.

Why should we be concerned about self-esteem? School life inevitably establishes a hierarchy of perceptions among children about who is and who is not able to be successful. Dweck's (2000) notion of entity and incremental theories of intelligence (more popularly known now as mindset theory; Dweck, 2013), which divide learners into those who believe they can alter and develop their ability to learn something and those who think they cannot, shows that, for some children, acceptance of a lack of progression in a subject is a potential danger.

Anxiety is also a potential problem in language learning (Horwitz, 2001). Many of us may experience, even if only temporarily, that tension and accompanying feeling of being 'tongue-tied' when we are in a situation where we have to use the target language. We know that we can say it, but it just seems not to want to come out. This was partly explained by Krashen's (1988) work on the 'affective filter' (a kind of barrier device), which related performance in foreign language production to levels of anxiety. Essentially, writing about more permanent characteristics of learners (which is in harmony with Dweck's thinking), he maintained that low self-esteem and anxiety can combine to raise the affective filter and create a mental block. When the filter is 'up' it impedes language acquisition as well as production. Experience of success will develop self-esteem and it is likely that motivation will be higher as a result, but anxiety will lower the levels of both. Therefore, we must avoid harming the good levels of motivation that we should find among our primary-age learners by not creating those anxious circumstances when they experience that tongue-tied failure to communicate.

The now common practice of regular and carefully constructed target setting in primary schools has started, in many cases, to move children's own perceptions of themselves as learners forward. Some will still hold the view that they cannot improve their performance, but very many schools have seen an increase in their percentages of children reaching Levels 4 and 5 (and now even Level 6) in the core subjects at 11 years (KS2 SATS) over the last five years. Much of this is due to a culture in which individual targets are set and groups of children receive special provision to boost their attainment. While some might argue convincingly this is test- and performance-driven and not about educating the whole child, it does seem logical that the more we can show children they can improve, the more their own self-doubt can be modified.

When children first encounter a foreign language they will not have such fixed notions in place for this new subject. The oral base for learning often encourages children who lack confidence in reading and writing to participate much more fully and enter into a cycle of confidence growth through success rather than confidence diminution through failure. So, for example in a Y3 context, when languages start to be learned, there is a levelling of established ability order perceptions. In the project reported in Hood (2006: 7–8), this was stated most powerfully in a Y6 focus group, the members of which had developed strongly established 'pecking orders', particularly in the core subjects, as they approached the end of primary education:

> Y6 Pupil 1 – I feel if you get a question wrong in French nobody laughs at you because they all know the same as you because we've all had the same amount of lessons but in maths and things you've got people who are good at it and people who are bad at it and they might laugh at you but in French everyone kind of knows the same thing.

If we look briefly at more general issues of self-esteem in schools and classrooms, we will find that language learning has this *potential* to augment levels of positivity among children and we hope that the rest of the book will give some examples of this in action. Both de Andres (1999) and Arnold (2007) mention a set of components of self-esteem listed by Reasoner (1982). These are: learners' security, identity, belonging, purpose and competence. Clearly we can use collaborative and active experiences to create a sense of belonging and purpose and, by planning carefully for enjoyable and meaningful outcomes by the whole group, we can emphasise competence rather than failure. By involving the learners in talking and eventually writing about themselves in another language, we are giving them space to consider and express their identities in a positive framework. The involvement of children in a set of enjoyable activities and the availability of choice – for example, in selecting songs and stories or roles – combine to create a secure feeling around language learning. Taking the positive sides of the 'difference' of French, German or Spanish lessons but still not sidelining them as being not part of the normal curriculum gives modern languages the best of both worlds in some respects.

Similarly, when writing about the more specific area of emotional literacy, Weare (2004: 90–1) gives examples of such potential contributions, noting several aspects commonly associated with language learning in her section on all subjects (for example, 'increasing emotional intensity through experiencing success, a sense of flow, laughter … celebrating learning' and 'emotional control, e.g. through waiting your turn … self-monitoring').

Pollard and Triggs (2000) present a very full survey (PACE Project 1989–97) of children's views gathered by means of longitudinal research. Extensive quotations from children show that issues of trust and ownership of practice, of independence and collaboration, of how they work and with whom are extremely important for their enjoyment of school and their avoidance of anxiety in some cases. They wish to be listened to and, especially in language learning, we should remember that the fine line between encouragement to participate and pressure, between challenge and barrier-erection is one that needs to be kept in focus. The particular mix of activity and experience held within good language teaching can build self-esteem very rapidly and very well, but can bring affective nightmares to some children if the balance is not right. We will reflect in a section on competition in Chapter 2 that less secure children should not be individually exposed in lessons and collaboration is often the best mode of organisation for activities. Finding out what children enjoy and offering it to them in a structured manner that combines fun with learning certainly seems to work. One eight-year-old boy summed up language learning as 'tingly and exciting' and that is clearly an effect we should all strive for.

Chapter summary

This chapter has attempted to set out the background to the growth of interest in primary languages over the last 15 years and the position of the Labour and coalition governments on the teaching of languages throughout young people's school experience. It has also looked at the role language learning and teaching (when planned and delivered successfully) can play in developing children's confidence and self-esteem.

Key reading

A still relevant work that addresses the position of primary languages is the DfES (2007a) 'Languages review' (The Dearing Review.) (00212–2007DOM-EN.) Nottingham: DfES. Available online at: http://webarchive.nationalarchives.gov.uk/20130401151715/www.teachernet.gov.uk/_doc/11124/LanguageReview.pdf

The current National Curriculum Programmes of Study for languages are available online at: www.gov.uk/government/publications/national-curriculum-in-england-languages-progammes-of-study/national-curriculum-in-england-languages-progammes-of-study

The international survey by Teresa Tinsley and Therese Comfort (2012) gives a comparative review of early language learning. This is available online at: http://cdn.cfbt.com/~/media/cfbtcorporate/files/research/2012/r-lessons-from-abroad-2012.pdf

If you are teaching children in EYFS or KS1, we recommend that, before you start to read about ML teaching and learning, you look at the document by T. David (2003) 'What do we know about teaching young children?' Southwell, Nottinghamshire: BERA. Available online at: www.bera.ac.uk/wp-content/uploads/2014/01/eyyrsp1.pdf

If you are interested in reading a recent summary about the theories around the critical period hypothesis, then you should look at an article by David Singleton (2005) 'The critical period hypothesis: A coat of many colours', *International Review of Applied Linguistics in Language Teaching*, 43 (4): 269–85.

CHAPTER 2

WHAT DOES LANGUAGE LEARNING OFFER A PRIMARY SCHOOL?

Chapter objectives

- To explore the nature of language learning at the primary stage.
- To suggest ways in which language learning can benefit children.
- To suggest ways in which teaching a language can benefit a school.
- To make links between Primary Framework English and language learning.
- To make links between approaches to English as an additional language (EAL) and approaches to language teaching.

Teachers' standards			
A teacher must:			
1			Set high expectations which inspire, motivate and challenge pupils
	b		set goals that stretch and challenge pupils of all backgrounds, abilities and dispositions
2			Promote good progress and outcomes by pupils

	b	be aware of pupils' capabilities and their prior knowledge, and plan teaching to build on these
8		Fulfil wider professional responsibilities
	a	make a positive contribution to the wider life and ethos of the school

Source: DfE, 2013a

Introductory vignette

I think for some children it's deeply motivating – they enjoy it because it's different. Whether it's because that's to do with the kind of lessons they are, because they're very oral and there's music and there's lots of games and so they see it as fun, it's nice that the whole school does it and the whole school is doing it together. We played some French music in assembly recently and they all noticed that it was French and enjoyed that. (Headteacher, 2005, in Hood, 2006: 6)

Comment

The headteacher quoted above introduced language learning into her school because, when she interviewed for teachers to cover the new planning, preparation and assessment (PPA) arrangements in 2005, she found that a language teacher was one of the two best teachers she saw. She was primarily interested in appointing people who could add value to the school. Because this was her approach, she considered languages to be an integral part of the curriculum from that point on. She had a real sense that language learning could impact the whole curriculum and the school experience of the children and, because the subject was given equal status with the rest of the curriculum and was well taught, it did.

Initial reflection point

Consider the two brief lesson scenarios that follow. Clearly there are differences, but what are they and do they matter?

Teacher A reads the class a simple story in another language about a boy who wants pizza for tea. The boy finds the ingredients in the supermarket.

There is a lot of repetition of the phrases for 'Here is …' and 'I like …'. Back at home, his mother asks him to unpack the bag and she checks he has all the ingredients – 'Do you have …?' He replies using 'Here is …' again. When the teacher reads it for the second time and pauses slightly at certain points, the class gradually starts to join in with the names of the ingredients, if they are not too hard, and the key phrases. By the end of the second reading, the children are all able to say, 'Yes, here it is!' and 'I like …'. The teacher then makes a three-ingredient pizza using a large card 'base' and chooses which three by asking the class to vote for their favourite ingredients. Individual children then create their own four-, five- or six-ingredient toppings by adding other items. If they have forgotten the word for an item or if they want an extra item not in the story, they ask for it in the foreign language.

Teacher B has selected the key vocabulary for the pizza ingredients and teaches them to the class using flashcards and asking the children to repeat each of the words several times, using different tones or speeds or emotions to give variety. The teacher plays some flashcard games – for example, using a noughts and crosses grid on the board with the flashcards turned away and children in teams competing to guess the right item and make a line of three. The teacher then adds the phrase for 'I would like' and plays pizza bingo with the class. Afterwards the class practises the word set again in pairs, asking for certain items from each other.

Comment

You could see something like both of these approaches in primary language classrooms all over England. The point of comparing and contrasting them is not to decide which is better, but isolate what the children get from each 'lesson' and whether or not that meets your objectives as a languages teacher. In deciding what they get from each approach, we need to think about the immediate learning and the more invisible acquisition that may be occurring. We also need to consider both immediate and longer-term motivation.

Follow-up reflection

In which of the two lesson scenarios above would children be most motivated and in which would they remember more words? Would either approach lead to a greater longer-term motivation and would either embed language in their minds more strongly if used regularly?

Comment

There are still no 'right' answers to these questions, but you may have formed a strong view and this might reflect a personal standpoint (for example, a memory of successful language lessons when you were younger) or a deep knowledge of how primary children learn. This chapter, and indeed the whole book, seeks to offer a range of interpretations of how language learning might look, viewed from the standpoint of the children, the teachers and the school.

Some important ways of looking at the issue involve thinking about the purpose of language learning. What is language learning *for*? What type of language do we have in mind? Is the focus on learning the language, learning about the language or learning via the language? What about culture? What is culture? Is it (to echo a previous series of course books) a matter of onions, sausages or castanets, or something deeper?

The teacher's objectives and how they shape what language learning can offer

We can start this dialogue by asking what appears to be a very basic question. When you, as the teacher, walk into the classroom to start a language lesson, what are your objectives? We can paraphrase and widen this by asking , 'What do you intend to do? What do you intend the children to know, understand and be able to do by the end of the lesson? Why are you doing this?'

There are some very different possible answers to this set of questions that relate to the summary at the end of the comment section above. For example, on the one hand, you may see language learning as equipping children to survive in an authentic context, such as a visit to a target-language-speaking country. Perhaps they will link with a class they have been writing to, even stay a couple of nights with a family there. If so, you may have an agenda that is about teaching and practising functional language around topics such as greeting, eating, exchanging essential personal information, expressing preferences and simple emotions. On the other hand, that may not be a likely scenario just yet and you may instead feel that, to start the process of language learning, you need to address some basic vocabulary areas, such as numbers, colours, families, food/drink and favourite leisure time activities.

In both of these cases, you are very firmly in the language learning camp, with the 'doorstep intention' of presenting a specific set of vocabulary and phrases, mainly via aural/oral means and with the intention of equipping children to use them orally in structures such as dialogues. Your desired outcome is probably that they can use this body of language when they receive certain stimuli such as simple questions. You may decide to find out if you have been successful in this by 'testing' the class orally (or perhaps in writing with older children).

Alternatively, you may feel it is still important, even in the primary context, that children start to build a grammatical awareness of the language they are learning. This might take the form of either some overt grammar or another literacy-linked aspect, such as strategy use. An example of the first could be awareness of parts of speech and their behaviour (agreement and position of adjectives in French or first-/third-person verb forms in German) and, in this case, it is possible that a lesson might be more expository with some rules being explained. The second might be accomplished more inductively, by using a 'language detectives' approach (as used by West Sussex Grid for Learning materials, 2006 and 2008). In our earlier example of the 'pizza' lessons, a third scenario might involve the use of a menu in the target language with a task centred on children trying to work out what the items are and give reasons for their choices. Clearly, if you adopt such approaches, you include learning *about* language as a major purpose.

A third scenario could have a completely different set of intentions at the threshold to the classroom. You may be using authentic texts (a story or song, for example) and think less about giving children a particular set of items for comprehension and reuse and more about their overall experience of the sounds of the language. There would probably be some inherent repetition contained within the story or song, which they would begin to catch and rehearse more informally. It might be that you want to offer the children the chance to construct meaning by looking at context (perhaps with the visuals associated with the text) and, although they will not understand the literal meaning of every word, they might laugh or feel suspense or anticipate a particular ending. You might want to deal with non-fiction and link something in the foreign language with work they are doing in mathematics, science, geography or art. You might hope that, in this way, they will experience some reinforcement (in a different form) of some of the concepts you have been dealing with at other points during the week or term. Later, you might teach them, in the foreign language, something from one of those other areas that is completely new. If you have these intentions, you are working within the approach that involves learning *in* or *through* the language.

We want to be clear that the options above are not described with a view to you choosing one of them as an approach that you will use. Of course, a single teacher might have that range of intentions, either with different classes or even with the same class, over a period of time. It is probably healthy for any subject to be tackled from different directions and in different ways across a whole primary school and even across the four years of KS2. The advocates of embedding the languages element into the whole curriculum (including ourselves) need to remember that there is a separate language curriculum based on authentic experience of life among mother-tongue speakers of that language – in other words, 'survival' content – that children need to learn. We need to recognise that, just as the National Curriculum for English includes elements of grammar, so a foreign language curriculum lasting a minimum of four years needs that, too. All teachers of languages at primary level, however, need to consider how children learn in general and how a focus on learning *via* the language can certainly offer other sorts of gains, as research has shown (see Chapter 9). We will now look at the nature of that learning from the child's as well as the school's perspective.

What do children enjoy about language learning? What can language learning offer children?

One survey of a whole primary school where all children were learning languages from Nursery through to Y6 (and where they had all started the process at the same time), found that the most popular element of learning French was songs. This was noted by 75 per cent of the children in the school.

In Hood (2006), we explored some early impressions of language learning from focus groups in the same school. In the plenary at the Primary Languages Show 2007 (Hood, unpublished), we presented further data from that school which showed the children were able to identify the benefits of challenge, very willing to show what they knew in the form of singing authentic French songs and strongly involved in taking the language home.

So far, this chapter has not mentioned the F-word. Many people associate learning languages with the fun element and we need to address this now because fun *is* certainly something that language learning offers children and schools. Fun can emerge from a range of approaches: from lively active teaching and learning, from a real mixture of stimulating resources, from creative activities that use the language, from genuine contacts with speakers of the target language, and from games that involve problem-solving, collaboration and competition.

It is vital to distinguish the fun that emerges from having a variety of stimuli and challenge from the fun arising simply out of the games and simply out of the fact that, for many children, language learning, being so orally and game-based, is not 'real work'. That sort of fun seems to evaporate as repetition sets in, progression is more limited and challenge seems never to materialise.

When children say that something is hard and then you ask them whether 'hard' is a good or a bad thing, very many will say that it is good, because 'hard' means you are learning. Similarly, 'easy' – implying a lack of challenge and a lack of thinking – is not often held up by learners as something positive. Above all, they want work addressed to their own maturity level. This is illustrated by a Y10 boy on work experience in a primary school who, at the end of a Year 3 lesson, approached the teacher and said, 'I wish we had done languages in primary school, because then in Year 7 we could have done some real work.'

Language learning should be active, have a large proportion of orally-based activities and relate to a range of aspects of children's lives, including their interests, social life, beliefs and learning. This should guarantee that, among different motivational qualities, it contains genuine elements of fun. In fact, fun should permeate the subject and not be a separate planning aim. Often, in the early stages, a combination of physical activity and rhythm and language can be stimulating and enjoyable. Incorporating some thinking into this type of activity is always possible, creating both fun and challenge. A Y1 boy asked his French teacher who was supply teaching one morning that was not intended to include French: 'When are we going to do the fun thing, I mean French?' This teacher believed that challenge was vital in all her activities, so this is evidence that fun can be a broad phenomenon.

Figure 2.1 Qualities offered by language teaching

We will now consider (Figure 2.1) the importance of some other qualities that language teaching, like all good teaching, can offer children. Conveniently, these qualities can be expressed in a series of words that begin with 'c':

- culture
- communication

- content
- challenge
- cognition
- collaboration
- competition.

We will look at each of these in turn below, show how they link together and offer practical classroom examples through an activity or resource. We will also ask you to reflect on an aspect of each element.

Culture

Culture may seem to be an obvious component of learning a language. The 'Languages programmes of study: Key Stage 2' document for the National Curriculum in England does not detail what culture might mean beyond mentioning different types of texts, but the opening sentence is, 'Learning a foreign language is a liberation from insularity and provides an opening to other cultures' (DfE, 2013b: 1). 'The Key Stage 2 Framework for languages' (DfES, 2005) had intercultural understanding as one of its three equally important strands, with a full set of objectives for each year group in the phase. Both French and Spanish, which are currently the major languages in primary schools, have the advantage of being global languages, spoken on three or more continents. France, Germany and Spain are themselves also multicultural societies. So, 'culture' can include a fascinating range of aspects concerning daily lives in schools and in a multitude of different homes, cities and villages that have some resemblances to and some key differences from the experiences our children will have there. Also, of course, our own children will come at alternative cultures from a wide variety of different standpoints, many of which will not be British in origin.

The potential richness for the whole curriculum of encouraging interaction on a cultural level in language lessons is immense and some authors have approached this notion in the context of language learning and cultural competence among older learners. The breadth of vision around culture that we will see in Byram's work, for example, is worth remembering, as an eventual aim, however. He has a model of cultural competences based on different types of 'knowledge' (Byram and Zarate, 1994; Byram, 1997):

- *savoir comprendre* – knowing how to understand
- *savoir apprendre/faire* – knowing how to learn/do
- *savoir s'engager* – knowing how to engage
- *savoir être* – knowing how to be/behave.

This is useful in that it gives us a sense of true intercultural understanding leading to both knowing *what* to say and *how* to say it because we have a deeper understanding of the people with whom we are interacting. In other words, it is eventually about understanding what makes people the way they are.

At primary level, we need to start with the realisation that many of our children will not have actually experienced different cultures and we can unwittingly set up stereotypes if we dwell too much on stating overly simplistic differences and unintentionally inviting 'horror' (frogs' legs, snails and horsemeat come to mind!). This starts with the power of image, which gives a stream of messages that we are not even aware of. In *Reading Images: The grammar of visual design*, for example, Kress and van Leeuwen (2006) explore the many ways in which different cultural images, including those in children's picture books, communicate their meanings. A complex mix of existing cultural concepts, juxtapositions of visual material and conventions, such as the direction of 'reading' (inherently left to right in Western cultures), create out of a simple picture an image that has as much power as dense text. We only have to look at some of the cultural 'loading' in our media (associations with Second World War uniforms, drinking beer and lederhosen for Germany, for example) to see that we are in constant receipt of stereotypical imagery.

For all these reasons, when evaluating materials for use with primary age children, it is very important that teachers consider their cultural content and the power of the imagery. If a book, DVD, picture material or an online resource makes extensive use of line drawings, clip art, neutral photographs, then its contribution to cultural understanding is very limited and might even be negative. If, on the other hand, it has authentic photographs showing children of an equivalent age in natural settings, then this encourages children to notice and ask questions about apparent similarities and differences. Many current resources use video extracts to present language and, as with Early Start Languages (www.earlystart.co.uk/index.html), for example, even a short clip of children eating lunch, being at school or shopping can open up the possibility of culture-based conversations. The short sequence in Early Start French 1 of a French family eating at midday shows a range of differences that exemplify some cultural attributes (for example, French children often eat lunch at home in a more formal lunch setting, there are different patterns of 'courses', collaborative laying, or clearing, of the table). While there is still a place for cartoon characters in stories and for all the fantasy possible with such images, they should be combined with strong, authentic, culturally accurate representations in any good set of materials.

In the last 20 years, crossover culture has been very strong and this leads to a need to reappraise what we mean by 'culture'. Spain as a holiday destination has continued to grow in popularity and, as a result, many children are familiar with much of the obvious features of Spanish life, such as some of the food, the climate and coastal landscapes. We can delve deeper, however, and present more traditional food and issues from the climate and less familiar landscapes if we plan this in carefully. More concrete examples can develop this theme. While food is an obvious cultural aspect of interest, there is much less value now than there was in offering learners of French a French breakfast as an activity, though this was common in lower secondary just a few years ago. Our supermarkets offer *pain au chocolat* and *brioche* as standard items, as well as *baguettes* in plenty. French yogurts are commonly advertised on television and hot chocolate is a more common breakfast drink than before.

We need to look at shopping habits, eating habits and a wider range of food items and make the point that French food has a strong North African influence, rather like ours has (among others) an Indian influence, and for at least some similar reasons. In sport, the premier league has brought not just French footballers into common view but also a host of French-speaking players from Africa. Countries such as Côte d'Ivoire and Sénégal are known to older primary children, some of whom may have seen scenes from Africa on television, watching African Nations Cup football. Spain and Portugal bring with them strong associations with South America, such as Argentina and Brazil. Access to less superficial cultural material is potentially more manageable if we can build on that initial basic knowledge. The Arsenal FC's Education programme The Double Club has created materials across the curriculum, including non-British origin players speaking in their own languages.

Many might see this as a partial diversion, however, because surely children cannot handle these conversations in the target language? As with everything connected to target language use (we deal with this in more detail in Chapter 3), we should look hard to find ways in which it might be possible before we opt for the safer English route. Scaffolding can be used to support children's use of the target language and this can take the form of a series of questions that offer language and support its reuse to express real opinions. By Y6, this should be possible at a relatively high level.

Example from practice

In a PowerPoint presentation we created, which used some material from an Oxfam website, a young girl's daily routine in rural Burkina Faso was explored very simply. She had to get up early, have her breakfast, then she walked for an hour to get to school, fetched water, had a day's lessons, walked home, helped her mother to cook and clean, then spent the later evening with family and friends, making their own entertainment.

Apart from some useful French language, this was tapping in to citizenship and environmental themes. Here is a sample teacher's scaffolding script:

'Alors, Mariam se lève à cinq heures, prend le petit déjeuner et elle marche une heure (soixante minutes!) à l'école.' (This sentence is said more than once, with the PowerPoint or other visuals in support. The figures '1 hour = 60 minutes' can be written on the whiteboard while pointing at the clock or a watch.)

'Se lever à cinq heures, c'est bon? Marcher une heure à l'école, c'est bon? Ça serait bon pour toi ou un problème pour toi?' (Use mime as well as images

(Continued)

(Continued)

and elicit an answer from one child then ask several others so that repetition occurs. Do this in a natural manner, with a range of children being genuinely asked for their opinion. They will, after all, have different opinions, so this dialogue is for a real purpose, both individually and collectively.)

'OK, ca serait un problème pour toi, mais pourquoi? A cinq heures tu es trop fatigué/e? Après une heure de marche, tu es trop fatigué/e?' (Giving vocabulary such as *après* and *trop* in a definite context is important because connectives, prepositions and adverbs often allow children to express more shades of meaning. They need to encounter these words in sentences that have a real purpose and not just learn them as isolated items. Note that the 'push' from the teacher here is to ask for reasons. The question 'Why?' needs to appear early and be used regularly in any target language.)

With these questions it is possible to respond in very simple or slightly less simple ways. This means children can self-differentiate, but still participate – the emphasis is on communication and finding real answers to questions where the answers are not known in advance.

It is also very positive to encourage children to experiment with using familiar language in different ways. Here they might want to express something about carrying things to school or the weather. If they are used to you as the teacher wanting contributions and supporting, making half-sentences into full sentences, then they may draw from previous work and offer: *j'aime ...', 'parce que le sac est ...'* or *'il pleut ...'*. If you then supply a word such as *dormir, lourd* or *souvent,* they will have the satisfaction of having made an original contribution and a chance of remembering the new item because they heard it and put it into a real context that belonged to them.

The PowerPoint then led to a more challenging worksheet suitable for older KS2 learners with more depth of language learning behind them.

Culture, then, can be brought directly into the fabric of the language teaching lesson – it can *be* the lesson and is certainly not an add-on, something the teacher includes from time to time as a topic that gives a change from language work. The new National Curriculum does not exclude this kind of work and encourages authentic use of text.

Reflection point

Think of an aspect of life in a target-language-speaking country – preferably arising from experiences you have had personally – that would be an interesting cultural element for your teaching. What resources might you look for that would engage children and allow them to explore differences in the right spirit and, preferably, using the foreign language? Write three questions you might use to help children notice and react to the aspect you have chosen.

Communication

Communication is obviously an essential part of language learning and teaching. Ask most modern language teachers if they have a style or method to their approach and they will reply that they are 'communicative' language teachers (see also Chapter 9 for a full discussion of this theme). The essence of the communicative methodology is that learning occurs via authentic communication – real messages for real purposes, using authentic language and authentic stimuli. This involves real menus, real transport timetables, real estate agents' details of houses, real penfriend letters from real children and real school timetables. The accepted curriculum is survival topics, which, for example, have always featured in the modern languages examinations at the national GCSE level, taken normally at age 16 in England, Wales and Northern Ireland.

Clearly primary age children need to learn how to identify themselves and survive (with adult support) during a stay in a target-language-speaking country. It now seems common sense that we should achieve this by helping them to learn by using the real materials they will encounter when abroad and allow them to practise dialogue which could take place there. In doing so, we should look to techniques from drama (for example, hot-seating or giving participants in a role-play 'secret' circumstances for the dialogue) to make the communication more inherently interesting and enjoyable. Even so, there is a danger in fashioning an entire language-learning curriculum around survival, especially when a concept such as van Ek's 'threshold level' (1975; van Ek and Trim, 1991) can become diluted to a syllabus consisting of vocabulary, grammar structures and topics.

Van Ek (1975) listed the themes or topics needed as foreign language knowledge to survive in another country. With these he included the language functions, grammatical understanding, key vocabulary required, but also how the language worked as a system of communication, socially and culturally and how speakers might compensate when their competence was limited. The 'syllabus' was one for survival, but in a sophisticated, linguistically competent way rather than what might be termed as at 'phrasebook' level.

In fact, in addition to those elements, discourse competence, sociocultural competence and compensatory competence all appear in van Ek's work and indicate the inclusion of genuine rather than staged (and stilted or mechanistic) communication. Even if GCSE examination boards maintain that this has been a part of their design, the reality is it has not been tested at any but the highest levels. Examinations are notorious for setting the standards, objectives and 'feel' of teaching and learning (Volante, 2004; Menken, 2006) and it would appear that GCSE ML has done this. Ironically, the low levels of thinking and creativity, the formulaic demand of role play and prepared questions, the endless listening and reading to spot contrived shades of meaning (that is, the lack of challenge) have resulted in the examinations being perceived as more difficult than those in other subjects. Difficulty in securing real motivation appears to have led to difficulty in fulfilling examination demands. One young secondary learner complained that her ML lessons were dominated by the unit tests and, in the unit tests, they had to learn what they were going to say or write and had no opportunity to respond using their real opinions and experience. This led to a slightly ludicrous situation where she had to write that she had visited the Louvre in Paris, when, although she really had been to Paris, she had not been to the Louvre. The option of writing the truth – that she had been to the Musée D'Orsay – was not allowed!

Of course, being able to use the language competently in a foreign country is a vital aim of language teaching and we should all equip our children with aspects of that skill, but if this is their *only* diet, it is not surprising that by KS3 learners have often tired of it. So, to explore communication more fully, we need to think what it is that learners are communicating *about*. This leads us to the next 'C' and shows us that communication as a concept, when used by itself, is limited.

Content

Content is often ignored in language teaching, where there is a tendency for the 'medium to be the message'. In other words, the content is the language itself rather than something else learned *via* language. As we saw above, if the content is an abstract global concept such as 'survival', there is a danger that processes can become mechanistic as learners try a range of parallel ways to reach a laudable but intangible aim. So, objectives might focus on a list of vocabulary or a grammatical structure or a skill such as complaining politely or the ability to give directions to a particular place. The problem with this is that it appears to learners that they are mostly either simply learning something for its own sake (for example, a list of words) or as relatively trivial content, unless a visit is imminent and they can see its immediate real purpose.

Using language is much more important than *knowing* language or knowing *about* language. Clearly, to use language effectively you need to know some language and have some kind of overview of how it works as a system, but if objectives stop at the *knowing* or knowing *about*, it might be harder to move on to *using*. If the objective is to use the language from the start, then the other factors will take care of themselves and the *purpose* of language learning will be unambiguous from the first lesson. Dropping learners into a target-language-speaking country and asking them to survive *is* authentic and does have a meaningful content, but recreating that in a classroom with learners who all share a different language from the one being used and expecting reality to be suspended is less convincing. Alternatively, learning about something else (which may be cultural) has the effect of deflecting attention away from overtly practising the language and towards solving a problem or establishing a new concept. An example of what we mean by this follows and the original of the worksheet we are referring to is available in the *A La Française* pack (Tobutt and Roche, 2007).

Example from practice

Les monuments de Paris

Materials

- Pictures of la Tour Eiffel, le Musée du Louvre, la Cathédrale Notre Dame
- Facts (formatted in boxes, they can also be cut up and used as a classification activity):

C'est une église.

C'est un musée.

C'est une tour.

La construction a duré de 1163 à 1345.

La construction a duré de 1887 à 1889.

Il a été construit en 1594.

Elle a été construite par Gustave Eiffel.

La hauteur est 324 mètres.

La hauteur est 69 mètres.

La pyramide à l'entrée est 21 mètres haut.

Il y a plus de 12 millions de visiteurs par an.

Il y a plus de 6 millions de visiteurs par an.

Il y a plus de 8 millions de visiteurs par an.

Ici on peut voir La Mona Lisa de Leonardo da Vinci.

La tour a été construite de 18 038 pièces métalliques.

'J'aime les arts.'

'J'aime l'histoire.'

'Je suis sportif! Je prends l'escalier!'

Activity

The activity here is to match the sentences to the monuments. The objectives include learning some information about the three monuments, but also aim to

(Continued)

(Continued)

broaden the knowledge of the children about the kind of historical sights Paris offers, to reinforce a historical awareness that modern cities have features that originated at very different times. Language objectives are mainly about receptive language (that is, comprehension) and include, for some or all, using contextual reading to infer unknown vocabulary items, using grammatical information (il/ elle and grammatical gender). Depending on the level and experience of the children, the class could also be asked to reason in French. *'La cathédrale est plus agée que la tour'*, *'La tour est plus populaire que la cathédrale, n'est-ce pas?'*, *'La Mona Lisa est une peinture – c'est dans le musée.'* So, active language use as well as the receptive processing of language can be involved in an activity like this. Children will learn something (a non-linguistic content) and will have used language to do so, reinforcing vocabulary, pronunciation and possibly grammar.

Reflection point

Take any three common language teaching topics and list next to them three dimensions of content that you could involve in presenting the essential language to primary children. An example might be:

Colours – What are the primary/secondary colours? Which colours do we use to express different emotions? Do a survey of colours of family cars or the children's bedroom walls or pets.

Challenge

Challenge sits in the centre of our list of seven terms. It is especially connected with what we have just said about content and clearly links into the next 'C', cognition. All the other 'C' words have a link into challenge, however, if we interpret them in that way.

Children generally welcome being challenged because they acknowledge that they are in school to learn and this process is often more stimulating when it is harder than when they simply coast. This is where excess repetition can be harmful, especially over time. If the content remains trivial and the curriculum is repetitive (the previous National Curriculum and GCSE survival topics have always tended to operate in a spiral that recurs at various points), if the activity types consist of short, undeveloped tasks with unsubstantial outcomes, then we should not be surprised if motivation drops. We can challenge our children in many ways, and the later chapters of the book will all deal with this as one of the constant themes. The main emphasis should always be on children discovering rather than being told, making connections for themselves that, admittedly, we may have set up for them, using language naturally and creatively and being inspired to go off and tell or teach someone else.

One Y4 boy, responding to a questionnaire, wrote the comment in Figure 2.2.

7. What do you most enjoy in French lessons?

Figure 2.2 Response from a Y4 boy

The *type* of challenge is, of course, important and the same boy added this (see Figure 2.3) to a later question (we think 'tingly' might be the intention of the third word).

10. If you chose strongly agree or agree for Question 5, can you write *how French lessons feel different* in this box.

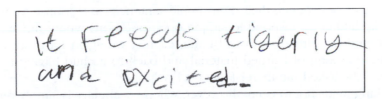

Figure 2.3 A further response

Children often like things that are 'hard' rather than 'easy' and one comment that showed this came from a Y3 focus group: 'When things are hard you learn it quicker.' A Y6 boy commented on why he liked to do topic work in French: 'You've got a challenge to do rather than doing just what you already know.' Many good language teachers report comments from parents that children teach parents or siblings foreign language expressions while walking home from school or at the table having a meal. It is obvious that to do this they must first care about what they have learned and also see a purpose in knowing it in the first place or else why would they bother?

Cognition

Cognition, then, links to this discussion because, essentially, what we need to do in language lessons is make children think. This is at the heart of the learning process everywhere else, so it should not be surprising that it is central here, too.

Thinking can be at different levels and in different guises. In commonly used language topics, thinking can be rather difficult to engender, because, often, the way these topics are approached is via fairly descriptive rather than analytical processes. When asking about likes and dislikes, for example, children may want to express more subtle shades of opinion and you may wish to ask them why they have certain opinions. This raises more difficult vocabulary and structures.

We could argue, however, that when languages are linked with other subjects, thinking is easier to manage. It can start at the level where children make a single, simple decision while using language in comprehension mode. Questions that operate like this might be, 'Did the Vikings have glass? Did they have chocolate? Is this sound from a violin or clarinet? Is this bridge made of wood or stone? Which of these animals is depicted in this collage?' This level of vocabulary (that is, single words) does not need to be presented separately, or pre-taught, as the simple format of asking 'Is it x or y?' or 'Was x true, yes or no?' actually teaches that vocabulary while the learners' minds are focused on the question being asked.

Thinking continues in the process where children make meaning from text, often as a group or whole class, as we showed in the example of the French monuments. It is present again when children are asked to reassemble sentences or generate their own simple sentences in response to pictures. If we ask children to respond to simple open questions where the answer is personal and not already known by the teacher, we again move away from formulaic parroting of learned material and back to a child having to think, 'What has she asked me there? How do I respond?'

Thinking tends not to occur, however, when vocabulary is simply repeated or when very tightly controlled pair practice or role play is used, especially if the children's own views or experiences are not elicited by the task.

The limitations of some common language learning activities should now be clear. An example might be flashcard games that have a place in the learning cycle but will become formulaic and tedious if used at the same point in every new topic. Partly this is due to repetition of a format but also partly due to the nature of the format itself. Excessive practice of common topics, such as personal information, is a further example. If we rehearse questions to which we know the answer too often and everyone else in the class knows the answer and the pupil we are asking knows that everyone knows the answer, then the motivation to give that answer becomes minimal. The worst example of this is the type of question that goes, *'Stephen, cómo te llamas?'*

but asking ages in a single-year class is similar, unless you are investigating proportions with birthdays at different points or establishing an age order, in which case you need years and months. Even asking about brothers and sisters more than once falls into this category and needs another dimension. One good way to sidestep all of this is to ask children to take on a different identity and keep it a secret. All of the same questions can then be asked but none of the answers will be known in advance. If we do not think about this, then, in the worst scenario, any real level of thinking can be absent from the entire learning cycle.

Reflection point

You have used a café menu to introduce a number of drinks. You do not want to play flashcard games with these items now, so need to consider some other activity that will involve some thinking as well as the use of the vocabulary. What could you do?

Collaboration

Collaboration is vital in language learning because language use generally involves some form of communication between two or more people. This might seem obvious given the amount of talk associated with the ML curriculum at all levels, but we do need to think beyond the obvious. Talking to a formula is not strictly collaboration and talking to a rigid formula makes the fact that two are involved in a dialogue almost superfluous. So, by 'collaboration' we mean that a pair or group of children are working for a real purpose (Oxford, 1997; Crandall, 1999; Dillenbourg, 1999; Fisher, 2002). This might be to make something, solve a problem or exchange information in an authentic way. You might even combine all three if you decide to instigate a survey about pets to find out the average number of pets per pupil then create a pie chart on pet popularity and perhaps push a little further by asking the children if they have had a pet who has died. While many children do know some other children's pets' names, colours and bad habits, this still contains a very real chance to find out unknown facts, use the information for another purpose and involve a more affective issue that is all too real for many children.

We are not just talking about talking, though. Children nearly always respond positively to being asked if they prefer to work collaboratively in general and, within the area of language learning, this is especially true of reading. They tend to make much more of a text when reading in a pair or group and also enjoy the reading more. In a group, it tends to become a matter of collective 'finding out', of argument and it carries a greater (because more public) sense of task completion and satisfaction. Reading is also much more immediately accessible as an activity when carried out collaboratively. So we can ask children to read earlier and read more if we do it this way. In an unpublished doctoral thesis (Hood, 2000), we looked at lower secondary age children reading individually and in groups and found clear evidence of higher levels of performance when they were working in the collaborative mode.

Competition

Very many children really love both playing games and solving problems and, in so doing, competing either individually or in teams. Competition can be healthy and involve high levels of collaboration. We just need to be careful to ensure that the focus does not move so much on to competition that it leads to a desperation to win and shortcuts too much the language and the process of using the language. It can also lead to anxiety among some children (Crandall, 1999; Oxford, 1999; Pollard and Triggs, 2000; Ortega, 2007). Ortega, particularly, deals with the relationship between competitiveness and anxiety and offers a set of classroom procedures to ensure a healthy ethos. Whole-class games, such as identifying vocabulary on the whiteboard as fast as possible, have the inherent danger of involving a very small number of children and leaving the majority on the sidelines at any one point. When using a whole-class format, therefore, it is important to issue something (for example, a card with a number or vocabulary item) to everyone and then carry out a team competition where an item is called out and the first person to stand up, show the card and say it correctly wins a point. This means anyone can be involved at any point. Group-based games have the advantage of involving lots of children relatively continuously. An example of this (available in the *A La Française* pack, Tobutt and Roche, 2007) is an envelope game involving euros that has a distant similarity to the TV programme, *Deal or No Deal*. Board games, which can be based on snakes and ladders-type formats are popular, but tend to take more time to play. With these, it is vital to think about 'surround sound' social language (which will be seen in Chapter 9 as language for learning) and get as much target language activated as possible. This has to be prepared for as it will not happen by itself.

Competition between the teacher and the class is extremely popular. A number of guessing games (with a number of guesses allowed or set times allowed for the answer to be reached) can be played in the early stages as directly competitive and this has a certain motivational power, particularly if the children in the class are able to work together. There is also the advantage that if the teacher is trying to guess a cultural object, location or other item the class has chosen, he or she can use a good range of target language to ask questions and test out guesses, to which the children need only answer 'Yes' or 'No'. This has the effect of offering a good receptive language experience for the children without making impossible demands on them. Of course when the children start to want to take the teacher role, they should be allowed to, even though the quantity of language they have will be far less.

In summary, we might say competition that is firmly aimed at enhancing learning works very well. This can often be organised in teams, thus combining competition with collaboration. Competition purely for its own sake might be popular for a time and with some children or classes, but, in the end, it will wear thin as a motivator.

Reflection point

Planning activity

Take a language teaching lesson plan and evaluate it for *challenge* by annotating it with examples of the other six Cs from Figure 2.1 on page 20.

- Are any of the Cs absent? Were opportunities missed?
- Could you insert them easily without changing the plan radically or should the lesson be completely replanned?
- How challenging was this lesson and why do you think that?

From the review of the seven Cs above, we can now infer that any dangers might emerge from too much repetition or restriction of the children's natural desire to use language to communicate. If we rely too much on making it fun, we may run into 'fun fatigue'. It is not that natural repetition or some measure of control over language is not part of the learning process – we mentioned earlier how important enjoyment is – but we need to mesh these elements in to the seven Cs to create a truly stimulating environment. To explore this further, we will ask another question.

Reflection point

How can learning another language offer even more to a school (for example, by reinforcing the development of core skills, such as first language or English as an additional language (EAL), numeracy or reasoning)?

Learning another language has always been seen by teachers as a potential consolidation tool for learners with particular difficulties. For example, in Y7, teachers have often commented that 'doing the time' in a foreign language offers students who still have difficulties with this life skill to gain practice in a non-threatening environment with others who are also learning it for the first time in French, German or Spanish.

If we make comparisons between the core subjects and languages, we can see a potential two-way process, where the foreign language draws from the skills established for the core subject but also gives back to them, reinforcing and extending those same skills. This applies to all children, not only those with specific or special needs and establishes ML as a truly integrated subject. In this chapter we will look in depth at examples from literacy.

ML and the National Curriculum in England

The new 2014 National Curriculum organises the English curriculum under the headings of reading and writing, each with several subsections. There is also a global statement on spoken language at the beginning of the document with 12 bullet points (shown below). For reading and writing there are several statutory requirements for each year from Y1 to Y6. If the approaches to ML teaching echo those to first language or EAL teaching, there is additional credibility to the value of the learning. On this basis we will look at elements of speaking and reading to make analogies between the work that is possible in ML and relates to objectives in English.

Speaking

Pupils should be taught to:

- listen and respond appropriately to adults and their peers
- ask relevant questions to extend their understanding and knowledge
- use relevant strategies to build their vocabulary
- articulate and justify answers, arguments and opinions
- give well-structured descriptions, explanations and narratives for different purposes, including for expressing feelings
- maintain attention and participate actively in collaborative conversations, staying on topic and initiating and responding to comments
- use spoken language to develop understanding through speculating, hypothesising, imagining and exploring ideas
- speak audibly and fluently with an increasing command of standard English
- participate in discussions, presentations, performances, role play, improvisations and debates

- gain, maintain and monitor the interest of the listener(s)
- consider and evaluate different viewpoints, attending to and building on the contributions of others
- select and use appropriate registers for effective communication.

We can see immediately that beginner language learners at the start of KS2 will not be able to use the language at a level approaching how they use English, as a first or additional language, but it is important to establish approaches towards achieving that and aims for the first and subsequent years about progression in language use as well as language knowledge. If the language lessons are sufficiently broadly based and offer enough challenge, they will have encountered simple poems, stories and songs as stimuli. In joining in with more repetitive elements they will not just get words but also meaning, as conveyed via intonation and gesture, together with other visual support. They will also start to gain a sense of cultural context. In an ML class, most children will be at a similar level, so the teacher's encouragement to use richer language is crucial. In a Y1 class of Cantonese speakers in Hong Kong, for example, children who had heard the story from *We're Going on a Bear Hunt* (Rosen, 1993) in a morning lesson were seen in the dinner queue later playing a game in which they chorused 'We're not scared!' in just the right tone and context and they clearly loved playing a game with the language they had just had contact with.

If the language lessons include a measure of content, such as science, then sequences will be embedded in the work the children cover. Helping plants grow well as a topic offers the opportunity to create simple checklists, combining visuals and text with either simple lists or sequences of information. Figure 2.4 shows how such language might be stimulated and what the best children might produce, at first in spoken form, then later in writing.

Language learning is expected to involve giving opinions and, if introduced from the beginning of learning, this also makes it more connected to children's lives and more 'real'. One item in the Programme of Study for KS2 is:

- engage in conversations; ask and answer questions; *express opinions and respond to those of others*; seek clarification and help. (DfE, 2013b: 2, emphasis added)

Clearly, then, Y3 children should be able to meet contexts in which they talk about an item of personal interest and give some simple reasons for their preferences. This might involve food and healthy approaches. The key to making this happen is how it is stimulated and scaffolded. For example, a simple organiser to prepare for such conversations might be a matrix with four quadrants, labelled as shown in Figure 2.5. By locating foods onto the matrix children are ready to give simple opinions about healthy eating and the more able will be able to add some simple reasons. When this is put together into a paired comparative dialogue or a mini-presentation, we get material relevant to the third of our speaking objectives listed above.

Pflanzen brauchen , and

Zwei Pflanzen waren...

Eine Pflanze hat bekommen.

Zwei Pflanzen waren...

Eine Pflanze hat bekommen

WPflanzen brauchen: Licht, Wasser und Platz im Topf.
Zwei Pflanzen waren am Fenster. Eine Pflanze hat Wasser bekommen.
Zwei Pflanzen waren im Schrank. Eine Pflanze hat Wasser bekommen.
Nach einer Woche: die grösste Pflanze war am Fenster. Diese Pflanze hat Wasser bekommen.

Figure 2.4 Helping plants grow well

The use of more precise vocabulary is also simple to draw together. Language schemes of work often involve colours in the early stages, but at Y3 level children are already more sophisticated about their colour appreciation to settle only for the major primary or secondary colours with no qualifiers. It is not complex to introduce words for light-, dark- and even shiny, fluorescent and so more closely reach the expressions children want to use.

Grammar

Perhaps it will be felt that the speaking objectives will be a very easily accessible set for such comparisons. Grammatical strands are no more complicated, as the fact that children are focusing on such issues in English makes it very easy to

Figure 2.5 Conversation matrix for food and healthy approaches

focus on them also in a foreign language. They will naturally seek patterns and comment on what they find. This comparative approach gives extra support to both languages. We can, however, look for a more complex set to see if the case for a parallel focus between literacy and ML can really be substantiated.

Understanding and interpreting texts

Among the 2014 National Curriculum Y3/4 programme of study objectives we find:

Pupils should be taught to:

- develop positive attitudes to reading and understanding of what they read by:
  - o reading books that are structured in different ways and reading for a range of purposes
  - o using dictionaries to check the meanings of words that they have read
  - o preparing poems and play scripts to read aloud and to perform, showing understanding through intonation, tone, volume and action
- understand what they read, in books they can read independently, by:
  - o asking questions to improve their understanding of a text
  - o drawing inferences, such as inferring characters' feelings, thoughts and motives from their actions, and justifying inferences with evidence
  - o identifying main ideas drawn from more than one paragraph and summarising these
  - o identifying how language, structure and presentation contribute to meaning
- retrieve and record information from non-fiction.

As we will show later in the book, it is vital that children are exposed to text at a level commensurate with their experience in English from the very beginnings of their learning. Again, we should remember that an enormous amount of importance attached to text is signalled to them every day in literacy lessons. Therefore, it is illogical not to make parallels with French, German, Spanish or another language. So often the 'diet' we give learners is simply accessed by them as individuals at an appropriate level for their current development. Children in Foundation Stage who are really interested in letter patterns as a result of their phonics work and who pick out letters and sounds while listening to stories from a big book that they see in front of them, will naturally do the same in the foreign language. If they have not yet reached that stage in their work in English, they will not do this. By Y3, rhyming patterns in a poem, significant stages in a story or key words in the description of a town or village will be visible and 'notetaking' (probably orally and collaboratively) is more than possible. Again, from the beginnings of learning in F1 or F2, children listen avidly to stories in a foreign language, look closely at pictures, 'hear' intonation and emotion portrayed in the course of reading and so identify and empathise with characters or situations. At first, it may be preferable to talk in English about a story that they have heard in a foreign language, making the most of the foreign language experience of listening. As with the grammatical objectives, learners focusing on text organisation in English will be able to make similar comments about foreign language informational texts and use that structural understanding to help them identify and infer the meanings of words.

Perhaps these objectives are best considered from the point of view of a single theme – an example might be endangered species. The webpage www.linternaute.com/nature-animaux/animaux/dossier/especes-menacees/top-10 gives access to short dossiers that a teacher could use to produce visuals and simple facts for a theme of *Sauvez ... !* For example, from the card about giant pandas, the 'start text' is:

> *Panda géant: où vit-il?*
>
> *Dans les forêts humides et froides qui couvrent les versants des montagnes*
>
> *du Tibet et du sud-ouest de la Chine, dans les montagnes situées au*
>
> *Sichuan, au Gansu et au Shaanxi, à plus de 2000 mètres d'altitude.*

The teacher can elicit the real key words by asking the class collaboratively to supply possible endings to the sentence, *'Le panda géant habite ...'.* They might offer:

> *Les forêts; les montagnes; Tibet / Chine; 2000 m*
>
> *Les forêts sont humides et froides*

This can lead to poster work – *Sauvez les pandas géants* – where design is informed by the preceding language work and some Y4 shaping text objectives about persuasiveness are anticipated. Using story books linked to the theme allows it to be located in the child's wider work – even if these books are for younger children, such as Eric Carle's *Panda Bear, Panda Bear, What do you see?*, told in the target language. At a very simple level, teachers could show, by means of simple poetry, for example, how the language can *sound* different with different intentions. Ideally, this could involve poems on the endangered animals theme written by children who are native speakers.

The two examples given of ML work associated with National Curriculum English objectives are not contrived to make a link that does not really exist. They demonstrate that a modern language *functions as language*, just as English does. We also need to see the *role* of the language in our teaching, as well as the language, as a teaching end in itself and we need to encourage our children to communicate in and play with the language as well as 'learn' it.

 Reflection point

The previous Literacy Framework in the Primary National Strategy, which was replaced by the 2014 National Curriculum in England, had separate objectives for listening and responding. The strand objectives for Y1 and Y2 were as follows.

Y1

- Listen with sustained concentration, building new stores of words in different contexts.
- Listen to and follow instructions accurately, asking for help and clarification if necessary.
- Listen to tapes or video and express views about how a story or information has been presented.

Y2

- Listen to others in class, ask relevant questions and follow instructions.
- Listen to talk by an adult, remember some specific points and identify what they have learned.
- Respond to presentations by describing characters, repeating some highlights and commenting constructively.

Which of these could you imagine being used as ML objectives for a Y3 class by the end of the year? Make a few notes about how you might approach one of them.

What differences are there between 'language lessons' and the experience of a child coming into a school with EAL?

To complete the final point from the previous section – that language should be used to serve our teaching and not be an end in itself – we can make a further analogy with EAL. This is the term used to describe the context of a learner who does not have English as a first language. We will explore the research base to content and language integrated learning (CLIL) and EAL in Chapter 9, but it is important to note at this stage that teachers working with children with EAL operate a sophisticated model of scaffolding and differentiation within what is for the children with EAL an immersion framework. Being surrounded by the language and set carefully planned, purposeful tasks with clear outcomes should ensure a positive learning context for all to gain from it what they can.

These skills are very close to what is needed by language teachers and language learning should be as broad as this. The answer to the question is therefore that the differences should be of context, not so much of experience. The contextual advantage for teachers of a foreign language is that most members of the class will probably know a similar amount of the language as each other, whereas the parallel advantage for teachers of EAL is that they have native or near-native command of English. Clearly the competent ML teacher who also has experience of EAL has the best of all possible starting points!

Chapter summary

What can language learning offer primary-age children and what can it offer a primary school? We hope this chapter has demonstrated that learning a language can play a very full role in a primary school and the experiences of its children.

As ML enters the compulsory primary curriculum, it is difficult to see it as just another foundation subject. It needs to be timetabled regularly and this is not a status offered to most other foundation subjects, except physical education (PE) and perhaps personal, social and health education (PSHE). The embedding across the day and week, in registration, classroom organisation and management, routines and, perhaps, music in assemblies, means that it *could* almost stop having an overt focus being put on it. Certainly, some schools, feeling the intensity of time pressures, will look to account for a major part of ML provision by embedding it in other subjects in this way, with only a smaller official amount of time being allocated to it. This will not serve anyone's purposes in the longer term, however.

It may sound greedy on our part, but such embedding should not be seen as a part of the provision, but, rather, a way to prove that ML is a legitimate means of communication for real purposes. The way to 'save time' in the longer run is to give more but ask for more back. ML can contribute to the whole curriculum by taking some of that content in every single subject (including English!) and presenting it to children and asking them to work on it in the target language. First, however it has to be established as an aspect of school life that has real status and real support from all staff, no matter what their capability. In return, the school and the school population should see an increase in confidence, self-esteem and an opening out towards the new horizons that greater cultural exposure can provide. School linking, backed by two-way language use, is so much more satisfying than the realisation that both sides just have to use English and we cannot quite deliver what the other school seems able to do.

The chapter has tried to provide very practical strategies to offer a full range of experiences to children in schools. These have not been specific to age, ability or experience, but organised to demonstrate the importance of elements such as the seven Cs. The next set of chapters will look in more detail at specific ages or specific stages of development of the language curriculum and of children's competence in a school.

Key reading

To see alternative views of how the curriculum can be visualised, look at both The Cambridge Primary Review conclusions (Alexander, 2009) and the 'A big picture of the curriculum' visual at: www.ncca.ie/en/Curriculum_and_Assessment/Post-Primary_Education/Junior_Cycle/Junior_cycle_developments/Documentation/English_curriculum_framework.pdf

For an interesting view on foreign language materials, culture and tasks (written with secondary learners in mind), see D. Allford (2000) 'Pictorial images, lexical phrases and culture', *Language Learning Journal*, 22 (1): 45–51.

To see practical examples from an EAL context, visit: www.naldic.org.uk/Resources/NALDIC/Initial%20Teacher%20Education/Documents/KS1-2-The%20Multilingual%20Classroom.pdf. Follow the link to the teachers' media video. This shows how teachers can be sensitive to the language needs of learners without sacrificing challenge and cognition.

CHAPTER 3

HOW MIGHT I STRUCTURE LANGUAGE LEARNING IN THE EARLY YEARS FOUNDATION STAGE (EYFS)?

Chapter objectives

- To summarise how children of three–five years learn.
- To explore how children can best access another language.
- To establish what makes them successful learners of the new language.
- To offer some sample activities for each area of learning.
- To look from a teacher's perspective at how to plan ML into a stimu-lating curriculum.

Teachers' standards			
A teacher must:			
1			Set high expectations which inspire, motivate and challenge pupils
		a	Establish a safe and stimulating environment for pupils, rooted in mutual respect

	b	Set goals that stretch and challenge pupils of all backgrounds, abilities and dispositions
	c	demonstrate consistently the positive attitudes, values and behaviour which are expected of pupils
5		Adapt teaching to respond to the strengths and needs of all pupils
	a	know when and how to differentiate appropriately, using approaches which enable pupils to be taught effectively
	b	have a secure understanding of how a range of factors can inhibit pupils' ability to learn, and how best to overcome these
	c	demonstrate an awareness of the physical, social and intellectual development of children, and know how to adapt teaching to support pupils' education at different stages of development
	d	have a clear understanding of the needs of all pupils, including those with special educational needs; those of high ability; those with English as an additional language; those with disabilities; and be able to use and evaluate distinctive teaching approaches to engage and support them

Source: DfE, 2013a

Introductory vignette

Emily (five years, giving out fruit): *Une orange?*

Edwin (five years): Thank you.

Emily: *Qu'est-ce que c'est? Merci!*

Edwin: *Merci!*

This short and entirely spontaneous conversation between two children in a Reception class (F2) took place only six weeks after the children had started to learn French. What does it demonstrate? The children are happy to interact with each other in French; they even remind each other of conventions of politeness using the new language. In this case, the daily fruit time was used to integrate the ML into class routines very effectively: after only a few weeks of learning, the children did not just respond to the teacher's questions but

Figure 3.1 Child-initiated play in Reception class

were also able to use a complex question form themselves naturally and with clear purpose.

 Initial reflection point

What might the children shown in Figure 3.1 be doing and how might it connect with language learning?

Response

The children are playing with two of the puppets regularly used in French lessons. They are singing a French song together that they have previously learned. The activity is both authentic and spontaneous. They have not been asked to do this by the teacher, but have themselves asked to play with the puppets as part of child-initiated play.

How do children in the Early Years Foundation Stage learn?

> The ways in which the child engages with other people and their environment – playing and exploring, active learning, and creating and thinking critically – underpin learning and development across all areas and support the child to remain an effective and motivated learner. (Early Education, 2012: 4)

The 'Characteristics of Effective Learning' (Early Education, 2012: 4–7) interconnect with all areas of learning (prime and specific) and centre on a child's engagement (playing and exploring), motivation (active learning) and thinking (creating and thinking critically). The skills defined in these pages are at the heart of good provision and should build on research-informed practice, as detailed in works by Fisher (2013), Nutbrown (2011), Wood (2013) and Broadhead et al. (2010).

The origins of the thinking about the EYFS are the Rumbold Committee's report (DES, 1990: 9), which summarised the relevant characteristics of learning in the Foundation Stage as follows.

- Children are active learners, operating most effectively through first-hand experience.
- Children are naturally curious; their imagination can be nurtured by responding to their curiosity.
- Interaction with others is crucial. Learning should take place in a social context.
- Talk is central to the learning process.
- For the early years educator, therefore, the process of education – how children are encouraged to learn – is as important as, and inseparable from, the content – what they learn. We believe that this principle must underlie all curriculum planning for the under fives.

The most current government policy on the birth to five teaching and learning context is the 'Statutory Framework for the Early Years Foundation Stage' (DfE, 2014, available online at: www.gov.uk/government/uploads/system/uploads/attachment_data/file/299391/DFE-00337-2014.pdf) and 'Development matters in the Early Years Foundation Stage (YFS)', which is not statutory (www.early-education.org.uk/sites/default/files/Development%20Matters%20FINAL%20PRINT%20AMENDED.pdf, Early Years, 2012).

It is important to see policy documents against the background of academic writing underpinned by research and interrogate them to establish which are the more reliable in terms of the motivating forces that might drive them. In 2003, members of the British Educational Research Association's (BERA) Early Years Special Interest Group published a research summary (still available at: www.bera.ac.uk/wp-content/uploads/2014/01/eyyrsp1.pdf) and there is a signalled intention to update this in 2015. Also on the same website is a short research review article (David, 2003, at: www.bera.ac.uk/ wp-content/uploads/2014/01/eyyrsp1.pdf) on how young children learn that addresses the themes of pedagogy, curriculum and assessment and adult roles. In addition to these documents, works by Edgington (2004), Riley (2007) and Moyles (2010), as well as the volumes listed above, all deal with approaches to good teaching and learning for the age range and, more importantly, they also address the developmental issues that ground the pedagogy in terms of child psychology. Those researching the three to five stage of education seem to be united on the values, approaches and desired outcomes for this age group and place a strong emphasis on the role of the professional practitioner as the interpreter of attainment.

What stands out from all of the writing about this stage is the accent on creativity and independence. Far from being vessels to be filled, children in the three to five age range in school are given and exercise an enormous amount of choice in how and where and when they learn. The onus on teachers is to plan for this choice.

There is an expectation that the whole curriculum can be delivered both indoors and outdoors, for example. Children are expected, for at least some of the time, to initiate activity, fashioning their own tasks out of the resources they find and so control their own learning. They are given roles that start to establish collaboration, community and understanding of others. Children need to be engaged by teachers and other adults who have this enormous responsibility to provide stimulating learning environments because, at this stage, children are not especially gifted in rationalising *why* they have to do something. Even when there is a strong government dictum, for example, regarding the teaching of reading (Rose, 2006) and material to support this emerges, such as the various synthetic phonics schemes, successful progress is highly dependent on gifted practitioners who can make the activities fast-paced, varied and highly active and so draw children into the learning cycle. If the children enjoy the work, they will learn to read, but, if they do not, they will not. Synthetic phonics by itself is not the recipe. How practitioners use synthetic phonics is the key.

Given that the *process* – how children learn – is as important as the *content*, we should not separate the learning of a new language from the rest of the curriculum but aim for an approach that integrates ML naturally into activities which encourage children's learning. In fact, ML can provide opportunities for both whole-class or larger group work, such as singing or listening to a story, *and* more spontaneous free choice activity, such as in the role-play area or outdoors, which a small number of children might choose to do. In this sense, it can perform a full role in the EYFS curriculum, developing concentration and communal self-discipline at some points and firing children's individual imagination at others.

Reflection point

We are now going to take a look at a few short activities based on the names of colours as one example of something that is often introduced in the early stages of language learning. What are the children in each scenario doing? Are they actively involved? Are there elements of curiosity? Are the children interacting? Does the learning take place in a social context?

1. In the first scenario, the teacher uses traditional language methodology, saying the names of the colours while holding up different-coloured flash cards or objects. The children listen and are encouraged to repeat the names of the colours. They might then put the different-coloured cards or objects in a bag and pass it around in a circle while music in the target language is playing. When the music stops, the teacher asks the child who holds the bag to take a certain colour out of the bag.

In the second scenario, the teacher chooses two toys, two characters from a story the children have read and three different-coloured bags. The teacher then hides the toys in the different bags, asking the children to try to remember where they are *'Où est le petit chien? Dans le sac bleu, dans le sac rouge ou dans le sac vert?'* The children respond by saying the colour of the bag.

2. In the third scenario, the teacher is setting up an art and craft activity for making a dragon's mask. The children start by choosing the colour of their mask, with the teacher asking, *'Tu voudrais faire une masque rouge ou verte?'*

Response

The third scenario makes the most purposeful use of language as it is entirely focused on the art activity and uses language merely to establish how the children are going to start (by choosing the colour of paper they want to use). In the second scenario, the teacher is using a 'flow' of natural language to pose a question and is offering a choice of answers so that the children can respond at any level they wish. They might just nod at the right option or say a colour or produce the whole phrase. It does not matter which they do as the main purpose is that they understand the language used and understand as well they can make a choice. In the first scenario there is a real focus on 'fixing' the vocabulary by repetition and, at this point, there is no real purpose involved except to learn the language. The circle game offers more of a separate rationale as children enjoy playing guessing games and finding objects.

As teachers, we need to be clear in our own minds what we are doing and why. These scenarios might all be used at different points, but we should perhaps ensure that we do find a balance. If we only used the type of activities indicated in the first scenario, the children might lose out on some essential roles of language.

Using the target language

Our aim is very much for children to be able to communicate in the foreign language, not just recognise and recall lists of words. This can be achieved by exposing children from an early age to rich language and the use of new language for different purposes of communication.

Since the advent of the National Curriculum (KS3 and KS4) for ML in 1992, there has been a strong recommendation from government, CILT (National Centre for Languages), teacher educators, LA advisers/consultants and OFSTED for teachers to maximise the use of target language in the classroom. This stems partly from the ideas of Krashen and Terrell (1983) that if we mirror immersion techniques we will more *acquire* (a natural process) than have to *learn* language (an artificial one). Understandably, teachers with lower levels of confidence find this one of the most daunting aspects of starting to teach ML in primary schools. There are two very different but very important ways to address this.

In the first instance, because a teacher cannot suddenly 'magic up' language competence or confidence he or she does not have, the school should look at resourcing the start-up of the subject with multimedia materials that have audio support, such as DVD materials – the French resource *Mon Âne* (Le Notre, 1999) is a good example. The advantage of these materials is that they contain native speaker-recorded stories, songs, games and, in many cases, video extracts, all of which save the teacher from having to manage the language input independently but also provide a model so that the teacher's own command of the target language can steadily and invisibly improve. The resources can be used via data projectors and are colourful, well-paced, lively and provide very good models. The younger the children, the easier they find it to discriminate and produce very good target language pronunciation and intonation, so the resources also play an invaluable role in starting the children off with very good models to emulate.

The second route is one for the teacher to work on. Many native speakers admit that they find it difficult to modify their language sufficiently to prevent confusing children with too rich a language diet. Hitting the middle path between stilted, overly repetitive, even unnatural, target language use and completely unstructured use of anything and everything that comes out of a native speaker's repertoire is vital. We need riches but not a surfeit! Non-native speakers are often far more able to stand in the children's shoes and select forms that will be more accessible, perhaps because they contain more cognates (words which resemble each other in each of the languages) and the children will recognise, make sense of and start to internalise these relatively quickly.

So, teachers should script out a range of expressions (see below) and use them regularly in a natural rhythm and at a natural speed. All common classroom instructions can be given in the foreign language – introducing a few at a time, but then using them often. This can happen throughout the week, not just in the slots where the teacher focuses on whole-class language work.

To make the change between languages clear, it has proved successful to use a puppet that the children can associate with the new language. Whenever the teacher speaks in the ML, he or she can use the puppet, to make the change clear to the children. Research into bilingualism (Baker, 2006) has highlighted the importance of children associating each language with a certain person (or group of people) who should persevere using that particular language. A puppet can take on this function of indicating the change to the foreign language. In addition, the children can familiarise themselves with the idea that the new language might only be used in certain situations or with certain people. If the children then integrate the puppet into their role play, they will understand that they can only use French when they want to interact with the puppet. First, they will use greetings and simple songs or perhaps finger rhymes that they have learned, but they will soon feel the need to express more.

One boy in a Reception class was observed having a conversation with the French puppet, Croco the crocodile, offering different fruits from the shop in the role-play area. Owen (five years old) was familiar with the question, '*Qu'est-ce que c'est?*' and he knew the names of some fruits in French from his regular exposure to French during fruit time. He now put the two elements together, asking the puppet, '*Qu'est-ce que c'est une orange, Croco? Qu'est-ce que c'est … une banane, Croco?*'

After a while, he came over to the teacher and asked, 'How do you say "Would you like" in French?' The teacher modelled the use of *tu voudrais*, but Owen didn't go back to the puppet – Croco had eaten all the fruits he'd been offered and he was full up – so didn't use the new structure this time. He might be able to recover it on another occasion or he might not remember it.

With this age group, simply telling them the language is not enough. The important element in this incident is that he realised he needed more language and asked for it. It also shows how children respond when they feel the need to use language for a real purpose and how adding new language can most successfully be based on real communication for real purposes. Only this will, in time, create independent learners and, ultimately, confident users of the new language. If the teacher sets up the puppet as speaking *only* the target language, then the children readily accept that they need to try to understand what the puppet says and try to use the target language to speak to the puppet.

The teacher can also use stories and songs as sources of expressions, phrases and sentences to be used elsewhere if the context arises. Similarly, 'commentary' language may also be spoken in the target language. For example, some new sand appearing in the sand tray might seem a stronger colour. Using the foreign language to comment on this – *'Le sable est très jaune aujourd'hui!'* – reinforces a colour *and* the words for sand and today without it being a specific learning point. In these circumstances children will often reply in English and this does not matter. The intention at this stage of using strong target language is to set up the flow and the natural process of interpreting.

A vital language skill is to be able to select from a stream the key words that carry significant meaning. This is not easy, but, unless it is on the agenda right from the start, it will become a barrier frighteningly quickly. Perhaps because children are still developing their mother tongue strongly at three to five years stage they are unconsciously accustomed to making sense of words being used in new contexts and even of completely new words. They continuously integrate the learning of language with doing something else (hearing a story, singing a song, playing a game) and this is shown by the way they naturally also play with sounds and words at this age. It appears from our observations that children in EYFS find hearing a foreign language much more natural and can cope with the unknown much better than older children can. As long as the global meaning is clear and they know what they have to do and as long as they understand enough of a stimulus 'text' to enjoy it and participate, they do not worry about each individual word. This should encourage teachers to tap into the resources available so children hear a mix of native-speaking voices and teachers themselves slowly increase their own skills in using the language.

Some practical examples follow of how we might embed our use of language into routines. These tend to have, as we have said above, a teacher-initiated, receptive learner focus. The children more often act on the instruction than use the language themselves, but the scope is there for them to start to use the language, too. We saw in the introductory vignette and with the incident with Croco that some children will readily use the language for their own play or at those times when they briefly become the 'responsible adult', such as distributing the fruit.

Whole-class routines

- Taking and responding to the register in the new language can be at the level of a simple greeting, but can sometimes be extended to asking how the children feel. One teacher recounted how she met a child coming towards the school office and asked her in French how she was. The child responded in French that she felt ill today – in fact, she was coming to lie down as she had a stomach ache. This shows the true communicative power of the work they did on a regular basis – the response to the foreign language in the foreign language was entirely natural.

- General instructions (sitting down, getting in a circle, finding a partner, getting ready for play outside, lining up, washing hands, tidying up) can be introduced and built up gradually. In each case, the teacher can use gesture and modelling to support understanding until the children recognise the instructions and will then find that the support can slowly be dispensed with.
- Handing out milk or fruit gives children the opportunity to name the item they want in very simple language, but also, as we saw, to 'be the teacher' and use some additional target language themselves in those interactions.
- Giving praise. Children will sometimes also imitate this among themselves.
- General display in the classroom with labels in the new language will expose the children to the written form from an early age.

Using these familiar routines, the new language can be integrated in a natural way the children will soon adapt to. If practitioners feel concerned about confusing the children and, as we explored above, if your primary aim is to use language purposefully – that is, to communicate meaningful content – it should not matter which language is being used as long as the children feel safe and supported.

Reflection point

Take three of the routines listed above and script the language you think you will need to use to ask the children to carry out the routine. Consider how long the words and sentences are that you choose and look for ways of shortening them, but keep the language as authentic as possible.

Using the language for the routines is not enough, of course – we can go further! The next section looks at how teachers can plan to embed ML activities into the EYFS curriculum.

Embedding ML activities into the EYFS curriculum

The EYFS curriculum is organised into seven areas of learning and development – three prime areas and four specific areas (DfE, 2012):
The prime areas are:

- personal, social and emotional development
- communication and language
- physical development.

The specific areas are:

- literacy
- mathematics
- understanding the world
- expressive arts and design.

These areas of learning provide the basis for all planning and the children's learning. ML should be no exception, but integrated as far as possible into any activities. It is vital that specialist ML teachers working in the Foundation Stage, but not specifically trained for it, are aware of the EYFS curriculum structure and teaching methodologies in order to adapt their language work and integrate it into the children's learning. The following sample activities for each area of learning should exemplify the type of language activities that could be integrated easily into the curriculum.

Personal, social and emotional development (PSED)

Circle games can be played in the new language. These will encourage the children to work in small or large groups and support their social development, such as turn taking and sharing with others. During a simple but very popular circle game, one of the children has to leave the room while one of the other children is hiding a certain object (in this example, sea animals) behind their back or in their lap. The first child is then called back into the circle, where he or she has to find the hidden object by asking the children in the circle, 'Have you got the fish?' ('As-tu le poisson?'). The children asked can simply reply with 'Oui/Non' or add more language, such as 'No, I'm sorry' ('Non, désolé/e') or by saying that they haven't got it ('Non, je n'ai pas de poisson'), depending on their level of confidence. The game can be played until the child in the middle has found the object – perhaps count how many children have been asked or decide at the start how many 'goes' each child should get.

Other circle activities could involve counting and simple decision making. Put a range of objects into a bag and two hoops in the middle. All the children sit in a circle and count while passing the bag on to the next child. When they reach a certain number, they stop counting. The child holding the bag takes an object out of the bag, hears a question from the teacher and decides if the object should go into the 'Oui' hoop or in the 'Non' hoop. The teacher can control the language input in this case by using any relevant question associated with the current topic focus and the object the child has taken from the bag, such as, 'Le lion habite dans la mer? Oui ou non?' Children can be asked if it is the correct response. Other turn taking could involve children choosing a song that they might sing at the start of a language session or a small group game, such as bingo with mini cards.

A carefully prepared role-play area can provide opportunities for play and learning to experience different cultural backgrounds.

Certain stories with themes around friendship (*Die kleine Maus sucht einen Freund/La souris qui cherche un ami* by Eric Carle – *Do You Want to be My Friend?* (1979) in English) or being frightened in the dark (*Lilou a peur du noir* by P. Romeo, 2006) can be read in the target language to contribute additional support to children's emotional development in these areas. Children often reveal through their responses just how much they do follow of a story read in this way.

Early learning goals for the end of EYFS that can be supported in the foreign language include the following (DfE, 2012: 8).

> **Self-confidence and self-awareness:** children are confident to try new activities, and say why they like some activities more than others. They are confident to speak in a familiar group, will talk about their ideas, and will choose the resources they need for their chosen activities. They say when they do or don't need help.

> **Managing feelings and behaviour:** children talk about how they and others show feelings, talk about their own and others' behaviour, and its consequences, and know that some behaviour is unacceptable. They work as part of a group or class, and understand and follow the rules. They adjust their behaviour to different situations, and take changes of routine in their stride.

> **Making relationships:** children play cooperatively, taking turns with others. They take account of one another's ideas about how to organise their activity. They show sensitivity to others' needs and feelings, and form positive relationships with adults and other children.

Communication and language

Learning a new language can also underpin children's development of skills in English by widening their overall experience of a range of sounds by means of the foreign language. If songs, stories and rhymes are used regularly and the children are exposed to rich language from the start, they will experience listening to a range of new sounds and a different intonation. Far from confusing them, this will add value to their ability to discriminate and underline how important it is to listen carefully, with concentration. Listening to stories, joining in with songs and rhymes is a familiar style of learning for the children and offers a completely separate dimension to this valuable activity. Being encouraged to join in when they are ready, the children experiment with sounds during whole-class story telling and singing. Natural repetition in stories will encourage children to participate and they will be able to do this both individually if they are very confident or as part of a group if they are less secure. If you watch EYFS-aged children listening to a story or singing, you can see how often they look around to see what other members of the group are doing and then often start to join in. Additionally, the children experience not just the new language but often also a different culture first-hand while engaging with a story.

Teachers might want to start using simple stories first, such as a 'lift the flap' book of the likes of *Où es-tu, maman?*, which uses a comparatively small amount of language, but has a repetitive structure that invites the children to join in very quickly *(Oui ou non, Où es-tu? Toc, toc, qui est là?)*. Children can be encouraged to sustain concentration and active listening by responding to certain words or phrases using a physical response, such as touching parts of the body if they hear them mentioned while listening to the story – for example, *Va-t-en, Grand monstre vert!* (*Go Away, Big Green Monster!* by Ed Emberley, 1993), or joining in with the actions and sounds while listening to *La chasse à l'ours* (*We're Going on a Bear Hunt* by Michael Rosen, 1993). A story read in the target language can also provide the starting point for literacy activities, such as sequencing pictures of the story, focusing on beginning, middle and end. Teachers should choose a story that fits in with the theme as far as possible and should not worry that the children might not understand every word as long as they can follow the story line. It is important to not translate but let children engage with the story, whether in English or in the target language, and use gesture, mime and visuals to support comprehension. Stories can be used for active listening or simply for enjoyment.

Songs can be excellent opportunities to engage with the different sound system of the new language. Teachers should choose songs that, as far as possible, allow children to be active while singing. Good examples would be *Savez-vous planter les choux* (pretending to plant with different parts of the body), *Meunier, tu dors* (movements of different objects or animals), *Tourne, tourne petit moulin* (slow and fast turning of windmill), *Petit escargot* (actions for parts of snail and rain). The words of these songs are all available on the French-language Momes website (at: www.momes.net/comptines/comptines-chansons.html) and some also have midi-file-style music with the words so you can learn the tune.

In the early stage of synthetic phonics programmes, rhyme is an important device to help focus on sound, because being able to discriminate as to whether or not two words rhyme is a good first step towards being able to hear different sounds accurately. Younger children in an EYFS setting also really enjoy playing with words in this way. Teachers can also explore rhyming words in the foreign language in authentic songs and rhymes, such as French comptines, including *Bateau, ciseaux*, in which the teacher uses pictures to stimulate the use of the rhyming words and can alter the sequence to ensure that the children are actively involved.

We can see, then, early learning goals for the end of EYFS that can be supported via another language can include the following (DfE, 2012: 7–8):

> **Listening and attention:** children listen attentively in a range of situations. They listen to stories, accurately anticipating key events and respond to what they hear with relevant comments, questions or actions. They give their

attention to what others say and respond appropriately while engaged in another activity.

Understanding: children follow instructions involving several ideas or actions. They answer 'how' and 'why' questions about their experiences and in response to stories or events.

Speaking: children express themselves effectively, showing awareness of listeners' needs. They use past, present and future forms accurately when talking about events that have happened or are to happen in the future. They develop their own narratives and explanations by connecting ideas or events.

Physical development

This provides a good context in which a foreign language can be used for instructions for physical activity. This can include basic aerobic-type activity, such as 'walk, run, jump, hop, go faster, go more slowly, stop', and so on. The children can also count their heartbeat during warming up and cooling down exercises. They are limited as to how high they can count of course, but it is possible to monitor if it is 'fast counting' or 'slow counting', which allows them to see the difference. Action songs can be chosen so that the children can use movement and drama while singing. Good examples of this might be (in French) *'Le fermier dans son pré'* or *'Promenons-nous dans les bois'*, both of which can be found at the Momes website mentioned earlier in this chapter. Children often like to learn simple dances or clapping rhymes, which can also contribute to a more cultural appreciation of a target language-speaking country, especially if a video can be shown so that they gain a sense of other elements, such as traditional dress.

Early learning goals for the end of EYFS that can be as well supported by such activities in a foreign language as they can be in English are as follows (DfE, 2012: 8):

Moving and handling: children show good control and coordination in large and small movements. They move confidently in a range of ways, safely negotiating space. They handle equipment and tools effectively, including pencils for writing.

Health and self-care: Children know the importance for good health of physical exercise, and a healthy diet, and talk about ways to keep healthy and safe. They manage their own basic hygiene and personal needs successfully, including dressing and going to the toilet independently.

Literacy

It is with this area of learning that we should tread carefully. As we have seen, exposing children to books is an essential aspect of the ML diet for the youngest learners, too, but we should resist the temptation to focus at all overtly on actual reading or writing in the foreign language at this stage. Similarly, we should not engage with foreign language phonics.

It is usually believed that children best establish literacy in one language and can then apply it in other languages. Children may well want to take a foreign language picture book and 'read' it and they may want to 'write things' in the foreign language as well. They should not, of course, be forbidden from doing this, but it should not be part of the planned programme in the EYFS phase.

Mathematics

Numeracy work in the new language can support children's mathematical skills. A boy with autism was reluctant to join in with whole-class counting in English. Having learned a finger rhyme and a simple song in French that involved movement, he was observed later counting in French while he was lining up the engines of a train set. This even constituted a basic level of evidence for his EYFS Profile as it was clear that he was counting properly – that is, with a sense of the meaning of number.

Teachers can also use the target language and encourage children to use it while carrying out sorting activities, such as 2D shapes *(C'est un cercle/un triangle/un rectangle/carré).*

There are very many opportunities to use a foreign language during normal everyday numeracy work, such as putting the correct number of fruits and so on into baskets, adding missing numbers to a number line, looking at the colour patterns of beads, finding as many ways as possible to colour in trains with three carriages, using only three colours as part of a simple investigation and so on. Teachers can also use EYFS numeracy websites, such as materials for the interactive whiteboard and simply talk about them in the foreign language. They can play domino games and board games in the foreign language, too. In this way, the foreign language can be used whenever the teacher (or the children) wish to – it does not have to remain in its set slot.

Examples of French finger rhymes *(jeux de doigts)* for counting include the following.

Using the five fingers of one hand in turn:

Un bonbon

Deux bonbons

Trois bonbons

Quatre bonbons

Cinq bonbons

Miam, c'est bon!

Tapping increasing numbers of fingers on the palm of the other hand:

Un petit doigt qui frappe

Deux petits doigts qui frappent

Trois petits doigts qui frappent

Quatre petits doigts qui frappent

Cinq petits doigts qui frappent

Un, deux, trois, quatre, cinq Et voilà ma main

Early learning goals for the end of EYFS that can be supported via a new language include the following (DfE, 2012: 9):

Numbers: children count reliably with numbers from 1 to 20, place numbers in order and say which number is one more or one less than a given number. Using quantities and objects, they can add and subtract two single-digit numbers and count on or back to find the answer. They solve problems, including doubling, halving and sharing.

Shape, space and measure: children use everyday language to talk about size, weight, capacity, position, distance, time and money to compare quantities and objects and to solve problems. They recognise, create and describe patterns. They explore characteristics of everyday objects and shapes and use mathematical language to describe them.

Understanding the world

This area contains a range of what we see elsewhere as separate National Curriculum subjects. Science, history, geography, religious education (RE) and information and communication technology (ICT) are all subsumed into this general area. There are numerous ways in which this area can be brought into foreign language work, depending on the current topic that is being used to plan the curriculum activity. Some examples within the science and geography areas follow.

The teacher can use the target language for instructions and to elicit simple responses, such as in sorting activities (for example, toys according to size – big or small; materials that are hard or soft; warm or cold liquids). The children can suggest the correct habitats for different wild animals or different animals for different habitats. For example, 'Where does the tiger live? Which animal lives in the desert?' The children can experience hot and cold by holding ice cubes until they melt and offering reasons for this, such as, 'Because my hand is hot.'

Early learning goals for the end of EYFS that can be supported via a foreign language are as follows (DfE, 2012: 9):

People and communities: children talk about past and present events in their own lives and in the lives of family members. They know that other children don't always enjoy the same things and are sensitive to this. They know about similarities and differences between themselves and others, and among families, communities and traditions.

The world: children know about similarities and differences in relation to places, objects, materials and living things. They talk about the features of their own immediate environment and how environments might vary from one another. They make observations of animals and plants and explain why some things occur, and talk about changes.

Technology: children recognise that a range of technology is used in places such as homes and schools. They select and use technology for particular purposes.

Expressive arts and design

If we look at the EYFS guidance set out in 'Statutory Framework for the Early Years Foundation Stage' (DfE, 2012), especially the early learning goals, it is evident that, in some respects, the creative arts, such as music, art and dance are themselves viewed as languages. Children are encouraged to express themselves using alternative modes and not just by means of words. Therefore, a foreign language can be as easily used to create the stimulus and give simple instructions as English. Here, the teacher should try to provide resources from a variety of cultures associated with the language, including music, dance and art. Again, the teacher can use simple language to set up practical activities and so use language for a real purpose.

Early learning goals for the end of EYFS that can be supported via the target language are as follows (DfE, 2012: 9):

Exploring and using media and materials: children sing songs, make music and dance, and experiment with ways of changing them. They safely use and explore a variety of materials, tools and techniques, experimenting with colour, design, texture, form and function.

Being imaginative: children use what they have learnt about media and materials in original ways, thinking about uses and purposes. They represent their own ideas, thoughts and feelings through design and technology, art, music, dance, role play and stories.

Example of medium-term planning – integrating a foreign language into a topic

This section of the chapter (see Table 3.1) offers planning for a topic on wild animals. It is important to stress that the class is taking wild animals as its

Table 3.1 References to foreign language activities in a medium term plan on wild animals

Area of learning	EYFS learning objectives	Possible experiences	Resources
Personal, social and emotional development	• Be confident to try new activities	• Play circle games (hide and seek – *As-tu le pingouin? Un, deux, trois ... qui est dans le sac?*) • Play 'Loto' *(Qui a deux chameaux?)* • Encourage children to take turns	• (Finger) puppets for role play • Toys/objects/'feely bags' for circle games • Bingo game with animals
Communication and language	• Listen attentively and respond to stories	• Set up role-play area as a vet's practice • Use puppets to act out stories • Use a selection of non-fiction books to find out about different habitats	• Stories: *'La souris qui cherche un ami'*, *'Je veux ma banane'*, *'Petites chouettes'*, *'Bébés chouettes'*, *'Le petit pingouin'* • Songs: *'Tourne, tourne, petit moulin'*, *'Petit escargot'*, *'Les petits poissons'*, *'Renard, renard'*, *'Promenons-nous dans les bois'*
Physical development	• Children show good control and coordination in large and small movements	• Respond to story *'La chasse à l'ours'* • Play playground game *'Promenons-nous dans les bois'*	• Story: *'La chasse à l'ours'* • Song: *'Promenons-nous dans les bois'*
Mathematics	• Count objects to ten • Children use everyday language to talk about size to compare quantities and objects and solve problems	• Play counting games • Sorting small/big animals	• Counting equipment • Compare bears large and small
Understanding the world	• To know about similarities and differences in relation to places and living things • Make observations, explain why some things occur and talk about changes	• Place animals in correct habitat *(Le chameau habite dans la mer ou dans le desert?)* • Make ice cubes and let them melt in hand	• Laminated pictures of different habitats (and visuals on interactive whiteboard)
Expressive arts and design	• Begin to build a repertoire of songs and dances • Explore colours, experiment to create different textures • Manipulate materials to achieve a planned effect	• Learn songs and accompany with movements and instruments • Make animal mask *(On fait des masques)* • Create 'hot' and 'cold' pictures *(Il fait chaud ou il fait froid? Les couleurs chaudes/froides)* • Paint and weave 'Elmer' patterns	• Songs: *'Tourne, tourne, petit moulin'*, *'Petit escargot'*, *'Les petits poissons'*, *'Renard, renard'*, *'Promenons-nous dans les bois'* • Coloured card, paper, glue, crayons, paint, sand, sugar • Musical instruments

overall topic and the work in the foreign language forms a part of this. In other words, it is not a discrete foreign language topic on wild animals. Rather, activities in a foreign language will be embedded into a broader approach that also involves existing planning for the topic in English.

The following are some typical activities associated with the topic. Many of them can be set up in a foreign language and the teacher can use a number of stories. Many of those mentioned here are available in English as well as French, German or Spanish. It is probably best to use a story in only one language rather than both.

Example short-term lesson plan

For the story *Va-t-en, Grand monstre vert! (Go Away, Big Green Monster!)*

Learning objectives

- To listen attentively and respond to the story *Va-t-en, Grand monstre vert!* (Communication and language)
- To know some parts of the body (Understanding the world)
- To create a collage (face of monster) – explore colour, texture and shape in two dimensions, to manipulate materials (Expressive arts and design)

Lesson outcomes

- Children will join in with story
- Children will place cut-out parts of body (head/face) in the correct places
- Children will make their own 'monster' mask collages

Sequence of activities

Starter

- Warm-up – singing of familiar songs. Children take turns to choose. Teacher asks: *'Qui veut choisir une chanson?'*

Main activities

1. Teacher reads the story *Va-t-en, Grand monstre vert!* for the first time, using mime, gesture, variation of voice, pointing to visuals in the book to support understanding. Invites children to join in with the repetitive phrases *'Partez!'*, *'Va-t'en!'* (supported by gesture).
2. The teacher has an empty head shape on the board and asks the class where the first item (for example, eyes) should be placed. Then volunteers come to place parts of the face in the correct places on the board. Teacher asks questions such as, *'Où est la bouche? Où sont les yeux? Viens et mets la*

bouche sur le visage.' Teacher asks, *'C'est correct?'* to encourage children to join in, evaluate, be involved, even if seated in the group.

3. Half of the members of the group create their own monsters (free choice for others). Teacher models the process and gives instructions in French: *'Tu veux faire un monstre rouge ou orange? Prends les ciseaux. Prends un crayon et écris le nom. Prends la colle et colle le nez sur le visage.'*

End of lesson

Children put on their monster mask collages and show them to each other.

In the lesson plan above, we can see that the teacher uses specific language at specific times and always with a purpose. The children are generally engaged in responding using actions or simple language. An observation of this sequence showed that some children were unsure about where to place the eyes or mouth on a blank face, so they were learning this aspect of knowledge, too, while engaging with this material in the foreign language, so were not just 'doing French'.

The total repertoire of language needed to accomplish this is actually quite small. In the starter activity, it is the stock question, used always in a warm-up where the children will sing. In stages 2 and 3 of the main activity, there is a mix of commonly used classroom phrases – such as 'Where is?', 'Get ...', 'Write your name', 'Stick ...' – together with the vocabulary set for this topic – in this instance, the parts of the head and face. In the story reading section, the book provides the 'script' of course so the teacher does not have to learn all of that language by heart. In between, the teacher might well be using other familiar classroom instructions – such as 'Listen!', 'Sit quietly!', 'All stand up!' – but again this is language familiar to both the teacher and the children.

As we have said before, the children may respond on a number of levels. They may simply nod or shake their heads, echo phrases or speak more spontaneously in the target language. This does not matter because the important issue is whether or not they understand and feel part of what is going on. The teacher should always, of course, look round the group during a story reading. The children's expressions, reactions and general behaviour will reveal whether or not they are engaged. Their comments, often in English, will show that they are understanding. At the end of the *Va-t-en, Grand monstre vert!* sequence, where the monster gradually appears and then gradually disappears, a comment (in English), such as, 'He's gone now', shows that the sense of what has happened in the story has been fully comprehended, partly through pictures, partly through text. The subsequent activity will use individual vocabulary items from that story and underpin the purely language element of the story. The monster masks will again reflect the sense of what the class has been working on. If the children subsequently choose to hear the story again (and they often do), it will be even more meaningful on a second reading precisely because the different linguistic and creative activities have contributed to a richer understanding.

Reflection point

If you are in a position to plan and teach a lesson using a story, use the planning approach above to embed the story into a lesson that has an outcome for the children, such as the monster masks. When you have taught the lesson, make evaluation notes about what the children enjoyed and any issues that arose.

If you are not yet in a position to do this, select a story in the foreign language and make two sets of notes:

- write suggestions for yourself about how you will read it (think of speed, intonation, emotional aspects of your reading, repetition)
- summarise how it might link with other types of work (which could come before or after it).

Chapter summary

In this chapter we have tried to stress the importance of making the foreign language work as part of the overall integrated structure of the EYFS curriculum. We have spoken about how children learn and shown that the children do not easily separate out their experiences into different segments (apart from into enjoyable and less enjoyable categories). We have suggested that children naturally enjoy joining in with songs and stories and this is often the source of much of their learning. They can, however, in some cases, also be remarkably independent in their language use because they do not feel any inhibitions – language is language and is to be used. We have seen examples of children beginning to use the target language when interacting with each other (during role play, when playing with puppets, during everyday routines, such as giving out fruit).

For all these reasons, to make the ML element deliberately 'different' is not really justified. The children themselves speak about their ML experience and integrate it into their wider lives, as we see when we hear comments such as these:

'I love this song. I always sing it in the bath.' (Lizzie, five years)

'Isabella always sings French songs at home and she speaks French to her brother who is in Year 8.' (A mother about her five-year-old daughter)

Another mother reported that her daughter was teaching her younger brother, aged two, songs in French!

'I really like playing with le poisson.' (Owen, five years, showing that languages can be mixed in a way that is similar to what happens with bilingual children, but this is not significant to them – it is a form of playing with language that underpins language learning.)

We have also tried to show, by means of a series of practical examples, how, even with limited language, a teacher can achieve this integration. Teacher vision is needed for the planning and the conceptualisation of integration, in the sense of how to interlock different activities both with each other and with the general ongoing topic, but the demands in the terms of the language are much less than some teachers fear. A good EYFS teacher can be a good ML teacher, too.

We must remember that children of this age have an intriguing blend of 'innocence' – by which we mean the ability to suspend reality and use their imaginations – and 'experience' – by which we mean the ability to see reality as it is. When listening to a group of Reception children talking about how much they liked the crocodile puppet, we asked the question, 'Can Croco speak English?' Daisy (four years old), gave a withering look and replied, 'Well, it's only a puppet. It's the teacher that makes it talk!' We can really enjoy children's creativity and imagination, but we ignore their capabilities and their sophistication at our peril!

Key reading

Below are links to two key government policy documents for the Early Years in the UK (the second is non-statutory).

DfE (2012) 'Statutory Framework for the Early Years Foundation Stage'. Runcorn, Cheshire: DfE. Available online at: www.education.gov.uk/publications/standard/AllPublications/Page1/DFE-00023-2012

Early Education (2012) 'Development matters in the Early Years Foundation Stage (EYFS)'. London: Early Education. Available online at: www.early-education.org.uk/sites/default/files/Development%20Matters%20FINAL%20PRINT%20AMENDED.pdf

An American view on early language learning and its long-term benefits can be found in J.H. Stewart (2005) 'Foreign language study in elementary schools:

Benefits and implications for achievement in reading and math', *Early Childhood Journal*, 33 (1): 11–16.

A Norwegian view on English in the kindergarten can be found in P. Elvin, E. Maagerø and B. Simonsen (2007) 'How do the dinosaurs speak in England? English in kindergarten', *European Early Childhood Education Research Journal*, 15 (1): 71–86.

CHAPTER 4

HOW SHOULD I BEGIN TO OFFER LANGUAGE LEARNING IN KS1 AND KS2?

Chapter objectives

- To explore how we might start to teach a language by reflecting on languages in the community, how languages are learned and how to include aspects of culture from the beginning.
- To suggest appropriate activities for language learning in the first year and to note any differences between ML in KS1 or at the start of KS2.
- To establish throughout the strategies that are likely to make children successful learners of a new language.
- To offer some sample activities.
- To look from a teacher's perspective at how to plan ML into the curriculum.

Teachers' standards			
A teacher must:			
1			Set high expectations which inspire, motivate and challenge pupils
	b		Set goals that stretch and challenge pupils of all backgrounds, abilities and dispositions

(Continued)

(Continued)

2		Promote good progress and outcomes by pupils
	b	be aware of pupils' capabilities and their prior knowledge, and plan teaching to build on these
4		Plan and teach well-structured lessons
	e	contribute to the design and provision of an engaging curriculum within the relevant subject area(s)
5		Adapt teaching to respond to the strengths and needs of all pupils
	d	have a clear understanding of the needs of all pupils, including those with special educational needs; those of high ability; those with English as an additional language; those with disabilities; and be able to use and evaluate distinctive teaching approaches to engage and support them

Source: DfE, 2013a

Introductory vignette

Tristan (eight years old): 'My favourite lesson is maths and my second favourite lesson is French.'

After pausing for a few seconds, Tristan changes his mind: 'No, my third favourite is French, my second favourite is maths and my favourite lesson is maths in French.'

Comment

This comment by a child in the first year of learning French shows that children's enjoyment of learning languages can, from the start, be linked to the wider curriculum. When introducing languages, we should resist the notion that this is a 'separate' subject. While it might be appealing to create an exotic flavour around French, German, Spanish or other language we are offering, this difference can become counterproductive in time. Add-ons are rarely seen as positively as integral components. Rather, like other accessories, they may be discarded or replaced.

   ### Initial reflection point

Consider the following description of a classroom activity. What are the children doing? What are they learning?

A group of Y3 children look at a Spanish website showing schoolbags (for example: www.elcorteingles.es/tienda/papeleria/browse/subcategory_horiz_show

Case.jsp?categoryId=999.511&productId=&navAction=push&navCount=0&men
u=left) or toys (for example: www.ludomecum.com/index.php, choosing 6–8 age
range and clicking the *Tipo de Juguete* button for a dropdown menu, where you
can choose from a range of categories of toys), so that they can say in Spanish
whether or not they like the items and colours. They may also look in more detail
at the layout of the website, discussing what certain links may be and exploring
them to see what is there.

Response

The children may use limited active Spanish while doing this task, but they
will gain in other ways. They will have access to the culture of children of
their own age and discover that they have very similar tastes and interests to
their own, but there are also some differences. By exploring the links, they
will meet some key words in Spanish and use their own knowledge of the
merchandise they see to infer some of the descriptive language. They will
meet vocabulary that interests them and over which they have some control.
Similar websites could be used with Y1 classes, preferably in a whole-class
context, with the teacher guiding the conversation, but the children still managing the choice of links.

How do we start with complete beginners in Y1 or Y3?

We offer here a suggestion for how you might like to manage the first two
lessons.

Language learning should not happen in a vacuum, but should be connected to the class context in as meaningful a way as possible. In cities in
England, children in schools have had access to a number of languages for a
long time and that now applies much more generally to all regions of
England. From current data, available on NALDIC's website (www.naldic.org.
uk/research-and-information/eal-statistics/eal-pupils), we see that, in 2013,
18.1 per cent of all primary-age children have a language other than English
as a first language (up from 7.8 per cent in 1997) and, in London schools,
there are more than 300 languages spoken. The figures for England are substantially higher than those for the rest of the UK.

Although this book has used French, German and Spanish for its examples,
it is very important that we appreciate the languages children already know
and, in some schools, community languages are chosen as the languages all
children learn. As with all learning, we should build on children's existing
knowledge and this includes locating the learning of a language in a context
where languages are real, used and vital. In order to develop an interest in the

culture of other nations, we should acknowledge the interest and insight children might already have gained outside school, from family, culture, religion or holidays. Even in the most common context where a conventional European language is the one chosen for the school, a good starting point for the more general appreciation of the importance of all languages is to carry out a survey of which languages are already spoken in the school.

This visible proof that cultural diversity in school is valued and regarded as a source of learning easily leads to a discussion as to why it is important to learn other languages. From there you may also like to talk to the class about how babies learn language in the first place. By eliciting from the children that *listening* is the key element and babies have to work out what things mean by watching, listening and thinking as well as imitating, the key components of language classroom activity will start to become clear.

Of course this should not be too time-consuming. An abstract discussion, either about the importance of language learning or about how we best learn language, is no substitute for learning some language and enjoying the process. It is still vital, however, to find a way to start children thinking about these very important elements as they begin. Leaving it until later will mean that, in some cases, a restricted view of language learning may be instilled at the start, so later may be too late.

Embedding culture and content into an early lesson plan

One way to achieve a number of these aims from the beginning is to start with a strong cultural focus. This is probably often achieved by means of a geographical theme for a very early lesson. Look at maps, begin to establish where your target language is spoken. Limit the vocabulary, but still use full sentences for comprehension and extensive visual support. For Y1, this would probably just include France, Germany or Spain to begin with, but, with Y3, you could extend this to world language coverage. Satellite images are a very good way of demonstrating this, as their reality often excites children (the glacial deposits in Norway, Iceland and Switzerland usually draw comments). Using Google Earth to find a specific location is a further progression that reinforces for the children the reality of other countries. A progression from the Western hemisphere into Europe to highlight the UK and Spain, but then back out again to show South America and a focus on the number of countries where Spanish is spoken allows the wider importance of the language to emerge for older children. The KS1 and KS2 geography Programmes of Study demand a non-European comparison with the local area for KS1 and a European one for KS2, so, with both French and Spanish, the countries 'zoomed in on' can be appropriate.

You can then move to showing pictures of places from these different countries, but, of course, avoiding stereotypical images (the croissants and castanets phenomenon). Pictures of urban, rural, coastal and inland Spain, for example, already offer contrasts and challenge stereotypes. If you add to that the different landscapes of South America and the urban and rural populations of diverse societies such as Argentina, Peru and Mexico, you have a powerful and exciting montage. Also, depending on whether you are working with Y1 or Y3, you can restrict and expand the number of pictures you show and do this with the satellite images by building on prior knowledge or teaching something new.

This activity needs to be approached sensitively as we are certainly not suggesting you overwhelm the class with too much too quickly. The associated language can be limited to the names of countries and continents (and possibly oceans) in Spanish (which all underpins National Curriculum geography or builds on some prior knowledge), some very simple material, such as using simple description relating to the images, but highlighting adjectives such as *bueno, bello, estupendo, grande, pequeno* and maybe some colours. Those words that you might use to praise the children can be included in both contexts from the start. For a Y3 class, you could introduce some numbers by comparing the time zones and give an opportunity to move from saying *'hablan espanol'* to *'y yo hablo espanol'*. There will also be a range of comments and questions in English, some of which you might be able to respond to at least partly in Spanish.

In these ways, you achieve, at the very beginning of language learning, the cultural link – the fact that language is a vibrant medium by means of which you learn things. As a result of the questioning and very simple commentary, where possible, on the pictures, you will also give a sense of joining in and having fun using the language.

How do we start to use language and teach language? What types of activities and what materials should we use?

A book such as this should not set out to recommend any particular commercial material. We have occasionally referred to the resource pack *A La Française* (Tobutt and Roche, 2007) for examples of activities because it is mainly authored by one of the writers of this book and, therefore, exemplifies our own practice. It is important that children starting a language experience a good variety of material, so all teachers will undoubtedly wish to choose resources that offer stimuli they themselves cannot easily provide. A good example of this is authentic video material and we also referred to the course 'Early Start' in a previous chapter because it centres most units on some material filmed in the country and it is available in French, German and Spanish. The use of such video materials can only enrich language learning and rationalise it for children who perhaps do not actually visit any of the countries where the chosen target language is spoken.

Any resource that offers such video materials should be considered as an option for classroom use and we recommend that teachers seeking commercial resources look for this element above all.

The teacher's own use of language is bound to be a very important factor from the beginning if the classroom is to feel connected to the language and the culture. For that reason, we start the rest of the chapter with the language of routines.

The language of routines

The language of whole-class routines can be established gradually from the beginning. When children need to be brought back together to listen or look during these first lessons, using *'escuchen'* and *'miren'* with appropriate gestures will establish those words quite quickly. We saw in Chapter 3 that the whole structure of the day has potential to be used regularly in the target language, from lining up to go elsewhere at change-points, to giving out fruit (still relevant in Y1 at least), to moving from carpet to tables, to choosing equipment for tasks.

It is important that the children do not simply fall under a completely unstructured blanket of language and we plan how we might introduce each of these activity types. At the earliest stages it is useful (for both the teacher and the children) that the language used is scripted. For less confident teachers, scripting is also a means of being secure that, in the spontaneity of the classroom, you can deliver what is needed at the right speed and with maximum benefit. This is also important for specialist teachers, however, as it will focus you on what you want to use and prevent the children from being exposed to too much language or too many variants on a theme. Fluency can have its drawbacks!

Basic verbs, such as 'listen', 'look', 'read', 'write', 'draw', 'take', 'choose', 'give me', 'show me', as single word items (in Spanish at least) become known quite quickly. Lists are obtainable from sites such as TES Teaching Resources (www.tes.co.uk/teaching-resources) and can be assembled into a wall display for Y3 classes, with the visual and label placed together so that children can quickly check when they hear an instruction, although with non-verbal cues this would rarely be necessary.

Classroom objects to go with these words are often taught as a topic and you can move into referring to these when you tidy up before a lesson starts. Stationery is often not needed in the early stages of learning, but can still be brought into the conversation as most teachers want tables clear of pencils, rulers and rubbers so they will not be a distraction. Your aim is to move towards using only the target language for all areas of organisation and management in language lessons and expand this by having bursts of language time at other points in the week. Morning registration could become Spanish time, for example, or fruit could always be given out using the language. By trying out a couple of new instructions each week and ensuring you maintain the non-verbal support for as long as it is clearly needed, you should comfortably achieve your target language classroom within the first half of the year. If you know you need certain instructions, then you also know that you will use them in a purposeful context. Children are more likely to learn to respond, and in some cases use such phrases, if they actually mean something to them in the reality of classroom life.

Apart from the language of classroom routines, the importance of the children using language for interaction right from the start cannot be overemphasised. Expressions such as *sì/no, me gusta, pasame, por favor, gracias* can begin simply by means of natural repetition, but children need to be able, even with very little language, to react and interact, not just to repeat what they hear, so the teacher should listen for examples of children using language more spontaneously and praise and reward them.

Using a puppet

As with children in Foundation Stage, the introduction of new language using a puppet that only speaks that language is a useful tool. Y3 classes are often still 'young' enough in ethos and imagination to enjoy this, too. Certainly, those who have learned a language in Key Stage 1 are reluctant to give up the puppet as they enter Y3.

The puppet has two distinct functions. As a 'native speaker' of the language, it can introduce new language to the children either directly or by whispering things to the teacher. As a stranger to the school, it might not know things the children and teacher know (for example, all the children's names and ages) or it might not be able to read very well (especially if it is an animal puppet of some kind). A crocodile puppet, for example, probably would not know the names of the fruit even in its own language because it does not eat fruit. When the puppet makes mistakes, the children tend to enjoy correcting it and, of course, they have to do this in the target language because the puppet does not speak English. In the early stages this can generate practice in giving names and ages because the puppet can name the children wrongly and be corrected, either by the child *(me llamo Chloë)* or by another child *(se llama Martin)*. This means that the more mechanistic practice of topic vocabulary, such as eliciting personal information using questions that everyone knows the answer to, is avoided. Because the teacher can have a dialogue with the puppet, he or she can model both questions and answers and can encourage the children to imitate the questions, too. Within this imaginative space, some children will be more willing to speak and they will start to internalise the language because they are using it.

Stories

We have so far indicated the need to limit the amount and kind of language used to what is manageable and not too overwhelming for the children, but an important factor in this is the context in which the language is used. Too many or too complex instructions from the teacher, which can cause anxiety because a response is expected, are likely to have a negative effect on confidence and eventually on motivation. Children are much more likely to manage more challenging text if it comes in the form of a story or song that invites them to listen and either join in as a class by singing or not respond unless they wish to. It is via this kind of material (repetitive stories, songs and rhymes) that children are exposed to rich language and hear or sometimes read more than they can produce. A story can at first engage, stimulating emotion and curiosity, then allow the class to meet new language, then provide a base for further connected but distinct activity within a topic. In this sense, we are mirroring exactly how stories are used in English, especially as part of a topic-based curriculum. Alongside this there is the potential to pre-empt literacy development in the foreign language by means of phonological awareness activities and the following section picks up this theme separately.

One example of easily accessible story and associated activities appropriate for Y1 and Y3 is Eric Carle's (1979) *Veux-tu devenir mon ami?/Die kleine Maus sucht einen Freund* (*Do You Want to Be My Friend?* in English) Other Eric Carle books are equally effective and some are also available in Spanish. In KS1, this story can be used to introduce the names of different animals and children are likely to become involved in the story in two ways. Because of the repetitive pattern, where the little mouse asks other animals *'Veux-tu devenir mon ami?'*, they will naturally start to echo, join in with and at times even lead the chorus as it appears on each new page. They will also meet and begin to remember and say the names of the animals as single word items. Even if the children are not ready to join in with the longer question, the layout of the images allows them to guess which animal is being asked next. This is also a valid experience as only a fraction of the image is seen before you turn the page, so close observation is encouraged. While going through the book, the teacher can also easily use the story to involve the children by asking simple closed questions, such as *'C'est un crocodile? Oui ou Non? C'est un lion?'*, before the full picture is revealed on the next page. At this point, the animal is named again, but in a meaningful sentence as part of the ongoing story. In this case, the text is, *'Le lion dit "non, merci".'*, which is fully comprehensible and will generate further repetition and probably some imitation outside the context. It is very useful that the children can focus on individual words at some points but not lose the overall flow that this is a story, so it also has a value apart from the learning of some words in French.

After a couple of readings, follow-up activities in KS1 could include the sequencing of the story. The children could place cut out mini cards with pictures of the animals in the correct order while the teacher retells the story. Later in the year, this task can also be used by confident children who might wish to retell the story in very simple language, using the cards as a prop.

An example of a follow-on task, drawing on the same theme, is to use the animals that the children have met in the story and for groups to place them in the correct habitat. If this is done at first visually, the teacher can use the language items as part of a collaborative review and so move the vocabulary base to other areas of the animals topic. The fact that the children have made choices about where the animals should go means they will want to know if they are right. If the way to find this out is to access the foreign language vocabulary for these habitats by hearing the words along with non-verbal and visual support from the teacher, they will willingly participate, as long as the process is active, lively and comprehensible. So the teacher can ask, while showing the appropriate visuals, *'Le lion habite dans le désert ou à la savane? Dans le désert, oui?'* to elicit *'Non, à la savane.'* This process causes children to hear new words, process them and think of a response, but in a completely unambiguous context. If they have placed the animal correctly, they will hear the right word and repeat it very happily. If not, they will focus more on content and learn the correct habitat. This is entirely proper as we should not be teaching vocabulary without the concepts being established at the same time. This method can do both these things almost simultaneously.

If the same story is used in KS2, the activities given above could still be used if this happens early in the year. With a Y3 class, there might be a greater emphasis on introducing the written word to support the children's literacy development in the new language. You could focus on the 'i' phoneme in French, first discriminating the sound and identifying it in words such as *ami, crocodile, lion, souris, petite* before making the phoneme/grapheme connection. If we want children to be able to access language independently, we need to make them aware of the different phonetic system that will enable them to decode new words and also develop their ability to encode with increasing independence.

The story can also be used as an introduction to classifying animals into herbivores, carnivores and omnivores, explaining what different animals eat. Again, the teacher would need to exemplify this sorting process, using the appropriate language and using extensive closed and then open questions to fix the vocabulary by means of natural rather than forced repetition. From here, if this material is used later in Y3, the children can use short texts that the teacher might find giving information about the animals, their habitats and their diet.

Songs

Children of all ages in the primary phase seem to enjoy singing as long as the choice of songs is made with an eye to their age, interests and 'maturity'.

With Y1 and Y3 children, the important issue is to choose age-appropriate songs that have a real origin in the cultures of the countries concerned. While it can be a useful learning aid to sing language items to the tune of well-known English soap themes or, for that matter, to the tune of 'Frère Jacques', it is far better to offer them a song that has a story, uses rhythms they respond to or has accompanying actions. Song words can seem very complex, but children can absorb messages and sing with enjoyment without having each of the words in their active vocabulary. It is important that they do not just sing with no understanding, of course, and this is where modern DVDs can be very supportive. For example, *Mon Âne* (Le Notre, 1999) is a very popular French resource, which uses animations to reveal the gist of the songs. One Y6 pupil was quite shocked at the 'cruelty' in 'Alouette', for example. She still enjoyed singing it and, importantly, was able to draw out key words without needing an exact translation – the key message had certainly been understood!

For Y1 children, the very simple songs that were described in Chapter 3 are still relevant and it is just as important in both year groups that children are given a chance to choose which song they want to sing. Something very simple, such as 'Tourne, tourne petit moulin' for French (words and tune obtainable from the French language Momes website at: www.momes.net/comptines/comptines-chansons.html) is popular with younger learners because they can perform it confidently after a few practice sessions and it feels good to them not to be 'on the spot' but feel able to sing with the class and enjoy joining in. There are many other websites offering a range of songs, including for German (http://ingeb.org/kinderli.html) and Spanish (http://pacomova.eresmas.net/paginas/canciones_infantiles.htm), though the latter is perhaps more suitable for Y1 as there is a link to some songs with video performances on this site.

In the first year of learning, it is nearly always worth using actions with songs because it appears that, for many children, melody and movement really do facilitate and consolidate learning (Davies, 2000). The power of music for memory is easily demonstrated. Children sometimes need a push at the start of a song, but if the teacher sings the first line or just the first word, they can often take it from there and complete it independently.

Y1 language lessons, especially, benefit from a song as a warm-up, to establish that we are now using the target language as much as possible, or as a change activity for a few minutes in the middle or as a satisfying whole-class way of ending a lesson. Each of these is a valid use of time, helping to promote all of the positive attributes of learning a language and features of the KS2 curriculum, such as: participation, active engagement of memory and focus, active use of the language, collaboration with others, an intercultural dimension and enjoyment.

Phonological awareness activities linked to stories and songs

Developing phonological awareness in the foreign language is mentioned in the KS2 Programmes of Study, but this can easily be introduced earlier, such as in Y1, especially as now all children are experiencing phonics on a daily basis between the ages of three and seven.

As a language teacher, you can create your own version of phoneme displays as part of the learning environment. The flower pattern is especially useful as you can site the grapheme representing a particular phoneme in the centre of, say, a daisy shape, then add words containing that grapheme as petals around the outside. For this to happen the teacher needs to structure lessons that centre on particular phonemes and their grapheme equivalents. In such a lesson, the teacher will choose one phoneme that appears in a story or a song. First, the children will carry out discrimination activities, such as repeating the words that contain the phoneme in focus. They can then see the phoneme as a grapheme and identify words from the story that contain that grapheme. Finally, they will read independently new words that contain the phoneme/grapheme. Because this is an ongoing process, the children's attention can be called to it regularly by using the phoneme classroom display and this helps gradually to fix the concepts in their minds.

As we showed in Chapter 2, we can access other materials designed for literacy development in English. The earliest stage of 'Letters and sounds' (DfES, 2007b), the synthetic phonics pack, was dedicated to the development of phonological awareness with a whole range of suggested activities, as listed below, in the 'Letters and sounds' guidance document (available online at: www.gov.uk/government/uploads/system/uploads/attachment_data/file/190599/Letters_and_Sounds_-_DFES-00281-2007.pdf):

- join in with repeated refrains and anticipate key events and phrases in rhymes and stories
- listen to others one-to-one or in small groups when conversation interests them
- build up vocabulary that reflects the breadth of their experiences
- use a widening range of words to express or elaborate on ideas
- use talk to connect ideas, explain what is happening and anticipate what might happen next
- enjoy rhyming and rhythmic activities
- show awareness of rhyme and alliteration
- recognise rhythm in spoken words
- listen to and join in with stories and poems, one-to-one and in small groups
- begin to be aware of the way stories are structured

- show interest in books and print in the environment
- enjoy joining in with dancing and ring games
- sing a few familiar songs
- sing to themselves and make up simple songs
- tap out simple repeated rhythms and make some up
- explore and learn how sounds can be changed
- imitate and create movement in response to music
- engage in imaginative play and role play based on own first-hand experiences.

Clearly most of these activities (items two to five are less appropriate at this early stage of language learning) are also suitable for foreign language classes at Y1 and still at Y3 level. They can be linked to a song or a story very easily with joining in a very natural occurrence and rhyme and rhythm being picked out for special focus on some readings or 'singings'. The noticing of sounds in the target language absolutely underpins phonic skills for English as well, as it is the noticing process that is so important to establish. For most children in Y1 and even more in Y3, this noticing will be well established and the skill will be applied readily to the new sounds, but this is another example of where children with language development issues can only benefit from such a fresh and added opportunity to take part in a phonic discrimination activity in a non-threatening, collaborative, socially and academically equal context. The fact that there are some *new* sounds also highlights for all children the differences from known sounds and, therefore, consolidates those known sounds in English at the same time. The more independent stage of singing individually or as a group will also demonstrate some mastery of pronunciation, intonation, rhythm and fluency and will be carried out by some children before others. Even this, however, is not necessarily determined by ability, but can be as much linked with enjoyment of music, a capacity for using an ear for sounds and personality.

Games

Children in Y1 and Y3 clearly greatly enjoy playing games. The potential in language lessons is almost limitless, although, of course, we cannot use anything in the earliest stages that depends on the children using a lot of language. We have mentioned several times the desirability of avoiding parrot-style repetition, even if we dress it up with elements such as repetition with different emotions or in different voices. In certain circumstances, however, this can be beneficial and, as with all approaches, if a teacher perceives value for the children in using a particular method, then he or she should try it. For example, if a particularly difficult word has come up that the children in the class can see they are having problems with, then asking them to repeat it six times as a deliberate device to fix it in their minds and as a special method because it is difficult is often successful. Something you might need regularly, such as *¡Feliz cumpleanos!* or, in German, *Herzlichen Glückwunsch (zum Geburtstag)*, can be usefully repeated as a game when first encountered. The best technique here is to ask for six repetitions that become quieter with each one, ending in a whisper. The reverse is not to be recommended!

On a similar theme and undoubtedly popular is a repetition game in which the class has to repeat the word after the teacher, if the teacher has said the correct word. The teacher may point to a visual and name it correctly, in which case all the children should repeat it and, since this is easy, there are no points available for doing it! If, however, the teacher says the wrong word, everyone in the class must be silent. If they are, they gain a point, but if even one person repeats the wrong item, the *teacher* gains a point. The first to five points wins – it is usually the class!

Hiding or finding games are also popular with these younger children. This might be an image within a set (the well-known secondary game with flashcards held to the teacher's chest) or it might be an object in the classroom. Of course, further up the school the 20 questions format can be used as, by then, the children will have the vocabulary they need, but, in the beginner groups in Y1 and Y3, it is more likely to be a single object. This may be something among other objects, such as stationery on the teacher's desk, which is located by the use of simple questions such as, *'Ist es ein Bleistift?'*, *'Ist es ein Gummi?'*, *'Ist es blau?'* If it is something actually hidden, then the limited set questions might be, *'Ist es in einer Tasche?'*, *'Ist es unter einem Tisch?'*, *'Ist es in einer Hand?'* together with *'Ist es hier?'* (referring to a section of the classroom).

All normal guessing games are possible in the target language and usually need no materials. They can sometimes be planned in for specific reasons or can be used spontaneously, rather as we said with songs, because the teacher feels a game would be a healthy way to bring the class together and inject a short change activity into the middle of a lesson. They can also be used as a filler in non-language time, such as just before home time, giving children more exposure to the target language.

One way to consolidate a group of vocabulary items at an early stage is to play *Je pense à (une couleur)* / *Ich denke an (eine Farbe)* / *Penso en (un color)*. Although this game is normally started by the teacher (and we explored the competitive aspects of that in Chapter 2), we have noticed how keen some children are to volunteer to lead as they enjoy having a brief moment as the teacher. They can often manage turntaking very well and this allows you to observe who is really contributing and if any members of the class are less motivated or less secure in the language.

When children can read, chain games are also popular. These work by each class member having a card with one answer and one unrelated question on it. When they hear a question that they think they have the answer for, they stand up and read it out. That child then asks the question on his or her card to keep the chain going.

In Y3, an aural discrimination game that has very good potential for progression is the simple idea of a team game in which children have a word to listen for (stimulated either by the word on a card or a picture of the item if appropriate). Each team will receive the same set of cards so that, when the teacher says the word, the first of the two children who has the item must stand up and say it. This means all members of the class are involved as they have to listen carefully to each new item. The game can be moved on to include the word plus an adjective, such as colours, so now two on each team might have the same noun, but a different adjective, meaning concentration is even more important. It can also be moved on further still to sentence level, so the word needed must be heard within a longer flow of language.

A version of battleships that it is certainly possible to play with Y3 and perhaps later in Y1 uses a grid with squares labelled with objects rather than letters and numbers. Figure 4.1 gives an example that combines shapes and colours. The children play in pairs and each 'hides' an object in one square and then they take it in turns to call out a 'grid reference'. The first to find the object wins the game.

Figure 4.1 Grid for a version of 'battleships'

Beginning to link – working with art and mathematics

When the children are showing an initial confidence with the language of instructions, it will be worth trying to achieve a greater impact in their own eyes by taking them through a whole process in the foreign language to achieve a completely non-linguistic outcome. This might happen early in the year if you, as a teacher, are determined to make it work or it might be left until later if it seems more daunting.

If we imagine an art project with a collage as an outcome and a process involving choosing equipment, following steps and creating a finished work, we can see that there will be a series of short instructions, such as the following, needed to achieve it.

Prends le papier et les couleurs.

Colorie le papier.

Prends les ciseaux.

Découpe des formes droites et arrondies.

Avec toutes les formes, fais ta composition.

Prends la colle. Colle les formes sur le papier.

Et voilà, c'est fini! (*A La Française*, Matisse material, Tobutt and Roche, 2007)

This set of instructions needs to remain in the correct order and, with a Y1 class, the teacher would certainly use them with the class step by step, using realia at each stage so that the children *hear* the foreign language, but follow *visually*.

A great deal of natural repetition occurs when teachers give these sorts of instructions as children always operate at different paces, so the class will have a lot of opportunities to hear some key words, such as *prends, le papier, les couleurs, les ciseaux, la colle*. These words do not need to be pretaught as they will be known receptively by the end of this process. With Y3, it is possible to go further towards making the class more independent and a good way to use these instructions is on separate cut-up slips, asking groups to establish the order before they start to make the collage. In either case, children will have a completed collage at the end, which they will have made with no use of English for the instructions.

Art is often used for early cross-curricular work because it tends to involve receptive language, as we saw in the example above, but many teachers also use short maths tasks because they can be quick to set up and carry out (this builds on the notion of oral and mental starters at the beginning of the daily mathematics lesson, where the foreign language work can be easily located). Because maths is number based, it is also more language-free than some other subjects. Children can see the figures on the whiteboard and can calculate, without language, then retrieve the language for their response. Of course, larger numbers are difficult in most languages, so teachers need to be careful, especially at Y1 level, about what they attempt to do. Number bonds to 20 are still worth practising in Key Stage 1, however, and calculations that have an answer in the range from 1 to 20 could still be sufficiently challenging for Y3, especially if they centre on multiplication and division facts around the times tables set for that year group. Examples of such calculations might be $45 \div 3 = ?$, $? \times 4 = 48$, $36 \div 6 = ?$, $? + 82 = 100$. Each of the missing elements that the class must supply is still in the range from 1 to 20 and the teacher can talk through each calculation, asking for the missing number as he or she goes. In this way, especially if worked on quite regularly, the class will also learn larger numbers by hearing them and finding patterns. The Y3 mathematics objectives also include material on 2D shapes and, again, this is a good mini-topic for a foreign language.

Knowledge about language

Evidently there are differences between the capabilities and understanding of children in KS1 and lower KS2. Although children should be exposed to written language in KS1, ML lessons should concentrate on developing phonological awareness, as we showed earlier, introducing and identifying phonemes and so not really looking in detail at any grammatical elements of language. Writing can be given as an extension task, rather than as a norm for all children, and correction should certainly be avoided when children do write in the foreign language because they will still be at the emergent writing stage, perhaps even in Y3. Sometimes children will ask about language elements that they notice and this might include gender indicators, such as adjectives agreeing with nouns. There is no reason why a question should not be answered, but, in the first year, there is little reason to build lessons around grammatical points.

The new National Curriculum has a single bullet in the KS2 Programmes of Study about grammar, but the Knowledge about language strand in the former KS2 Framework (DfES, 2005) indicated certain themes (mainly addressing sound/graphic correspondence) and cross-referenced them to the main objectives within Oracy, Literacy and Intercultural understanding. See Chapter 7 for a full discussion of how to use the new National Curriculum alongside the former KS2 Framework. In other words, particularly for Y3, overt grammar should not be encouraged. That said, one of the reasons behind ensuring that children hear full sentences from the beginning is that they are exposed to the major word classes in context well before they begin to examine or discuss them.

Example topic: La Réunion

The full presentational material referred to here is available in the *A La Française* pack (Tobutt and Roche, 2007) and consists of a starter PowerPoint presentation that can be used with either Y1 or Y3, although, of course, any follow-up activity after that will be different.

The slides show a series of scenes from La Réunion, a French-speaking island in the Indian Ocean. They are intended to support the class topic, islands, which often focuses on islands in the UK, using the Katie Morag stories by Mairi Hedderwick both as a literacy starter and an organiser for the topic as it has a strong geography content. The purpose of the initial slides is to identify a possible hiding place for a butterfly, which is finally located

behind a flower. The question, *'Où est le papillon?'* and the follow-up suggestions, *'A la plage? Dans la mer? Dans le volcan? Dans la maison? A la
montagne?'*, establishes this key vocabulary in the course of the natural repetition by the teacher. As he or she puts the question to different children
(who may have different opinions), there is a chance for those children who
wish to speak to join in and use the vocabulary as part of this dialogue.

The presentation also includes a map of the island, drawn by a primary-age
child who lives there. At this point, the children can take cards containing pho-
tos of the scenes shown on the slides and bring them to the board to place in
the correct location on the map. For Y1 children, this represents a reinforcement
of their map skills, which the general topic is developing in English elsewhere
in the week. By choosing the correct card in response to the question, *'Où est
la plage?'* and placing it somewhere on the edge of the island where land meets
sea, they show that they have recognised the French word for 'beach' and know
a map showing an island is laid out as a view from above, with the sea surrounding the island and beaches at the point where land meets sea. Similarly, if
they place the volcano picture at the point on the map in the area to the east
of the centre of the island where there is shading to show higher ground, they
are again demonstrating a recognition of some geographical features.

Often in KS1 there are comparisons made between a remote and a more
familiar location and this activity also allows the landscape of La Réunion to
be compared with that of the UK or even with their own local environment.
The children could certainly draw their own maps of the island and label key
features and, as an extension, they could write a sentence about its location.

A poem about the carnival written by H. Jamy for children is available at:
www.ile-reunion.org/guetali/poeme/poeme.htm Visit the website and read
the poem before reading the next section.

With any such material, which may be pitched above the level of children
at individual word level, reading in pairs is usually a popular and successful
activity. If the children are given a more global task of finding out some
information and noticing elements of interest, they are motivated by the challenge and the fact that the task is open-ended rather than tightly prescribed
or quantified, so does not run a risk of failure. This is a good example of how
you can move beyond the narrowly defined topics, such as numbers, colours
or family, and into a context of real language use and real communication.
The message it gives – that we will rarely know it all, but we can certainly
work out some of it if we try – is vital in setting an early expectation of what
learning a language is really like.

Y1 children will not be able to cope with reading at this level, of course,
though they might enjoy hearing the carnival poems read, especially with
accompanying pictures. They can, however, undertake more practical and
less language-rich tasks, such as making masks and then using them for an
authentic dance. This still involves receptive language as, similar to the collage activity introduced above, the teacher needs to give instructions for the

design and technology activity in the foreign language, encourage the children to name their choice of materials using colour, material, shape, then teach the dance.

At both levels some work can also involve climate and weather. The Meteoconsult website (at: www.meteoconsult.com) is a very useful resource for French, Italian and Spanish (as you can select your language) and is best used on an interactive whiteboard as it gives detailed live forecasts for all parts of the world (select *'monde'*, if using the French service, then choose the continent and then the country) and for the next few days. La Réunion can be located within the site (via Africa).

Talking only about different weather and climates is a little limited, so teachers can look for opportunities to link the idea of more extreme weather, such as tropical storms, in music and drama activities, as well as pictures and video, if available. Again, in the first year of learning, some material in English that genuinely gives an insight into a different culture is still worthwhile from time to time.

Chapter summary

This chapter has attempted to describe and rationalise the range of activity teachers may wish to include in the first year of learning for either Y1 or Y3. It has shown that, from the beginning, we can offer children a whole-language experience, exploring richness of both culture and language where possible, but still with an emphasis on making the experience both enjoyable and non-threatening.

We have indicated that the children may be using the language in only very specific, manageable scenarios, while meeting a much broader range from the teacher and from commercial and online resources. We have recommended extensive use of texts and songs to ensure that this happens with the least pressure on non-specialist teachers. We have given examples of games. We have looked at the early development of literacy in the foreign language and at beginnings of linking with other subjects.

Key reading

The Early Language Learning in Europe (ELLIE) project produced a book chapter summary of its findings on six- to eight-year-old learners. It is available online at: www.ellieresearch.eu/docs/Szpotowicz_MihaljevicDjigunovic_Enever_Ch16.pdf

A document produced for the USA regarding EAL speakers in mainstream schooling has some interesting points about language learning in general. It gives a good view of the need for language learners to experience some form of immersion in the language. It can be downloaded from: http://fcd-us.org/sites/default/files/MythsOfTeachingELLsEspinosa.pdf

CHAPTER 5

WHERE TO NEXT? HOW CAN I EMBED LANGUAGE INTO THE SCHOOL DAY AND THE WIDER CURRICULUM?

Chapter objectives

- To consider briefly what psychology research says about the relative roles of ability and aptitude, motivation, attitudes, task setting and learning styles.
- To address the issues of differentiation and personalisation.
- To explore a range of different aspects of progression through examples from practice from both KS1 and KS2.
- To explore a model of progression through four levels of cross-curricular integration.

Teachers' standards		
A teacher must:		
1		Set high expectations which inspire, motivate and challenge pupils
	b	set goals that stretch and challenge pupils of all backgrounds, abilities and dispositions
4		Plan and teach well-structured lessons

(Continued)

(Continued)

		contribute to the design and provision of an engaging curriculum within the relevant subject area(s)
	e	contribute to the design and provision of an engaging curriculum within the relevant subject area(s)
5		Adapt teaching to respond to the strengths and needs of all pupils
	a	know when and how to differentiate appropriately, using approaches which enable pupils to be taught effectively
	d	have a clear understanding of the needs of all pupils, including those with special educational needs; those of high ability; those with English as an additional language; those with disabilities; and be able to use and evaluate distinctive teaching approaches to engage and support them

Source: DfE, 2013a

Introductory vignette

Two children in Y4 are learning about the Vikings in French. They practise offering each other a range of artefacts (photographs on card) as part of a bartering dialogue. After a couple of turns they begin again and one child decides she wants a sword – she has a malevolent intention!

A: *Tu voudrais un verre?*

B: *Non.*

A: *Tu voudrais une peigne?*

B: *Non merci!*

A: *Tu voudrais une épée?*

B: *Oui, oui.* (Takes the picture of a sword.) *Attaquez!*

The previous two chapters have each approached how to start language learning at particular points in a school and have aimed to provide an initial focus for a new teacher or for a school languages coordinator when starting to organise the teaching. From the beginning, however, it is important to see also where the subject should be heading. A clear and shared vision for the whole of the school's present and future language provision will considerably enhance that initial teaching.

This chapter looks at how initial progression might be viewed, while Chapter 6 deals with the aspirations a school might have for language learning at the end of KS2.

Initial reflection point

In a topic-based syllabus, especially one created by the teacher to fit with the needs of the class, there is a danger that progression will be limited. Each topic tends to start at the beginning with new vocabulary and structures and be practised in isolation from other previous topics. Published schemes of work – for example, the former QCA ones (2007) or the Catherine Cheater scheme (2006) – have addressed this issue to some extent.

What is your view on progression? Do you feel that children only need to do different topics across the four years because primary ML is about building a base for KS3 or do you feel that the language classroom in Y6 should be very different from the Y3 classroom? If so, how?

Does progression mean the same for all children?

Primary teachers are fortunate in that they see children across the week and across different subject and skill areas. Thus, they gain a comprehensive view of a child's complex personality and do not just see the child in a limited role. Secondary teachers are perhaps not as lucky as they may view a class and its children from a perspective that is determined by a time of the day or an influence from another lesson or teacher or by the fact that they teach the child a single subject. For this reason, personalisation (rather than whole-class differentiation into, say, three levels of work) is perhaps easier for a primary teacher than for a secondary colleague to visualise (although, of course, no less time-consuming to put into practice!).

This chapter will address ways to personalise and differentiate in its second section, but we need to be clear at the start about how we establish the criteria for any division into levels of work that we make.

Ability

When devising groups for literacy and mathematics work, good primary teachers currently balance the notion of an 'ability level' with other aspects, such as confidence, a need for support from an assistant, a preferred approach – visual or hands-on, for example – or a social special need. Perceived ability is probably still the major factor, but our understanding of what that means now includes other aspects. For example, in his review of individual differences and language learning, Dörnyei (2006: 42) notes that there are five major domains of these differences: 'personality, aptitude, motivation, learning styles and learning strategies'.

The phrase 'readiness to learn' is commonly heard in the UK context, often from the children themselves who are asked by teachers if they are ready to learn. There is a difference between this and the 'phase readiness' referred to by policy makers when they urge schools to make children 'ready for school' at age 4 or 'secondary-ready' at age 11. Each child needs to be ready to learn during each day at school, but the onus is also on the teacher to design a pedagogy that is suited to the child's particular *form* of readiness. It is this quality of readiness, stimulated by a teacher's use of approaches and resources to engage that counts, rather than simply the child's ability, as we will try to show.

Progression can be tied in to grouping in so far as teachers may provide different materials or even programmes for different groups. The previous government's document 'Grouping pupils for success' (DfES, 2006) itself offered a range of models and rationales. Some writers promote the use of full mixed-ability rather than ability-based groupings on the grounds that all children learn best when they are able to articulate their understanding and scaffold each other's learning by collaboration, while others support this approach more from a social justice perspective.

Ireson and Hallam (1999) challenge ability grouping in the form of sets or bands on a number of counts (including reinforcement of low expectation, unreliability of allocation, effect on self-esteem) and suggest that schools might like to look at different criteria for grouping at different times and for different needs. The 'learning without limits' group (Swann et al., 2012) created a powerful argument for not grouping and not labelling children and, in their case study school, The Wroxham School in Hertfordshire, conventional differentiation has been rejected in favour of levels of challenge that children select for themselves. Nevertheless, it is still common in many primary schools that have a two-form entry or bigger to 'band' for literacy and mathematics and then divide into ability groups within those banded classes.

Learning styles and ability

In the second section of this chapter and in the practice examples we will try to illustrate how learning styles might play a part in securing progression in different ways.

There has been a great deal of attention paid to the notion of learning styles in recent years and many teachers mention aspects of visual, auditory and kinaesthetic input/activity (VAK) or multiple intelligences (MI) theory (Gardner, 1985) if they speak about their approach to planning. We should remember, however, that neither VAK nor MI has any proven status in terms of the most recent neuroscientific knowledge.

Writers such as Sternberg (1997) or Riding and Rayner (1998) have explored learning styles in more detail, although a critique of this entire literature was supplied by Coffield et al. (2004). Techniques such as accelerated learning (Smith and Call, 1999) have been popular subjects for school INSET programmes, but the whole debate proves that it is now more difficult to determine why a child should be grouped with others and what the nature of 'ability' really is.

In terms of language learning, ability is a difficult concept. What was earlier called 'language aptitude' is now seen as a linked set of different factors (Robinson, 2002; Skehan, 2002) rather than a single quality that an individual has or has not. Research has shown that learners' actual performance level can vary and be determined by a whole range of elements (and often by these in interaction). For these reasons, we want to give a brief overview here of some aspects of the possible role of motivation and effort, attitudes to ability and task demands.

Motivation and associated elements

Tremblay et al. (2000) showed in a study on young adults that aptitude or ability was only one factor that determined achievement. They also found that motivation and effort, the attitude towards the teacher and subject and anxiety were all significant factors. These other aspects, of course, can be linked, so motivation will be greater if the attitude towards the teacher or subject is positive. While that may seem like common sense, it is important to note these other elements have been shown empirically to impact performance as well as motivation because this means it is even more an issue teachers should heed.

Lepine et al. (2004) looked at the interaction between what they termed 'stress' and performance among a young adult group and established stress in the form of 'challenge' could produce a positive effect that enhanced performance, whereas what they called 'hindrance stress' impacted negatively. So, it is important when we consider progression that we plan to both support children and offer the right amount of challenge and in the right way.

Cury et al. (2006), building on Dweck (2000), identified the importance of entity and incremental views of ability (in other words, whether or not learners think they have any control over their own ability levels and so can affect their own performance, which is the incremental view, or not, which is the entity view). They found that mastery goals (part of a more personalised and self-developing motivational structure that led to continuous individual development, irrespective of others) were associated with the incremental view and performance goals (those related to doing well against other members of the class) were associated with the entity view. An entity view, unsurprisingly, was less likely to generate a high level of intrinsic motivation. In her recent work, Dweck (2007, 2013) has used the term 'mindset' to explain these theories and this is now commonly used by teachers in schools. In Chapter 8, we will look at formative assessment for learning techniques that are associated with personalised mastery structures.

Teachers sometimes comment that a very bright child who has excelled at the more 'predictable' tasks offered in a subject can become anxious very quickly if the work becomes more investigative, more open-ended and, therefore, less predictable. Just as a child with learning difficulties can become acclimatised to failure and not believe he or she has the chance to improve, so an able child can become acclimatised to success, but only of a certain kind. That child may not be able to cope with a different and/or more demanding level of work, not because he or she has less ability, but because his or her self-belief is posited on being able to succeed without a real challenge. Clearly, this gives us the message that we should find ways to show all learners that they can act to affect their performance and achievement and we should not just talk about it, but prove it to them in concrete ways.

Children's existing views are difficult to change, but one of the positives about the fact that, no matter how well we integrate language learning, children still often see it as a little different, is we can set out a new classroom landscape when using the target language where established hierarchies and beliefs about ability are not as valid. If shown consistently that they can achieve, children will believe more readily that this is in their own realm of control. Once again, this underpins the need for teachers to consider more than ability when deciding what the individuals and the classes in front of them are capable of.

Motivation and how we generate this is clearly crucial. Dörnyei's very extensive work on motivation in language learning (for example, Guilloteaux and Dörnyei, 2008; Dörnyei and Ushioda, 2011; Hadfield and Dörnyei, 2013) has shown consistently that motivation is a vital component of success in language learning. It has personal, contextually situated and temporal aspects and is certainly not a fixed or single entity. Along with Gardner (1985), he identifies what is known as the integrative aspect of motivation as being crucial to language learners. This means they identify with a community (target language speaking) into which they wish to integrate and has been shown to be more predictive of language learning success than a more instrumental focus (for example, learning to get a job or impress one's parents). Again, we see here the importance of incorporating culture as an active and meaningful part of the programme, planning for it to permeate our materials and not be seen as an occasional add-on, because the culture that enters the classroom is, of course, more constant as an influence than the culture lying overseas. The culture of the classroom is equally important – joining in with that is also a part of the integrative motivation spectrum.

In a book on motivational strategies (Dörnyei and Ushioda, 2011), Dörnyei addressed at length the importance of generating initial motivation and then maintaining and protecting it. Much of this is a summary of good practice for working in classrooms, but he stresses the importance of clear goal-setting and success criteria, demonstrating genuine commitment to the subject and to the learners, making material relevant but also interesting (for example, via the intercultural dimension), varying the task styles and lesson structure, being aware of potential causes of anxiety and acting to lower or remove them from the programme, increasing both collaboration and independence while promoting higher self-esteem through success and opportunities to work actively and with confidence. He also included in this the notion that, with the use of learning strategies modelled by teachers, children could rise above their apparent 'ability' and learn better. It is clear that an enhanced ability to call on strategies will engender greater success, greater motivation and, hence, positively affect readiness to learn.

Writers on primary language learning will vary in what they think needs to be done to achieve the commonsense goals included here. Some will argue that caution is the way to not lose children from the learning process and enjoyment should always be highlighted, while others might say progression that is too slow will be equally problematic. To make sense of this, we need now to look at personalisation and differentiation techniques from a practical point of view.

How should I approach planning differentiated or personalised lessons?

In the first section of this chapter, we considered a range of elements that might prompt planning to include different levels of work available in a teacher-targeted or open-choice approach. Clearly, no teacher can think of *all* of these elements when planning differentiated work for a class.

A personalised approach is, in some ways, easier to plan for, as teachers who know a class well will be able to visualise how the whole class might react to certain stimulus materials and activities and how certain groups of children will be able to collaborate to enjoy and perform on different types of tasks. Certain individual children will come to mind because they need something a little different and this might involve suggesting a certain role within a group task to ensure they can succeed, the allocation of a teaching assistant to support them or even, on some occasions, offering something more individual.

The conventional models of differentiation are that the teacher should consider modifications of task, text, support and content interest. There is a danger, in the common planning structure with three-level learning outcomes of 'all will', 'most will', 'some will', that teaching can become too rigidly forced into having three different degrees of expectation and children will be channelled only into certain types or levels of achievement.

The rest of this chapter looks at concrete ways in which we can build progression into the second year of learning and is written to be supportive also of non-specialist teachers who feel less confident about moving on.

Progression in target language use by the teacher: embedding the language further into routines

Whether we are working with Y1/2 or Y4, a progression into a second year of language learning should feel like a move forward to the children. As we have indicated in the first part of this chapter, there will be more of a need to differentiate and personalise the further we progress – this is entirely normal – but, as we have shown, this does not need to come down to three different strands of work that are rigidly enforced.

We should find, as we move on from year to year, that more and more complex school and classroom routine language is used, but, of course, the earlier, more straightforward language will still be in use as well, thus offering completely natural repetition and reinforcement to all children. Because instructional language so often requires pure comprehension and a non-verbal response rather than one that demands target language use (which may generate anxiety), there is less pressure on less able linguists. In many instances, they will see the response, in terms of actions, from peers and will be able to follow it. The natural repetition will, over time, enable them to begin to respond automatically and personally to the instruction that will become familiar.

We should remember that this progression is sometimes daunting for the non-specialist teacher as well, so the examples given below are also intended to offer scaffolding for this eventuality. What we should be aware of is that the dialogue of the classroom offers countless opportunities to enrich the language experience – this may come spontaneously or may be semi-scripted. If a teacher simply thinks of possible events and prepares a few simple 'follow-up lines', they will be ready when needed.

Using the target language in bigger chunks

Some of the 'extra' language will come in the form of aggregation – that is, several familiar elements may be combined. For example, in the early stages of learning, you may give separate instructions to get up, go and get coats on and line up ready for playtime, lunch or home time. You may wait for each task to be completed and say the instruction several times in the target language, using mime to accompany it. In the earliest stages, the mime is so clear that you are actually teaching the language by using it, but, gradually, you will be able to stop using so much mime, yet still say the different instructions separately and generally keep them simple.

> *Levez-vous!* (Mime get up, by raising both hands, palms up.) *Bon, Chloë, Bon Viktor. Levez-vous! Levez-vous, Isaac et Molly!*

> *OK, maintenant, les manteaux! Mettez les manteaux!* (Mime putting on coat.) *Mettez-vous en file ici! Paul, Daniel, ici s'il vous plait! En file tous!*

By the second year of learning, you should be able to build on the familiarity of such routines by giving such a set of instructions together and weaving in more personalised comments when needed. This does not need to be done at speed and there can be repetition where needed, of course, but the class in general should be able to absorb the global message and act accordingly. After all, the children do know the routine – you are merely prompting it in the target language.

> OK, c'est maintenant la recréation. Alors, levez-vous vous tous, allez mettre les manteaux et après ça, mettez-vous en file devant la porte ici. Paul, tu as un manteau? Il fait froid aujourd'hui, n'est-ce pas? Timea, ne parle pas – tu peux parler avec Amy dans la cour – mets ton manteau, s'il te plait!

Building up the target language from the very simple to a more natural expression

Some early instructions that were pared down to a very basic level can ease towards more natural target language use and, in this way, the language of the classroom will gradually progress towards a richer experience. Again, these are often instructions that will be used very regularly, so the progression we are suggesting can happen gradually and be very well internalised. An example might be setting up some written work.

> Ici le titre – copiez! Ici la date – copiez! Soulignez le titre! Soulignez la date! (Here the teacher would point at the items and mime the action of underlining.)

We can see from this example that, in the early stages, the language used would be very clear because it is either visually prompted or close to English or both. If used at this level too much, the children may not actually internalise the language at all because they follow without thinking. If it becomes part of a more natural flow, however, this changes.

> OK comme toujours, il faut écrire le titre et la date – ils sont ici et vous pouvez copier. N'oubliez pas de souligner, s'il vous plait, comme toujours!

Using the written form

Some language can be added in written form so that children moving around the school stay aware of the presence of the target language throughout the day around the building. Many schools have labelled different rooms, some in a range of languages to reflect the languages used in school by different children from different backgrounds, but this can be taken further to include simple notices about conduct and behaviour, targets, the school's ethos, events (such as sports results). In a way, a 'notice' is more of a learning opportunity than a 'label', as children are more likely to engage with it, especially if it changes periodically. The disadvantage of room labels is that they sit there permanently and cease to be noticed.

Using assemblies

Assemblies are a real opportunity to build the language experience of the school. As we saw in the vignette that introduced Chapter 2, a head picked out the fact that the children could share that they were learning a language in an assembly piece of music. In another infant school where only the Reception class had French lessons timetabled, the Y1 and Y2 classes had a French assembly each Friday, where they learned songs and heard stories and also shared something that the younger children were experiencing. Of course, we can again build on the fact that children know the routines and will understand them in the target language readily if used in that context. From greetings, instructions and management to showing work or things brought from home (with a target language or culture connection where possible) and centred on the content of the assembly, a remarkably rich diet proved possible, even though the majority of children in the hall did not technically learn French! Again, this centres on the fact that the children are exposed to a manageable amount of the target language for comprehension and are supported in their own use of the language in these situaitons because it arises mainly from joining in with a song or with the repetitive parts of a story.

Managing behaviour

It is generally accepted that classroom behaviour management is more than possible in the target language. Some teachers take the view that a telling off in a foreign language will be clearly understood, but will probably not have the same confrontational feel for more disaffected children that a stern warning in English can sometimes have, leading to resentment and worse behaviour. This was perhaps well illustrated by a cartoon in a book on target language used by Jones et al. (2002). A teacher, speaking to two guilty looking boys cries, *'La prochaine fois c'est la mort!'* One boy says to the other, 'I don't know what she said, but if we do it again she'll kill us!'

Some critics of this claim that a teacher cannot generate a 'normal' relationship with a pupil in a foreign language and the use of the foreign language for management is likely to lead to more problems as the pupil may ignore the instructions or admonition. It is perhaps worth considering that some of the people who hold this view still feel that it is very important to use praise in the target language (yet there is little difference between the two functions, as both concern emotional aspects of the learning process).

Simple instructions can be used from the beginning of learning and phrases such as 'listen', 'look this way', 'be quiet now', 'don't touch', 'sit down', 'sit with…' will quickly be learned, as we saw in Chapter 4. While this is not intended as a general rule (we must not be mechanistic about either language teaching or classroom management), progression does offer the opportunity to go a stage further and name both the unacceptable behaviour and the desired alternative.

> *Sam, ne parle pas avec Finlay, regarde-moi!*

> *Chloë et Claire, ne parlez pas! Ecoutez!*

We can also sometimes offer reasons for the instruction to do things differently, so giving a good model for language use in other contexts, too. Here, we should still use mime and visual support to make the meaning clear. Five quick pieces of non-verbal language can easily accompany the following management instruction to make it absolutely clear.

> *Ben, ne touche pas les crayons maintenant, parce que tu dois regarder les images ici sur l'écran.*

Language use by means of dictionary use

A teacher who lacks confidence can promote the use of dictionaries very effectively if it is a regular classroom occurrence to look for a word together. Sometimes this will be spontaneous, but if a teacher has had to check a word while planning the lesson, he or she could consciously do this again during the lesson. This is a vital language skill and should not be seen as reflecting any lack of competence on the part of the teacher. As few classes will have a whole set of dictionaries, this is perhaps best done by the teacher with a different pupil each time.

As the children become more accustomed to using a dictionary, it can be extended by tasking a pair of children to locate a word. It is also possible to use an online dictionary so that the whole class can see and participate in this process (a dictionary for a range of languages can be found at www.wordreference.com). There is a whole skill involved here of course and the teacher should give guidelines as to what is being checked and what should be ignored to start with (for example, the grammatical notation that accompanies the entries). Later, perhaps in the last year of primary school, the full extent of dictionary vocabulary can be opened up so that children know whether they have found a noun or a verb, an adjective or adverb.

Raising the bar – drawing children further into the routine dialogues of the classroom

Another way to instil progression into the language use of the classroom in a scaffolded way is to move on from an acceptance of English in routine questions. Here, of course, a response from the teacher to a question in English should always have been in the target language so the pupil using English still has to process the foreign language to get the desired result. Instead, the teacher may start to project an expectation of target language use by the pupil. This means, of course, turning receptive into productive language.

This does not have to be done in that rather negative way of making the children say a complete sentence and possibly even repeat it several times before permission or a response is given. The children may use the language at various levels and, as long as there is a real desire to communicate, this should be both accepted and praised. So, a fairly common request may range from, *'Die Toilette bitte'* to *'Darf ich bitte zur Toilette gehen?'* and each is completely acceptable. Each, however, also gives the opportunity for the teacher to initiate by qualifying permission with something that has to be processed. For example, *'Aber nur zwei Minuten!'* or *'Wenn Lewis zurück ist.'*

Sometimes children will not have the right vocabulary for a particular function – negatives are often particularly difficult for children, for example – but this gives rise to two issues. First, we should accept and praise for effort any real attempt to communicate – for example, *'Nein Bleistift'* – before offering an alternative – *'Kein Bleistift?'* (accompanied, of course, by hand signals to show it is a negative). Other attempts to say the same thing might bring, *'Wo ist Bleistift?'* or one closer to what is needed, *'Ich möchte Bleistift.'* In these cases, a natural response is what is needed from the teacher.

While it is believed that simply recasting a response and echoing it to a pupil does not usually effectively repair language errors, except phonological mistakes (Lyster, 1998), we have to balance maintaining a positive learning atmosphere with a gradual move towards the use of accurate language. On seeing that children have started to try to express negative sentences, it would be worth devising a lesson that teaches them in context and preferably in a content- rather than grammar-driven way. The teacher may reveal to the class that he or she has left her bag with pencil case, packed lunch, books and phone at home and therefore does not have some essential items. This could then lead to a confessional (under amnesty of course) in which the children reveal what they have forgotten on that day.

Moving to more open-ended use of productive spoken language

If we give children opportunities to talk to both us and each other in the target language in non-threatening ways, we slowly create a norm of expectation that the language of the classroom is not English unless absolutely necessary. This can be achieved by setting up short dialogues and role plays, but in a way that some level of creativity is offered right from the beginning. Children will try to initiate if they have a chance, so we should avoid setting up drill-like sequences where the dialogue is purely mechanistic. We saw in the vignette to this chapter how at even the simplest level of language, children will take the opportunity to inject humour and have fun while using the target language. It is important to value these small instances, because they signal a desire to communicate spontaneously.

We have spoken before about the need to avoid asking questions to which the answer is already well- known to everyone in the room. Obviously in a primary class, personal information can fall into this category all too easily, but a lot of practising of this is possible if you move to taking on different identities. This can also be a very good opportunity to move towards more communicative and purposeful use of the kind of language that is often learned fairly early, such as name, age, family, pets, friends, likes and dislikes.

One way to make this contained but still spontaneous is to have a set of photo cards of celebrities (and perhaps school personnel) with key facts and then ask a pupil to draw one out and take on that identity. This may start as a whole-class collaborative activity with different children forming questions they feel confident of and all as a group trying to guess the identity. It is better, therefore, for the more able children to be the celebrities to begin with as they are likely to be more fluent, but they can be paired with a less gifted partner and work together to provide the answers. From there, you can evolve it into a team game, with competition to guess the identity, then to pairs of children being pairs of celebrities – the more unlikely the better – and eventually to playing the game in groups with the whole set of cards in use and more intensive practising involved for all.

An extension of this topic could result in the children carrying out a survey. This could be either still on the theme of the assumed identities, and with more people being involved, giving further repetition of questions and responses, or, with some extra unknown information, they could revert to their real identities. If this is the case, then there needs to be an outcome, such as a whole-class graphic summary of the data produced.

Some KS2 teachers opt to maintain the EYFS practice of having a role-play area in the classroom. If this is available, then it can certainly be used for the children to practise the target language and would best be linked to the class topic area. Not all children will want to be 'on the spot' in this way, but, equally, some will really enjoy the challenge of picking up a 'scenario card', which gives a situation for them to explain to a partner. The card, written in the target language, acts as a support in terms of vocabulary, but does not tell them what to say (in the manner of a GCSE role-play task card). If the class is working on habitats for science and humanities, for example, a scenario card might involve a brief vet/client dialogue about an injured wild animal. The beginnings of this might be possible for many children by the end of the second year of learning and we will present a longer example in Chapter 6.

Progression in literacy

We showed in Chapter 4 that we should not keep the written word hidden from children at any point. Even in the Reception class, more able children are often interested in how we write the words they are learning and may try to use phonics knowledge to do this for themselves. Certainly by Y3, children beginning a language have a very real engagement with literacy and it will seem odd if they do not encounter text in the target language. Of course, different languages make different demands on children, with Spanish and Italian perhaps being the least problematic of the four major Western European languages, and German being a lot more instantly accessible than French, which rivals English for obscure spelling patterns.

There is no reason why, from the beginning, core vocabulary should not be on display so that children can access it when they are ready. Those with more visual and language-based learning styles will gain a great deal from regular exposure to these key words. As we progress into the second and third years of learning, however, the displays will be able to fulfil different purposes – ones more akin to other classroom displays the children have available to them.

We can keep the core vocabulary that we feel they need, but add language from the current topic and move through the regular cycle of display in best practice classrooms, where the content of a topic is presented then harnessed into a more learning-orientated pattern (perhaps using questions and informational responses) and, finally, to a more celebratory purpose, where children's work is displayed. (If you want to explore this topic further in more general terms, carry out an Internet search using the search term 'purpose of classroom display' and you will find that there are numerous sites to stimulate thinking on this topic, including a mind map example at: www.mindmeister.com/39774624/the-importance-of-display-in-the-primary-classroom)

We can see how this progression might look by means of the example of a food and drink topic linked to healthy eating. From a display showing a range of breakfast items (see Figure 5.1), which still invites some thinking as the children need to make the links between the visuals and the labels (coloured string or ribbon can be used to do this physically), they can move to playing with alliteration in the language of opinions (Figure 5.2) and then to considering questions around healthy options by deciding on the health rating of five breakfasts before creating their own (Figure 5.3).

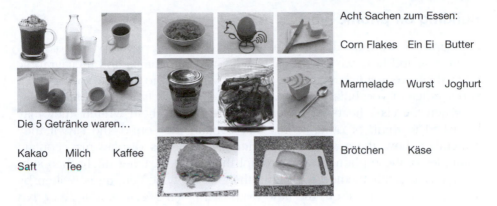

Acht Sachen zum Essen:

Corn Flakes   Ein Ei   Butter

Marmelade   Wurst   Joghurt

Die 5 Getränke waren…

Kakao   Milch   Kaffee
Saft   Tee

Brötchen   Käse

Figure 5.1   Classroom display showing range of breakfast items

Ich mag Milch

Tee ist besser!

Saft ist super!

Ich mag Limo!

Kakao hat Kalorien!

Kaffee hat Koffein

Figure 5.2   Adding opinions to the breakfast items

Ein gesundes Frühstück?

Mach dein eigenes gesundes Frühstück hier!

Wenn nicht, warum nicht?

Figure 5.3   Considering how healthy different breakfasts are

Building on phonic work

In Chapter 4, we looked at the need for activities that develop phonological awareness and how we might teach individual phonemes and their graphic equivalents. As reading increases, children will need to be able to decode a wider range of vocabulary and read aloud as accurately as possible.

When the class hears new words, before seeing them written, they may be asked to think of other words that contain the sound and say, if they remember, how these words are written. (The class display may contain examples of these phonemes to prompt them.) The teacher might then subsequently use this method for telling the class how something is written by saying, for example, about the new word *'seau'*, *'ça s'écrit comme l'eau, pas comme chaud.'*

Use of stories

By the second year, there is a great deal more potential for the use of stories. The issue of stories being age-appropriate may begin to have more of a role and every class is different in this respect. The enthusiasm generated by the teacher for a resource can be sufficient to 'sell' it to classes who are becoming more mature, but there is, of course, a danger in using material that the children will consider babyish. Teachers who enjoy creating their own stories by using PowerPoint or other presentational tools have the opportunity to design material that they know will appeal in terms of content and they know will challenge, but be essentially understandable with concentration, collaboration and support where necessary.

In the second year, you may like to consider the potential of a link between a target language reading stimulus and a piece of writing in English. A story, especially one with some mystery and an open-ended conclusion, may create a starting point for an imaginative piece of writing.

An example of a story available originally in English (Brown, 1992) but also in both French and German is Ruth Brown's (2001) *Une histoire sombre, très sombre/Eine dunkle, dunkle Geschichte*. It is not available in Spanish, although other works by the same author are. This story, which gradually progresses from the whole country down to a small mouse in a box in a series of snapshots, is clearly understood from the combination of text and visuals, so children do not have problems accessing it. The sentence structure is repetitive, which creates expectation and tension and so engages a class very quickly. The same structure also invites the children to join in, as they perceive the pattern, so the language moves from the receptive to the productive in the teacher's use of pauses, which encourage the class to supply the words before the teacher says them.

Sequencing activities that have been successful with this story include:

- arranging the visuals in order
- labelling the visuals with the correct sentences
- arranging word cards with the 'focus' of each page in order, such as *un pays, une forêt, un château* and so on
- extending the above so that extra items appear, such as *une ville* between *forêt* and *château* or using *grande* and then *petite* with *boîte*
- writing imitatory sentences then follows and even a complete new story (perhaps with photo illustrations is possible).

This can be linked with geography topics, where the big to small focus can also be used (as we suggested in Chapter 4, when looking at the first two lessons).

Use of informational texts (at different levels)

In the second year of learning, you can begin to use informational texts on topics the class is engaged in elsewhere in the week. The final section of this chapter looks in more detail at how you might progress with such curricular integration, while Chapters 6 and 9 give more detail on how and why this might progress further. At this point, however, we are looking at very simple text to move children on from language topics to a more general use of the language. Just as we saw in Chapter 4 that some work is possible in the first year of learning in areas such as art and mathematics, we can see a wider range of opportunities when the children have both more language and growing maturity in terms of study skills.

One source of material for short informational texts is schools' websites. Where the school has included information about class topics and examples of children's work, there are more likely to be appropriate levels of language and the motivation of seeing another young person's work. An example of a school's site with a great deal of material is http://rpi.ecole-st-jean.over-blog. fr, which has both video and text material relating to school topics. All such sites need to be carefully vetted before use since they sometimes carry advertisements at the beginning of the video material or elsewhere. In this case, there is video without text that can be used to stimulate talk once the material is known.

Short texts sourced from such sites can be gathered, laminated and given to individual children, either in whole-class or silent reading sessions. Teachers should develop a system for differentiating the texts by difficulty (although interest is also a highly significant factor) so that individual children can all read something at an appropriate level. This is also a possible source of individual extension work where needed, but reading should be available to all the children, not reserved for only the more able.

Developing cross-curricularity: four levels of integration

This chapter has emphasised how both challenge and integration should grow as children become more confident in their language learning and has attempted to set out how teachers could also progress in terms of using their limited but growing confidence and competence at different points.

This section now seeks to explore how to manage the progression in curricular integration on a planning and policy level. In Chapter 6 there is a continuation of how to achieve this towards the end of KS2, but the idea behind the progression is presented here because it is important, as stated already, that teachers (and children) have an idea of the direction in which they are moving.

We can see this progression in terms of four levels of embedding and integration:

- surface cross-curricular linking
- integrating language while building on semi-familiar content
- integrating language and new content
- immersion (full or partial).

In this scheme we can see that the third level is distinct from the second, in that where the second level recaps and extends material within a topic the third level addresses an entirely new topic. The second and third levels of this scheme, however, can also be seen as inextricably linked because we should never simply reteach something that the children all know in the foreign language and stop there. They will see no rationale for doing this as they have learned it already. We can (and should) recap on familiar material before extending into a new direction in the foreign language, however, and, in doing so, we may use more challenging language when the children are familiar with the content and less challenging language when the content is new. So, the second and third levels will not always be progressive in terms of language level.

The rationale for the progression is given as we more closely define each stage and, first, Table 5.1 sums up the differences by giving some practical examples.

Surface cross-curricular linking

This is probably where teachers with less confidence in their language competence or with existing language teaching experience with a more topic and vocabulary-based focus will begin. In its level of integration, this stage remains mainly language focused in its style and sequencing. As topics arise

Table 5.1 Summary of progression using practical examples

Subject/topic	Surface cross-curricular links	Integrating language and semi-familiar content	Integrating language and new content	Immersion (full or partial)
Maths	Numbers 1–31 used in addition and subtraction calculations in KS2	Numbers 1–31 used in more complex operations, such as ? × 10 = 170; 39 ÷ ? = 3; 45 ÷ 10 = ?; √64 = ?, or in a matching task, such as *Trouve les paires*: 75%; 0.67; 3/4, 0.25; 2/3; 25%	Teaching a Y4 class to construct different tabular/pictographic representations of data, using TL stimulus	The teaching of an entire subject in the foreign language, such as all the art and design curriculum, across several years. The subject becomes associated with the language. Comprehension of almost native speaker language becomes possible. This can be extended to other subjects so that a proportion or all of every day is taught in the target language
Geography – an aspect of a country where target language is spoken	The teaching of 8 compass points via imitation/repetition	The teaching of 8 compass points via a challenge to recognise and arrange them using prior knowledge and cognates or inference via factual information: *Voici quatre villes en France. Calais est dans le nord de la France, et Perpignan est dans le sud. Strasbourg est dans l'est de la France, et Marseille est dans le sud-est*	Use compass points in target language as part of a task where certain squares are identified on a grid (superimposed on a map). This in Y4 would be new knowledge	
Science: healthy eating	Teaching food/drink items and classifying them as healthy or unhealthy	Identifying healthy and unhealthy elements of sample breakfasts – expressing preferences and negotiating healthier options. *J'adore les pains au chocolat. Je prends deux pour mon petit dejeuner. OK je prends un pain au choclaot et un yaourt*	Teaching the food pyramid as a new item. The visual uses some food items already known and adds others, but the concept of the pyramid is new. Children come to understand the differing amounts of the different classes of food needed in the foreign language	

which allow some links with another curriculum area, they are explored through the language approach with sets of topic vocabulary taught in a more traditional way through imitation and repetition. The focus is more on the use of familiar activity types and limited language rather than allowing the chosen content topics to define language needs. The children will not learn any new content through this level of integration as the pitch is often on material which they learned some time before through English, but which is now revived so that they can learn the foreign language vocabulary associated with it. There is likely to be a 'listening and speaking' focus predominating, backed up with consolidation reading and writing. It can of course be gradually extended and one way of doing this is to use the question words 'Why?' and 'How?' more frequently, as these questions will start to build a greater demand for more complex responses and more thinking.

Examples of activities that may occur in this curriculum include:

- basic addition and subtraction calculations with numbers up to 30 with KS2 students, which do not therefore use mathematics at their current cognitive level
- as part of a topic on the geography of a target language country, the teaching of compass points by means of repetition; basic verb form 'to be situated' and then a drill sequence of questions/statements locating places on a map; weather, but at a simple sentence and descriptive, rather than 'forecast' level, and a subsequent weather forecast role play that operates on series of single format sentence-level units
- in a PE link, the use of simple commands, such as left, right, forwards, backwards, and parts of the body in aerobics-style activity, but without more specialist vocabulary being introduced
- in a science link, the exploration of the life cycle of a butterfly at essentially single word level, such as first the egg, then the caterpillar, then the cocoon, then the butterfly, or, in healthy eating, the use of the single items, healthy and unhealthy, to classify a vocabulary set.

Integrating language while building on semi-familiar content

This approach moves towards a more content-centred base, possibly via a whole-school topic – that is, drawing from different subject areas. It is unlikely to be used to teach an entire unit in another subject as that would imply substantially more new content. The themes may be chosen with language topics in mind, so vocabulary areas that the teacher wants to include in the languages curriculum can still be introduced at this point. There will be some coverage of content already encountered in the mother tongue, but it is important to build on this in the foreign language. The task styles may be drawn from both foreign languages and content subject methodologies.

There may still be some 'preteaching' of key vocabulary, but not in a conventional languages format. For example, as in Table 5.1, the children could be asked to identify and arrange correctly the eight compass points from a set of cards randomly stuck on to the whiteboard. This focuses them on the vocabulary, but they can only do the task by activating their prior knowledge that compass points exist and form a certain pattern. The compass points may either be introduced using the method indicated in Table 5.1 or with a map and photographs of towns as visual support and as parts of whole sentences: '*Voici quatre villes en France. Calais est dans le nord de la France, et Perpignan est dans le sud. Strasbourg est dans l'est de la France, et Marseille est dans le sud-est.*' In either method, the compass points vocabulary is therefore inferred rather than directly taught. The teacher will still give many examples and engage learners in questioning to provide necessary repetition (rather than chorus-style). He or she will establish whether the forms have been heard and internalised properly and a gap-fill reading or writing task will probably be used to consolidate the vocabulary with older learners. There can also be a development on this by using more complex reasoning, but still with simple language structures. For example (drawing in the weather, if known) by asking such questions as, '*Il fait plus chaud à Perpignan qu' à Paris – pourquoi?*', eliciting, '*Parce que Perpignan est dans le sud.*'

Other examples of such a level of integration include the following.

- More demanding numeracy activity that reflects recent or even current mathematics objectives. This could involve, for example, in KS1, number bonds to 20, simple multiplication calculations, identification of shapes. In KS2, numbers from 1 to 30 might be used as the missing part of more complex calculations, such as , $? \times 10 = 170$, $39 \div ? = 3$, $45 \div 10 = ?$, $\sqrt{64} = ?$, or in a matching task, such as, *Trouver les paires:* 75 per cent, 0.67, $\frac{3}{4}$, 0.25, $\frac{2}{3}$, 25 per cent. In these examples, the teacher can read out the calculation, but pause for the missing item, which the class will be able to offer.
- More demanding geographically situated tasks can involve simple comparisons of features in human or physical geography between countries or the reinforcement of facts about global geography (for example, continents, countries, capitals, mountains, rivers, oceans). If the weather topic is used, it is important to address some aspects of climate as well as weather and use authentic Internet sources for weather forecasting that involve the range of vocabulary (noun as well as verb forms concerning weather types). The encouragement to use strategies – for example, to infer *ensoleillé* from *soleil* – is vital and reflects an important aspect of the former KS2 Framework.

- In a science context, the life cycle of a butterfly can be addressed more fully and in more complete language forms by using the story *The Very Hungry Caterpillar* (Carle, 1995).
- Healthy eating is another very accessible topic area. Foods can be classified by fat or salt content, which are very visual and encourage the children to think. As long as the language used for the output is scaffolded, the children will cope both willingly and easily.
- Both the water cycle and photosynthesis are further topics that lend themselves to such a visual approach, perhaps using flash animations, and can therefore support exposure to richer language used as part of a scaffolded explanation and questioning sequence.
- If language topics provide the starting point for the curriculum, then daily routines can offer both citizenship and historical opportunities by, for example, looking at the daily routine of a child in a developing country, where lifestyles are very different, or by investigating aspects of the lives of children, perhaps during the Second World War.
- Finally, a friendship/anti-bullying theme, which often forms part of a whole-school focus, can also involve parallel foreign language activities that subsequently contribute to a whole-school display or recording of the week's work.

This level of engagement is clearly manageable for all schools, as long as planning addresses the vital issue of scaffolding. Chapter 9 offers more strategies for this in the section on the theory behind CLIL. Moving from the surface level to the second level is as much about wanting to do it as it is about competence regarding the target language. If you can do this as a teacher, you will start to offer the challenge that we are suggesting throughout this book is vital for children's continuing progression and maintaining their interest.

Integrating language and new content

When we introduce new content in the target language, we need to be especially mindful of the language demands we are making. The previous level could, in some ways, be more challenging linguistically because it was using previously learned content as its base, but taking on a new topic in a foreign language is, of course, rather daunting. It will take time and confidence before many teachers can easily move into this level of integration, although for a specialist language teacher, the move can be made as soon as the children are ready.

It is important to remember, however, that this is a curriculum focused principally on content objectives via content subject methodologies. It is truly a CLIL framework and, if multiplied sufficiently, will become an immersion framework (see the next section below). It will take linguistic issues into consideration when framing the ways in which learners meet the concepts and develop the subject skills. Learners will understand more language than they can use productively, but will be able to demonstrate that understanding as they complete tasks which are supported and demand less language.

It is likely that some revision of a previously learned content topic will begin a unit, but new material will then be included, probably with a focus on a target-language-speaking country. Table 5.1 shows ways in which our previously mentioned topics can be extended in this way. It can happen at any level, but, of course, needs to reflect the actual new content the children are scheduled to meet in that year group. Ultimately, it is the introduction of a new concept that sets it apart from the level before.

Other examples of topics that may occur in this curriculum and can still be linked to a relevant languages topic, also ensuring survival language progression, are the following.

- An extension from a familiar topic taught in geography or history to a new context. This demonstrates a natural progression from integrating semi-familiar content to integrating new content. For example, a historical character in a target-language-speaking country can be described and analysed after similar work has been covered in a revisited content context (such as, work on Henry VIII leading to work on Napoleon). This would also link to personal information/descriptive work in the languages scheme.
- A new topic taught in the foreign language, because there is a rationale for this. An example would be for part of the mountains unit in KS2 geography to be taught in French or German with an Alps focus or in French or Spanish with a Pyrenees focus. This also links to the world around us/environment topics in the languages scheme.
- A new topic that centres on practical activity for its understanding, such as a science topic with a strong experimental basis, in which data rather than abstract explanation provides the material that establishes knowledge and understanding, or areas of the expressive arts, PE, the design curriculum. This will link to the free time, house and home, food and drink, travel and transport or holidays topics in the languages scheme.

Immersion (single subject, partial or full)

This approach will also use largely content objectives and content subject methodology, framed with linguistic issues in mind and with an expectation that comprehension will exceed production in scope. The aim of the single subject model (most likely in the UK context) is to teach the National Curriculum content of one subject fully and facilitate language acquisition by means of a high-level exposure to authentic (although carefully controlled) fluent language.

When more subjects are added, the model becomes partial or full immersion. A large focus is placed on making the content comprehensible by using supporting material and the teacher's interpretation. Tasks are tightly structured to support the use of language individually and collaboratively and thereby internalise the content and language simultaneously. A pure language focus will be needed at some points to consolidate and rationalise language use, such as grammatical explanation, to ensure learners can manage the complexity of language demanded by the content.

Examples of subjects that may occur in this curriculum are:

- initially, areas of the expressive arts, technology and PE curriculum that emphasise doing rather than abstract knowledge and where the products can be, to a certain extent, 'language- free'
- subsequently, areas of the curriculum with high visual, or tabular, content, such as geography, mathematics and science
- finally, any subject.

Chapter summary

The chapter has tried in several different ways to offer:

- a rationale for progression (children need to see a deepening of focus or they will become bored)
- a discussion about how we manage that progression in terms of differentiation and personalisation
- concrete examples of how progression might look in linguistic terms, using both receptive and productive skills, oracy and literacy
- a concrete scheme for the progression in content terms, specifically by different levels of cross-curricular integration.

This has been an attempt to provide a signposted and differentiated route towards progression that does not simply operate on a language knowledge, language awareness or knowledge about language model. In this way, we have also attempted to ensure that language teaching and learning are pitched at both enjoyment and seriousness, both fun and challenge in a similar way that other subjects are defined by teachers and perceived by children.

Key reading

The DfES document, 'Grouping pupils for success' (2006), gives an indication of the issue from the perspective of the former Primary Strategy priorities. It is available online to download at: http://webarchive.nationalarchives.gov.uk/20110809101133/nsonline.org.uk/node/84974

Carol Dweck's work on children's perspectives on their own ability is important to bear in mind when addressing issues of ability and progression. Dweck's article with Heidi Grant is a recent work that looks at how self-evaluation and target setting can be used to offset a more negative self-view. See H. Grant and C.S. Dweck (2003) 'Clarifying achievement goals and their impact', *Journal of Personality and Social Psychology*, 85: 541–53.

Cable, C. et al.'s (2012) report on a longitudinal study of KS2 French, 'Language learning at Key Stage 2: Findings from a longitudinal study', *Education 3–13*, 40 (4): 363–78 (a primary languages special issue).

CHAPTER 6

HOW DO I MAKE SURE I REALLY CHALLENGE THE OLDER LEARNERS?

Chapter objectives

- To present a unit plan aimed at Y5 or Y6 that demonstrates how far language learning might develop in a three- to four-year programme.
- To suggest additional activity types that can build on established knowledge and skills in creative ways.
- To explore the range of ways in which language teaching and learning might play a part in the life of the school in upper KS2.

Teachers' standards			
A teacher must:			
1			Set high expectations which inspire, motivate and challenge pupils
	b		set goals that stretch and challenge pupils of all backgrounds, abilities and dispositions
2			Promote good progress and outcomes by pupils

	b	be aware of pupils' capabilities and their prior knowledge, and plan teaching to build on these
3		Demonstrate good subject and curriculum knowledge
	a	have a secure knowledge of the relevant subject(s) and curriculum areas, foster and maintain pupils' interest in the subject, and address misunderstandings
5		Adapt teaching to respond to the strengths and needs of all pupils
	a	know when and how to differentiate appropriately, using approaches which enable pupils to be taught effectively
	b	have a secure understanding of how a range of factors can inhibit pupils' ability to learn, and how best to overcome these

Source: DfE, 2013a

Introductory vignette

Y6 children talking about learning French:

'If you're in big business you have to travel the world, and if you went to France you could speak French to the people you were doing business with.'

'Some people come over here to work and you need to speak their language when you meet them.'

'It's good that it's quite hard, because if it was too easy we'd fall asleep and it would be boring.'

'You can join in more in French.'

Comment

By Y6, children are likely to see the potential instrumental gains of learning another language, as demonstrated above. They can often also see how they might be able to use it to make friendships with children of their own age. The children quoted above were still in their first year of learning French, so challenge was not greatly developed at this stage, but they were already indicating that, when it was hard, that was a good quality, as was the collaborative nature of the work. Other parts of this focus group interview emphasised the last two comments further as they identified various competitive, collaborative and problem-solving activities as the things they liked the most.

Initial reflection point

If your Y5 or Y6 class has been learning the target language for two or three years, how much language are you now using for routines? Is it enough? If it needs to be developed, how could you increase it? How much do the children use the target language for their part of routine conversations? How might you increase this?

Response

The previous three chapters have each dealt with the theme of target language use, with a view to suggesting a natural development , first of the teacher using the language, then of the children's use of the language, in instructions, management, organisation, resourcing and the questions that arise in classroom life. This chapter will not feature this aspect specifically, but the questions in the Reflection point above were asked deliberately to encourage you as the teacher to audit the extent to which the language is now embedded in your routines and has become natural and expected by the children. If you have inherited a class not used to this way of working or the children in upper KS2 have only just started language learning, then the sections in Chapters 4 and 5 on classroom language should be useful.

Planning for the Y5/Y6 topic: Tudor explorers – Les grandes découvertes

The first section of this chapter explores the next stage of progression in both content and language via a series of activities in the target language that are directly linked to a whole-class topic.

The following planning grid (Table 6.1) uses French (as that is how we have used it so far), but it could be recreated in German, Spanish or Italian as it is not specific to French history, but belongs to a more general Western European historical context. It was used as part of a whole-phase topic that classes in Y5 and Y6 worked on for half a term. The language content is approximately five hours in total, but, of course, this will vary depending on the class, the amount of time they have been learning the language and the needs of individuals.

The new National Curriculum programme of study for history limits KS2 topics to earlier periods than the Tudors, but KS3 geography allows for much of this content to be included. Additionally, the use of this material in a foreign language extends the non-core curriculum into a coherent and, we hope, engaging area that could act as a transition bridge to KS3 (see Chapter 8 for more on that important theme).

Table 6.1 Planning grid for the Y5/Y6 topic: Tudor explorers – Les grandes découvertes

Learning objectives	Learning outcomes	Teaching activities/language	Resources
To ask and answer questions	Identify geographical features and learn about places in different countries	Children see a series of images from francophone countries and note which ones are in France	Images from French-speaking countries around the world
To recognise similarities and differences between different places	Understand and name the continents and some countries	C'est en France? Oui ou non? Pourquoi? Pourquoi pas? C'est où? C'est en Europe/Afrique/Amérique du Sud/Australie?	
To understand question forms and negatives in spoken and written language		Display cut-out shapes of the different continents. Say their names for children to repeat, such as, l'Europe, l'Afrique, Amérique du Sud, l'Amérique du Nord, l'Asie, l'Australasie. Phoneme focus: que, je	Cut-out shapes of continents
		Display large map of the world. Call out names of continents and invite children to identify them on the map – Où est l'Afrique? and so on	Map of the world
	Use language cues to produce a practical outcome	Give a small card with a name of a continent to each child. Children walk around the room, finding other children belonging to their continent – Qui a l'Asie?	Pieces of card with names of continents
		Place one group of children in a certain place – Ici c'est l'Europe. Then ask other groups to find their correct place, reconstructing the map of the world – Où est l'Afrique?	
		Show satellite image of the world. Ask children to identify certain continents and features – Où est l'Australie? C'est quelle continent?	Satellite image of the world

(Continued)

Table 6.1 (Continued)

Learning objectives	Learning outcomes	Teaching activities/language	Resources
To listen attentively and understand more complex phrases and sentences	Develop understanding of past and present, historical change. Use and analyse a historical source. Make notes	Show a large image of a Tudor period map of the world. Let children look at copies in groups with a task – *Quelles sont les différences? Faites une liste*	Copies of map from Tudor period
To make simple sentences and short texts		Then repeat questioning as before, including, *Où est l'Amérique? L'Amérique n'est pas là*	
To practise new language with a friend		Write year of origin of the map on the board (for example, by Henricus Martellus, 1489). Note at that time, *L'Amérique existe, mais en Europe, on ne sait pas ça! L'Amérique n'a pas été découverte, n'est-ce pas?*	
To use context and previous knowledge to help understanding and reading skills		*Quels continents ne sont pas là? L'Amerique du nord, l'Amerique du sud, l'Australie* Then ask groups to look at the map again with these questions: *Où sont les pays de l'Europe? Quelles sont les autres différences?*	
	Read and understand short passages and identify key elements of a short text	Ask in plenary for the location of a range of countries. Include also more difficult items, such as, *Où est l'Inde?* Introduce some explorers, giving an image and a short description	Map of the world with navigation routes of different explorers
To read and understand the main points and some detail from a short written passage	Recall and practise personal information. Practise and use third person singular	*En 1492, Christophe Colomb découvre l'Amérique. Il arrive sur le continent américain le 12 octobre 1492, après 70 jours de navigation*	Short descriptions of explorers' routes
		En 1534, le navigateur français, Jacques Cartier, part à la recherche d'une route vers l'Asie. Il découvre le Canada	

Learning objectives	Learning outcomes	Teaching activities/language	Resources
To use context and previous knowledge to help understanding and reading skills		In pairs, children identify navigation route on map and colour code different routes of different explorers	
	Work collaboratively	Children work in groups to produce notes from the texts used in previous activity for a class timeline, such as, *En 1492, Christophe Colomb découvre l'Amérique. En 1534, Jacques Cartier découvre le Canada*	Cut-up statement of two explorers
To make simple sentences and short texts	Recognise, understand and use language about explorers' lives	Children work in pairs to classify statements about two different explorers, such as Columbus and Cartier	
Prepare a short presentation on a familiar topic	Recognise and practise use of third person singular	*Il s'appelle … Il vient de France/Genova. Il découvre le Canada*	
Write sentences on a range of topics using a model	Plan, prepare and present a short presentation	*L'Amérique. Ses bateaux s'appellent La Grande Hermillon/Santa Maria, Nina et Pinta*	
Apply knowledge of language rules and conventions when building short sentences		They then prepare and present a short presentation of one explorer to the class	
Perform to an audience			

In this approach, it is important to note that the topic mixes the second and third levels of the four-stage scheme presented in Chapter 5. Some of this material builds on (presumed) prior knowledge about the world and the continents and some on the ongoing work that the children were doing in English, but there are also new elements and the text material around the explorers and their lives was unknown and was not being covered at all in the part of the scheme delivered in English.

It is equally important to note that the topic is built up from early confidence-boosting activity that is neither linguistically nor conceptually challenging and is designed to settle the class into a positive and anxiety-free mindset.

The first activity expects the children will be able to recognise that some scenes in the pictures are not in France. This is then linked to some basic knowledge of the globe, with the names of continents and some relevant countries on either side of the Atlantic Ocean. The names in the target language can be taught by being used and not as separate vocabulary items, especially as they are cognate with English and will be related to prior knowledge by a majority of learners.

Not all learners will know accurately the make-up of the globe and the physical relationships between these areas, however, so there is both some consolidation and some teaching of new content here, depending on individual children. With all new content-based topics it is important (and also reflects standard good practice) to begin in this way, re-establishing prior knowledge and creating as close to a level playing field for all children as possible, but, at the same time, it is equally important to raise the game, conceptually, quite soon.

The scheme first does this by using an original source – the Martellus map – to provide an important piece of 'new' information – that is, in the late fifteenth century, no Europeans knew of the existence of America. Because the map is visual and linked to the immediately preceding work, the new concept is established *without* language (the children see the image and see that America is missing) and then *with* language. (Having gained the new concept, the language is then mapped on to that piece of knowledge and, from that context, any new words become meaningful immediately.) Both American continents and Australia are missing from the map and this can be established by questioning.

It also gives an easy opportunity to practise some of the countries that will be needed as origins of the great voyages. The European section of the map is mostly very recognisable, so identifying the UK, France, Spain, Portugal is easy, but the teacher can also ask about other differences between this map and modern versions. This is an important historical skill – to identify that things change and original sources help us track these changes.

The next stage is to introduce some text. In effect, the teacher has done this aurally by asking questions that have produced statements about the map, but the class has had this heavily scaffolded because the questions have been prompts for answers that, together, have produced a series of statements to constitute an aural text. Now the use of written text, which requires reading, makes the work progress and involves literacy in a different way.

It is vital in all of this to use group work to allow children to pool knowledge and scaffold each other. The role of talk in learning is established beyond any contention and whether we look to overriding mental schemes such as Vygotsky's (1978) zone of proximal development or more activity-focused interpretations such as Wells' (1999) dialogic teaching or Mercer's (1995) talk types, we know that asking children to talk together in a focused way will be valuable. If the overarching task is given in the target language and they need to report back in the target language, too, then even if the dialogue is in English, the learning will be secured and they will need to formulate their thoughts in the target language as part of the activity. So, for the group work on the map or on the text, we should ensure that the way we set up the task and the way we 'harvest' the work that they have been doing uses the target language and is manageable for the children. If we do this, their language will be enhanced and they will also be thinking in the ways they do in other subjects.

The use of short texts in this unit is designed to introduce a range of new facts to the children and allow them to internalise this new knowledge by engaging with those texts and manipulating the information. Importantly, this is done with the overall purpose of producing a short presentation for the rest of the class. Because different groups of children will work on slightly different texts, each of these presentations will also hold new information for some class members, so they can be designed as listening tasks, ensuring still further exposure to the key language in context.

The scheme is arranged with the teaching activities and language areas covered in the third column of Table 6.1. The content was the driving factor in the planning of the topic, but the language-related objectives also form part of the thinking as some key skills are included that link to both the new National Curriculum and the former KS2 Framework. Subsequently, an audit for breadth and to check that progression is contained within the unit or in terms of the year of study was made. As Chapter 7 deals with the planning process, using the new primary curriculum and the former KS2 Framework in detail, this aspect will not be commented on here.

The topic was then developed further by moving into a study of Canada, comparing features such as size, climate, wildlife and favourite sports in the UK and Canada. This was directly linked to Cartier's discovery of the country and its resulting bilingual nature. The children appreciated the opportunity to use language that would be useful to them (for example, relating to weather, animals and spare time hobbies) in other contexts as well as for the topic.

Reflection point

Using the Internet, try to find some simple text material that would support one of the themes mentioned above for the Canada topic. (If you are teaching Spanish, you may like to do this for a Spanish-speaking Central or South American country; if you are teaching German, you may like to look at Namibia.)

Once you have done that, think about the following questions. How difficult was it to find this material? Have you found images, tables or diagrams as well as text? Is the text in long sentences or short bullet points? Have you found any material on websites of schools in the target countries?

Response

Searching for material is an inevitable (and perhaps unenviable) burden on language teachers, but when we find good material we are always extremely pleased that we can offer children something more targeted to their interests and developing a better understanding of language and the target environment.

School websites can be useful as they sometimes offer material written by children and at or near the right level. In text searches generally, it can be fruitful to search using a small sample of the kind of text you are looking for, as this can throw up less obvious Internet sources. Using image searches is also important as you need visual material as well as text. Do not rule out target language versions of Wikipedia as it often contains tabular material or sites such as YouTube as they can offer some (appropriate) surprises!

The remainder of the chapter looks at the different types of work you may wish to include in your language learning scheme, either in addition to the topic work as described before or instead of it, if you are working separately from the rest of the curriculum.

Songs

We mentioned earlier that even at the top of KS2, songs are still a very popular element of language learning, according to the survey of a primary school reported in Hood (2006). By Y5 and Y6, although many children still actively engage in the authentic action-type songs we have been advocating right from EYFS stage, they will all also appreciate something closer to youth culture if we can offer this. There are singers who are frequently recommended by teachers, such as Henri Dès for French, Detlev Jöcker for German and Rosa Leon for Spanish. All of them have their own websites and CDs can be bought fairly easily from Amazon and others.

We found in our French teaching a very useful source in the singer Ilona Mitrecey, who started recording at the age of 12 and produced, at that time, genuine pop (techno-flavoured) music with a younger approach than is normally evident in chart-based music. You can hear songs such as *'Laissez-nous respirer'*, *'Dans ma fusée'* and *'Retourner à l'école'* at:

- www.youtube.com/watch?v=Bxan-qGoIHU
- www.youtube.com/watch?v=Le9Q7cy331A
- www.youtube.com/watch?v=UxjpNFWa_fk

Singing is not only popular but, just as for younger children, also supports learning and teachers will want to encourage the use of songs for this as well as cultural reasons. Mnemonic use of singing is very common among primary language teachers and there are various commercial resources available that have songs especially created for language learning, centred on topics and functional sentences. Teachers vary in their enthusiasm for such resources, but the rationale behind using singing of whatever format is not disputed.

Stories

Stories continue to engage learners at the ages of 10 and 11 and, although their reading in English is reaching quite sophisticated levels that cannot be replicated in the target language, it is important to keep an eye on the age-related aspect of material we offer them. Cook (1997) and Ellis and Brewster (2002) clearly show how and why stories are important for language development. In their full-length resource book, Ellis and Brewster explore the ways to read and tell a story and how this can impact language learning in L1, EAL and FL terms and they offer many concrete examples. In general, as with the songs, children are often very willing to read 'younger' texts, especially if the work that spins from it is more obviously age appropriate (see Chapter 7 for a scheme based on *Handa's Surprise*, for example).

Translations of Mercer Mayer's books have been used successfully with this age group. A good example is *There's an Alligator under my Bed* (1991) – *Il y a un alligator sous mon lit* in French, *Da liegt ein Krokodil unter meinem Bett* in German or, in Spanish, a parallel book is available entitled *Una pesadilla en mi armario* (1992). This book is *intended* for younger readers, but the language level in the target language is enough to challenge upper KS2 children and the teacher can evoke their memories of being scared when they were younger or their reflections on their younger brothers' and sisters' fears now. This injects some humour into the reading.

From a linguistic perspective, the story has three obvious features:

- it contains food vocabulary
- it is a narrative of events with a selection of first and third person verb forms that allow consolidation of the pronouns 'I' and 'he/she/it' by acting out, sequencing, retelling and recasting into a different story sequence
- it has a selection of prepositions, making it a useful contextual way of signalling how to say 'under', 'in', 'on', 'next to' and 'behind'.

As always, the story should be read for enjoyment first and foremost. It falls into three sections, with the initial problem (the alligator under the bed), followed by the solution (the boy entices the alligator into the garage) and, finally, the next problem that arises as a result (the boy's dad will find the alligator in the garage when he goes to work the next day!). This makes it easier to focus on the text in more detail after the initial reading and, by Y5 and Y6, we can read more intensively with the children, word by word – not through the entire story, but with a real attention to certain sentences and, perhaps, to some language forms, such as the first and third person pronouns. Pausing between sections allows some prediction and some summary in the target language (both with support frames offered by the teacher). After some more detailed reading, alternative storylines that are heavily based on the original can be created by pairs or small groups and these can be read or acted for others in the class.

Some non-specialist teachers feel that stories are quite daunting at this level and worry about issues such as their fluency of delivery, pronunciation or ability to cope with questions that arise during reading. A good solution to this is the use of electronic stories that are often part of larger courses. One popular set of such stories is 'Talking Big Books' (available online at: www. earlystart.co.uk/bb/index.htm#guide). These can be obtained in French, German and Spanish and contain the stories, teachers' notes, interactive activities and electronic flashcards.

Using resources such as these enables less confident teachers to enhance their own pronunciation and intonation and learn new vocabulary while working on these elements with the class. The story should remain the essential part of the activity and all of the techniques that primary teachers would say characterise good story reading should be used with such resources. The accompanying activities are a bonus that will support further consolidation of the vocabulary, although with an eye to the issue of cognition and challenge if necessary for upper KS2 children.

Books with a very small amount of language can still sometimes provoke thought and emotion. A good example of this (although only available in French) is *Mon cochon* by Jean-Pierre Blanpain (2001). The pig at the centre of the story does not like being pink, so imagines how he might be a range of different colours (*'Il aurait aimé être bleu comme le ciel … ou rouge comme une tomate'*). At the end, he reveals why he does not want to be pink – *Le rose, c'est la couleur du jambon*, which means because it is the colour of ham.

The story can be completely understood even though it is all in French because of the key words and the pictures, but it also has a useful sentence structure – 'he would have liked to be' – that can be reworked so it is in the first person and this can then be used to encourage some creative writing by the children who have read the story.

Reflection point

Choose a good storybook for use with an upper KS2 class. If you do not have easy access to material in your target language, choose an English resource that you might be able to find in a translated version (visit: www.amazon.fr, www.amazon.de or www.casadellibro.com).

Why might these books be good resources to use and what might be the pitfalls? How would you read them, with what specific focus? What kinds of activities might lead from this? How might they link with a wider topic?

Poetry

Poetry is both a good source of short texts to read and a stimulus for simple but fulfilling and imaginative writing as a follow-up activity. Finding the right poems is not quick or easy, but two useful French websites are: www.momes.net and www.tact.fse.ulaval.ca/fr/html/nathalie/poesiefinal.htm. Momes has a great deal of material to offer and is a superb resource, the poems being found in the *comptines* section. The second site gathers together poems written by younger children, plus other children have selected one they like and drawn a picture of it. Searches in German or Spanish will reveal similar sites. One small selection in German, for example, can be found at: http://theodorschule.lspb.de/Kinder/Gedichte/index.html#NACH_TITELN. Here, there are poems written by children either as *elfchen* (consisting of 11 words) or *rondell* (a round in which the first two lines are repeated to form the last two). Having a structure, like these or using the *haiku* form or, perhaps, an acrostic pattern, helps to make children think about their choice of words and limits, in a positive way, how much and how they write.

Because the children in Y5 and Y6 are accustomed to a variety of written material and reading for information and pleasure in English, they are often able to use strategies to make sense of material in the foreign language as well. This means that poetry reading is something very appropriate for paired or group reading. The texts are short and should be linguistically manageable, although, preferably, with food for thought or something that will generate an emotional reaction of some kind.

'*Sommerglück von Louisa*' is also available at the Theodorschule Paderborn website mentioned above, at: http://theodorschule.lspb.de/Kinder/Gedichte/Rondell/Sommer/Sommerglueck.html. Visit the website and read the poem before reading this next section.

This poem has some keywords that are instantly recognisable, such as '*Sommer*' (summer) in the title, '*Eis*' (ice-cream), '*Sonne*' (sun), '*Schwimmbad*' (swimming pool). It contains an expression, '*Das ist kaum mehr auszuhalten*' (It's hard to bear it any longer), that will not be known and is not easy to guess, but could be a useful expression to know and could be used as the centrepiece of a follow-up poem written by pairs or individuals. The word '*schwül*' (humid, oppressive) will not be known either, but could be given as a clue and might help to unlock the longer sentence, especially as both are part of the repeated sequence.

How much a pair or group would be able to make of the whole poem's literal meaning depends on their use of strategy. If the class has learned '*Hilfe!*' (Help!) the children may guess the end of the third line. They should be able to guess '*strahlt*' (shine or beam) because that is what the sun does and it is a poem about summer heat. Similarly, '*bei so einem Wetter*' should emerge clearly from the context.

You might ask pairs to perform the poem, taking a line each so it becomes a dialogue. You might also ask them to create an alternative version by giving them the phrase '*es friert so*' (it's freezing) to use instead of '*es ist schwül*' and substitute where necessary other items to make it read sensibly. They could also perform it as a dialogue. Finally, more able children might manage to create a non-weather version by retaining the long sentence of the repeated couplet and thinking of another situation where it is hard to bear it any longer.

An example of a new version that shows how effective a small amount of language might be is:

Fünf zu null	5–0
es ist kaum mehr auszuhalten	It's hard to bear it any longer
ich möchte ein Tor!	I'd like one goal
Fünf zu null	5–0
Sie spielen so gut	They're playing so well
Wir spielen so schlecht!	We're playing so badly!
Fünf zu null	5–0
es ist kaum mehr auszuhalten.	It's hard to bear it any longer.

Other resources

We can also be creative at this older level by using existing 'language-free' resources for foreign language teaching.

A very frequently used item from the previous Literacy Framework is *The Piano* by Aidan Gibbons (available online at: www.keystage2literacy.co.uk/film-narrative.html). This very moving two-and-a-half-minute animation of a man playing a piano while reminiscing about his life, which has been known to reduce children (and even teachers!) to tears, is intended, in Y5 literacy, to stimulate discussion about both its content (not completely defined so open to interpretation) and its technique (the filming, especially use of camera angles).

Like any language-free resource, we can make of it whatever we wish, but, given the realistic limits of language at Y5 or Y6, we suggest two approaches that have been successful, both used after the class had seen the animation during literacy time.

There is a timeline that can be inferred from the piece, but it is not obvious and can serve as a group-based language activity. The children can at first match sentences in the target language to the scenes of the animation and hold them up as it plays. They can subsequently arrange these in the order in which they might have appeared in the man's life (which is not the same order as the animation itself).

The emotions evoked by the different sequences are another potential topic, although, to do justice to the resource, we cannot simply use basic feelings such as 'happy' and 'sad' as the level of discussion that would be produced in English would be much deeper. Here you might encourage children to ask for words that they wish to use to express what they think the subject is feeling and locate these together using an online dictionary on the whiteboard. This clearly is a more demanding activity for both teacher and class, but could result in a collaborative paragraph written together to sum up the way that the class has reacted to the animation.

There is a German story, *Opas Engel* (Bauer, 2003), also available in a Spanish translation, as *El angel del abuelo*, which traces a similar and also serious theme and that could be a very strong follow-up to using *The Piano* with a Y6 class. Again, the language, in short and simple sentences, is limited to a few words on each page, so it is manageable and yet still thought-provoking.

Non-fiction material

An ideal source of non-fiction material might be a partner school in a target-language-speaking country because you could specify exactly what you are looking for. Certainly such a link could be used to activate material for a classroom display on a theme, which is one very good way to present and highlight for attention some key language about an informational topic (we will look at school-to-school linking in a later section of this chapter).

Without such a link, the best source of non-fiction material is real books or magazines you find during holidays in the countries concerned or via online bookshops that show sample pages. They generate texts of all types that you can use (by scanning them) for whole-class work, but are still available for groups to handle as books for more personalised reading tasks. Magazines are particularly good as they can be broken up and used as single pages, laminated or in plastic wallets. The Internet, of course, is a further source, if you have the discipline to surf without losing all track of time!

Using non-fiction material tends to highlight, initially, the skill of reading for information, the inference of unknown words from context and the learning of new information via the language. Reading challenging text in a second language and the use of reading strategies has featured in the work of many researchers – for example, Barnett (1991), Grabe and Stoller (2002) and Koda (2005). All of these writers agree that a self-awareness of *why* we are reading and *how* we might read are important elements that contribute to success. The sophistication of the objectives in the literacy strand Understanding and interpreting texts at Y5 and Y6 levels gives an indication of the mother tongue or EAL expectations of children.

You may not want to work with more complex texts in another language as a whole class too often because it can be very challenging, but it undoubtedly enhances language learning if you set it into that context. If you do find a variety of short texts, however, the approach also works very well as an extension activity for more able children and groups of children who enjoy the 'problem-solving' aspect of reading. In gathering this material, it might help to consider Figure 9.3 in Chapter 9, which raises the notion of different types of text and their levels of difficulty. Adaptation is, of course, sometimes required as what you find may not be exactly what you want.

For French, two sections of the Momes website can be used to locate non-fiction material, although it will usually be necessary to modify it a little as it is really intended for native French speakers:

- www.momes.net/dictionnaire/minidossiers/archives.html
- www.momes.net/education/introduction.html

The German online school web server is at: www.schulweb.de/de/deutschland/index.html and, by choosing a region and the type of school *(Grundschule)*, you can access a range of school sites, some of which have texts written by children and teachers that can be adapted for your purposes.

An example of a site in Spanish that has a range of material on the popular theme of endangered species can be found at: www.animalesextincion.es/articulo.php?id_noticia=60. We will use this example to suggest how quite challenging text about the jaguar (an animal found in Spanish-speaking countries) might be used at Y6 level.

Jaguar – CARACTERÍSTICAS

El color de la piel varía de amarillo pálido a café rojizo, con manchas blancas en el pecho y parte interna de las extremidades. En todo el cuerpo tiene manchas negras, que en los costados forman rosetas, y que pueden presentar una o más manchas pequeñas.

El peso de un jaguar adulto va de 45 a 130 kg dependiendo de la subespecie, pudiendo llegar a pesar 150 kg.

Su longitud es de 1.70 a 2.30 m, y tiene una longevidad de 20 años.

The best approach to a text such as this is a combination of working as a whole class with groups finding out and reporting back. It can be presented as a real problem-solving challenge, so the children know they are not expected to find it easy.

Although the vocabulary is difficult, a keyword identification task – highlighting words that the children think they may be able to guess – would start to produce a first level of understanding. The theme of the list itself acts as an advance organiser and the use of prior knowledge is clearly a support for this kind of reading. The children can also, for example, be asked to scan for familiar words in each sentence to start with – this gives several cognates that more able children will know and will start to be shared within mixed ability groups.

It is important to show children that they can get something out of complex texts, but also give support at the right point. So, a checklist in English, given after the first level of work, will start to focus the readers on further identification of vocabulary.

After the main meanings have been established for each sentence using this combination of group-based and whole-class detection, the teacher can take stock and perhaps even reveal a translation, in random order, as a checklist.

Follow-up work would include looking at another section of the text, for example 'HÁBITAT Y ÁREA GEOGRÁFICA', which appears further down the webpage, and/or looking at another animal in danger. An activity that is less challenging might include the making of a display on the theme *'animales en peligro'*. This would enable a range of work from listing animals to explaining what the danger is for them, with groups producing a good illustration or diagram for each one and then labelling it carefully.

Such texts can be approached as a whole-class task. If the children are told that they will find (for example) three different types of habitats in which jaguars can still be found (and one in which they think it no longer lives), it is possible, even if they cannot be sure about the precise meanings of these words, that they will be able to identify those which they think are the key words for a dictionary check. Groups can each choose a key word, write it on a mini-whiteboard and hold it up. The teacher can then check the three most popular choices first (if possible using an online dictionary, such as that at: www.wordreference.com), then go back to the text to see if more has been unlocked as a result. There may be some English in this discussion, but if the focus and concentration are firmly on making meaning from the Spanish, the effort is worthwhile.

It is often interesting to ask for a general summary of a text at the beginning and a further one at the end of a task such as this. In this way, the children can see clearly how much they have gained from the process linguistically and can also identify some new knowledge that they did not have before.

Reflection point

If you have less experience of using text in this way, try to locate something online about a current topic you are teaching to upper KS2 outside language time. Use the text in the ways described above. Talk to the children about the process and find out how they feel about challenging material.

Talk activities

In Chapter 5, we commented that one way to encourage more spontaneous speaking, going beyond simple dialogue tasks the teacher may set up for pairs or groups, is to use a role-play corner similar to that normally set up in the EYFS and, increasingly, KS1 classrooms.

For upper KS2 classes, it might be appropriate to use a transactional focus, including a counter, brochures of various sorts and a till. The introductory vignette showed that children of this age are more likely to consider the career applications of languages and such an area is clearly a very flexible setting in which to explore this. A travel agency or tourist information centre would probably offer the most potential to practise the language that appears in this stage of language learning.

Dialogues on countries, transport, entertainment facilities, times and costs feature in both these scenarios. As we mentioned in Chapter 5, scenario cards are probably the best way to stimulate dialogue. At this older level they should still be very clear and in simple language, so as to prompt the dialogue without setting translation tasks (keep them in the target language) or giving all the language needed as then they become merely scripts to read out. An example might be:

> *Vous êtes une famille de cinq personnes (et un chien!) Vous voulez faire des vacances sur un camping en Normandie. Une personne adore l'equitation, une personne adore la mer et une personne adore lire. Vous avez €1500.*

It is worth having some core phrases on display in the role-play area as testing is not the purpose of the activities here, but development of fluency is definitely an aim. *'Je voudrais'* clearly needs to be there, but other examples might also include, *'Ça coute combien?', 'Pardon, je n'ai pas compris', 'Vous êtes serieux/se?'*

Encouraging an injection of humour from the children participating is a very positive aim as it acts as a strong motivator for them to return to the area again and 'play with language'. Tarone (2000) and Bell (2005) both found that humour enhanced language learning among adults, as the processing of the language was more memorable when associated with something humorous. Cook (1997) also extolled the virtues of language play, making connections between first and second language learning.

This corroborates the benefit of jokes or word play for receptive listening or reading work, that they are a potentially productive part of the teacher's repertoire. It is evidently more challenging to visualise this with children involved in language production and it may be more likely to happen with the more able. Nevertheless, ensuring mixed ability pairs and threes work together is obvious good practice and sometimes it is the personality rather than the language ability that creates a potential humorous moment, which can then be built on collectively.

In the role-play area, recognised characters from TV advertising might be suggested as 'role models' or you may like to overlay an unexpected context on one of the roles. So, for example, the travel or tourist agency worker may be extremely tired or new to the job or the customer may be in a hurry to get the business done and go to another appointment. The children might exaggerate costs, offer unpleasant-sounding options or try out catch phrases from TV comedies, such as, *L'ordinateur dit "non"!'* Of course, it will not appear from nowhere – the desire to be funny will be there, but, before suggesting this angle to dialogue work, the necessary language must be prepared in other types of work.

European Languages Day – possible roles for older children

Each year on 26 September or as near to that date as possible, a day is designated as European Languages Day (visit: http://edl.ecml.at to see the current list of events). The events held on that day are tailored for all the different age groups learning foreign languages and some do relate to primary learners.

The most important intention of the celebration is that individual schools or local authorities arrange special events for their own children. This is a good opportunity to involve all of the children in the school in different ways. Children in upper KS2 classes can contribute by devising and taking part in the sorts of active cultural, fun-based and inclusive language activities that make up these events. This can also offer the older children a chance to help plan and run activities and add a different dimension to their experience of the day, especially if they have progressed up through the school, taking part each year.

One feature of many of these days is the celebration of the different languages present among children attending the school. Younger children who have a community or other language and who want to share this will find it difficult to structure a teaching activity to offer others, but older children can support this, drawing on their greater experience of learning a language to suggest ways of choosing what to teach and then having an appropriate activity to achieve this.

Younger children who want to run a café or sell items they have made that have a target language connection can advise both about the practical aspects of this and the language which might be used.

Older children can play a really key role in greeting and accompanying visitors and ensuring that languages are used to do this to make the whole experience memorable for everyone. Since language learning – in terms of the lesson experience – often has such a positive effect on children's self-esteem, it is thoroughly appropriate to enhance this still further by taking part in activities made possible because the school has a languages and intercultural curriculum, but it also has positive effects more generally, too.

Advantages of schools linking

A school link is often best organised with a strong focus on the upper KS2 children, simply because they have a little more language and are slightly more independent than the younger children. There is also more of a chance, perhaps, that they might travel to the country and meet children in their partner school.

The best starting point for setting up a new school link, if the LA does not have a partner authority in the country, is to use the British Council's 'Partner with a school' online partner-finding tool (see further information at: http://schoolsonline.britishcouncil.org). This gives both a search facility and a great deal of advice on linking schools and other international activities in schools.

Many school partnerships start with a single class-to-class link via letters, e-mail messages, an audio or videotape or videoconference event. In many ways, the more traditional communication medium of letters is still very positive as they give children a chance to experience real handwriting on real paper (often squared in France and Germany) and to know that another child has created this for them to read. Even the simplest letters can bring a great deal of pleasure and the teachers can negotiate about the language/s used.

It can be a good policy to start by letting the children use their own language, but encourage them to think carefully about the needs of a reader who doesn't have much of that language when they construct the letter. From there, a mix of languages or an attempt to write in the target language can be planned in. Frequent exchanges, although time-consuming to organise at first, are certainly profitable in that they quickly build the relationship and the expectation of making other kinds of contact desirable to the children.

Such links can be further developed by means of whole-class activities and some of these could even take place in English rather than in foreign language lesson time. If the class works together on the best format for a written presentation about the school, created as webpages and made accessible to the partner school via the Internet, this would meet some criteria for both English and the ICT aspects of computing. Because the language will need to be restricted, the use of images and sound files could be crucial in designing something that is comprehensible to the children in the partner class.

Working in this way validates communication with the partner school as a general curriculum activity, not just a foreign language task. As importantly, it also highlights the role of intercultural understanding as a whole-school issue. To make sure other classes recognise that the link exists and see what can be gained, the materials received from the partner school – reformatted electronically if they do not arrive in that form – can be presented in an assembly by the class that receives them. This may take two or three weeks of foreign language lessons to prepare, but the range of language skills involved (listening to and reading the original source, extracting and summarising material, perhaps into a PowerPoint presentation, creating and then rehearsing a spoken script, performing in assembly) more than warrants the time. The effect on the self-esteem of older children when they achieve this kind of presentational level is enormous. The message it gives to younger children about the progression that is part of language learning is wonderful.

Chapter summary

This chapter has set out to establish the range of activities that are possible by the end of KS2. It is not intended as a compulsory checklist and clearly different classes will have different interests, capabilities and preferences in terms of activities and materials.

We have shown that stories can still play a central role in how children meet new language and spark very positive follow-up work, even in Y6. We have stressed that age-appropriateness is an important consideration and will determine the way you use a resource, even if sometimes the resource is not at first sight aimed at this age group.

We have shown that teachers can be very flexible about how children use new language and that 'making it real' in as many ways as possible is even more important than with younger children. Chapter 7 will show in more detail how the new National Curriculum has some quite challenging expectations by Y6 and we have tried to echo that fact in this chapter.

In summary, we firmly believe four years' good teaching, even of just one hour a week, can bring children to such levels of receptive and productive ability that secondary colleagues will have the opportunity to plan exciting and challenging lessons in KS3 and this should ensure we overturn the so-called 'national language barrier' still persisting in the perceptions of some groups in the UK, even in the twenty-first century.

Key reading

The OFSTED page (at: www.ofsted.gov.uk/inspection-reports/our-expert-knowledge/modern-languages) contains the most recent OFSTED surveys relevant to languages across schools and also some case studies of good practice.

CHAPTER 7

HOW DO I DEVELOP PROGRESSION IN THE NEW NATIONAL CURRICULUM?

Chapter objectives

- To investigate the different strands set out in the National Curriculum for languages in KS2.
- To present and discuss a unit of work referenced to the National Curriculum.
- To consider the wider context of language learning when planning with the National Curriculum.

Teachers' standards			
A teacher must:			
2			Promote good progress and outcomes by pupils
		a	be accountable for pupils' attainment, progress and outcomes
		b	be aware of pupils' capabilities and their prior knowledge, and plan teaching to build on these

(Continued)

(Continued)

	c		guide pupils to reflect on the progress they have made and their emerging needs
	d		demonstrate knowledge and understanding of how pupils learn and how this impacts on teaching
	e		encourage pupils to take a responsible and conscientious attitude to their own work and study
4			Plan and teach well-structured lessons
	a		impart knowledge and develop understanding through effective use of lesson time
	b		promote a love of learning and children's intellectual curiosity
	c		set homework and plan other out-of-class activities to consolidate and extend the knowledge and understanding pupils have acquired
	d		reflect systematically on the effectiveness of lessons and approaches to teaching
	e		contribute to the design and provision of an engaging curriculum within the relevant subject area(s)
5			Adapt teaching to respond to the strengths and needs of all pupils
	a		know when and how to differentiate appropriately, using approaches which enable pupils to be taught effectively
	b		have a secure understanding of how a range of factors can inhibit pupils' ability to learn, and how best to overcome these
	c		demonstrate an awareness of the physical, social and intellectual development of children, and know how to adapt teaching to support pupils' education at different stages of development
	d		have a clear understanding of the needs of all pupils, including those with special educational needs; those of high ability; those with English as an additional language; those with disabilities; and be able to use and evaluate distinctive teaching approaches to engage and support them

Source: DfE, 2013a

Introductory vignette

Language learning should be planned as an integral part of the whole curriculum, adding a new dimension, rather than a 'bolt-on' extra. The [KS2] Framework exists to enable schools to build motivating and imaginative teaching plans and units, which deal with content of real interest and relevance to children (DfES, 2005: 8).

Comment

This quote from the former KS2 Languages Framework (still accessible at the time of writing at: www.primarylanguages.org.uk/policy__research/policy_ and_reform/key_stage_2_framework.aspx) makes clear the importance of planning activities that are integrated into the wider curriculum and stresses the need for the actual content and style of language units to be exciting. In our view, the National Curriculum for languages in KS2, which supersedes the Framework, should continue to act as an audit tool for teachers, ensuring that their planning achieves two major elements:

- a good coverage of a range of objectives across the four language skills, with the inclusion of a degree of authentic cultural material, reflecting a focus on knowledge about language and developing the beginnings of an ability to draw on language learning strategies
- a sense of progression across the four years of learning from the ages of 7 to 11.

 ### Initial reflection point

1. Read the following sequence of activities and reflect on what the children are doing and learning.

    A class of Y3 children are listening to the story *Le bonhomme de neige*. The teacher encourages them to join in with the storytelling by miming the actions every time they hear a weather expression. When they hear certain weather phrases for the second or third time, some children join in with the words as well as the actions.

    Having met the new language in the story, the children practise these expressions in a variety of activities, such as, *'Jacques a dit ...'* or *'Répétez si c'est vrai'* – a simple repetition game to reinforce pronunciation. The teacher chooses the 'oi' phoneme as a focus to develop the children's phonological awareness, making links with already familiar words, such as *'moi, toi, trois'*.

    At the end of the session, the children look at a series of images showing different weather conditions in a variety of French-speaking countries and they describe the weather, selecting a written phrase from a word bank displayed on the interactive whiteboard. Throughout the week, the children take turns in updating their classroom calendar, changing the date as well as the weather. Later during the week, the children paint hot or cold landscapes, adding a short description of their art work in French.

    (Continued)

(Continued)

2. In National Curriculum terms, the activities constituted work on the following points from the Programmes of Study (in bold below). Match up each of these to one or more of the activities above (DfE, 2013b):

- **listen attentively to spoken language** and **show understanding** by joining in and **responding**
- **explore the patterns and sounds of language** through songs and rhymes and **link the spelling, sound and meaning of words**
- **engage in conversations; ask and answer questions; express opinions** and respond to those of others; seek clarification and help
- **speak in sentences**, using familiar vocabulary, phrases and basic language structures
- **develop accurate pronunciation and intonation** so that others understand when they are reading aloud or using familiar words and phrases
- present ideas and information orally to a range of audiences
- **read carefully and show understanding of words, phrases and simple writing**
- **appreciate stories**, songs, poems and rhymes **in the language**
- broaden their vocabulary and develop their ability to understand new words that are introduced into familiar written material, including through using a dictionary
- **write phrases from memory, and adapt these to create new sentences**, to express ideas clearly
- describe people, places, things and actions orally and in writing
- understand basic grammar appropriate to the language being studied, including (where relevant): feminine, masculine and neuter forms and the conjugation of high-frequency verbs; key features and patterns of the language; how to apply these, for instance, to build sentences; and how these differ from or are similar to English.

Additionally, items from the former KS2 Framework (DfES, 2005) that centred on intercultural understanding are also featured:

- IU3.2 **Locate country/countries where the language is spoken**
- IU3.4 Make **indirect or direct contact with the country/countries where the language is spoken**.

What does the new National Curriculum ask from teachers?

In a speech about improving teaching given on 10 April 2014, the then Schools Minister Elizabeth Truss said:

> We're funding teaching schools to prepare for the new curriculum, and using the subject expert groups to identify potential gaps in resources for new topics. And there's the Assessment Innovation Fund, to help spread good assessment models. But we are not going to say 'here it is', as happened with the old National Strategies. Because heads now have the freedom – and responsibility – to ensure that what they use is effective – that it uses teachers' time to the best ends – and is well researched. It's about what works.

This statement is in line with other advice about the new National Curriculum and suggests that teachers have considerable influence on how they teach the subject.

As we write, there is much debate about assessment, as the previous models across the curriculum are discontinued. KS2 languages did not have a prescribed assessment format under the KS Framework and, although there was a 'languages ladder' system that linked into the Common European Framework and an examination scheme called Asset Languages run by one of the examination boards, these are no longer available.

We mentioned above that the National Curriculum can be seen as a means to audit your provision and, as it is just a set of simple statements, it offers a simple model for achieving this. In many ways, it should not be the starting point for planning. As our sample scheme later in this chapter will show, it is difficult to simply plan a series of activities around these objectives and meet them neatly one by one – that is actually not the intention of the National Curriculum's Programmes of Study, as it was also not expected by the former KS2 Framework.

Before discussing further how we might use it, here is a summary of its essential features. As we have seen from the list above:

- it does not prescribe the content (no 'topics')
- it is non-language-specific
- it is skills-based, but the statements are listed as discrete items rather than being seen as integrated
- progression across the four years is expected, but not specifically outlined.

That intercultural understanding is not included as a strand equal in status to that of language skills, which was the case in the KS2 Framework, is seen by many primary teachers as regrettable. In the new National Curriculum Programme of Study, there are references to stories, songs, poems and rhymes, but not to other forms of culture or links to target language societies, although, admittedly, the very first sentence of the document is, 'Learning a foreign language is a liberation from insularity and provides an opening to other cultures' (DfE, 2013b). There is a tendency throughout the short document to associate culture with literature.

Similarly, the manner in which, in the former KS2 Framework, the two strands of knowledge about language and language learning strategies were to be seen as cutting across the major three (oracy, literacy and intercultural understanding) and informing and supporting them but not having a separate existence, indicated that 'grammar' and 'learning to learn' were important, but only when integrated with other skills in a context that made them real, purposeful and directly relevant to language use. The new National Curriculum has a grammar bullet among the 12, but this does not emphasise a dimension to the other skills in quite the same way. Rather, it is seen to be part of the knowledge bank of another language.

Because progression is such an important issue and needs to be assured to avoid children transferring to secondary schools without a sense of having built up their knowledge and understanding of another language, we will now use the Oracy objectives from the former KS2 Framework (DfES, 2005: Part 1) to exemplify how the principle can work over a four-year programme.

Progression in the KS2 Framework Oracy objectives

Year 3

O3.1 Listen and respond to simple rhymes, stories and songs

- identify rhyming words
- perform finger rhymes and sing songs
- join in with storytelling.

O3.2 Recognise and respond to sound patterns and words

- listen with care
- identify phonemes which are the same as or different from English and other known languages
- speak clearly and confidently.

O3.3 Perform simple communicative tasks using single words, phrases and short sentences

- recall, retain and use vocabulary
- ask and answer questions.

O3.4 Listen attentively and understand instructions, everyday classroom language and praise words

- repeat words and phrases modelled by the teacher
- remember a sequence of spoken words
- use physical response, mime and gesture to convey meaning and show understanding.

Year 4

O4.1 Memorise and present a short spoken text

- learn finger rhymes, poems or a non-fiction text
- learn and say several sentences on a topic.

O4.2 Listen for specific words and phrases

- listen with care
- use physical response to show recognition and understanding of specific words and phrases.

O4.3 Listen for sounds, rhyme and rhythm

- identify specific sounds, e.g. rhymes, letters, phonemes, words
- compare different sounds.

O4.4 Ask and answer questions on several topics

- practise asking and answering questions with a partner
- devise and perform simple role plays.

Year 5

O5.1 Prepare and practise a simple conversation, reusing familiar vocabulary and structures in new contexts

- focus on correct pronunciation and intonation
- ask and answer questions
- use tone of voice and gesture to help convey meaning.

O5.2 Understand and express simple opinion

- agree and disagree with statements
- understand and express likes and dislikes.

O5.3 Listen attentively and understand more complex phrases and sentences

- understand the main points from speech which includes unfamiliar language.

O5.4 Prepare a short presentation on a familiar topic

- remember, retain and recall words, phrases and sentences
- memorise and present a set of instructions.

Year 6

O6.1 Understand the main points and simple opinions in a spoken story, song or passage

- listen attentively, re-tell and discuss the main ideas
- agree or disagree with statements made about a spoken passage.

O6.2 Perform to an audience

- recite a short piece of narrative either from memory or by reading aloud from text
- develop a sketch, role play or presentation and perform to the class or an assembly.

O6.3 Understand longer and more complex phrases or sentences

- re-tell using familiar language a sequence of events from a spoken passage, containing complex sentences
- understand and express reasons
- understand the gist of spoken passages containing complex sentences, e.g. descriptions, information, instructions.

O6.4 Use spoken language confidently to initiate and sustain conversations and to tell stories

- participate in simple conversations on familiar topics
- describe incidents or tell stories from their own experience, in an audible voice.

Clearly the major progression occurs in the following:

- the *amount* of material a child is expected to marshall and use – from remembering and using single words and short sentences to performing a sketch or role play to an assembly
- the *complexity* of types of material – from finger rhymes, words and phrases to pieces of narrative and conversations
- the interaction of *receptive* and *productive skills* – from repeating modelled phrases and remembering sequences or words to retelling, agreeing/ disagreeing and expressing reasons in reaction to language heard

- the *independence* with which the child manages this – from identifying, joining in and repeating to planning, developing and participating
- the *fluency* and *confidence* with which he or she expresses language, leading to the fluency necessary for performance.

This entirely accords with our presentation of progression through the central chapters, where we have tried to show the need to build in these same ways, from more receptive to more productive, from more language-orientated to more integrated curricular models and from more limited to more open-ended sources of input, either from the teacher or other sources.

 Reflection point

Although no longer current education policy, using the former Framework for planning allows teachers to reflect on different strategies relating to how children learn languages and how they acquire necessary skills to be successful language learners.

Four short teaching sequences follow. The first, which we are using as an example, has the Framework objectives listed immediately afterwards. It is important to see all the possibilities as we have done here, not in order to break a world record for objective linking, but because all of the objectives represent worthwhile focuses for the language teacher. Having a clear overview of those objectives in action will shape the teaching towards more purposeful activity and more focused plenary review.

After reading the example, try to make a parallel list for the other three activities, considering all five strands.

1. In Y4, the children have been studying the geography and climate of Canada. They now look at the most popular sports. In small groups they are matching visuals of sports and simple phrases (*'J'aime faire du ski. Je n'aime pas jouer au hockey.'*) Then they discuss how these sports are placed in order of popularity (*'C'est numéro 1? C'est le sport le plus populaire?'*)

In this activity the children match phrases and short sentences to pictures or themes (L4.1), they listen with care (O4.2) and ask and answer questions (O4.4). They also learn about some aspects of everyday life and compare them to their own (IU4.2). In terms of Knowledge about Language (KAL), the children recognise categories of words, use question forms, they apply phonic and whole word knowledge in order to decode text. They also use a range of language learning strategies (LLS) to carry out the task: they use context and previous knowledge to determine meaning and pronunciation, they practise with a friend, use gesture and mime to show they understand and practise saying new words aloud.

(Continued)

(Continued)

2. A Y3 class is watching a short video of children performing a finger rhyme, sent by the partner school in France.

   Voici ma main

   Voici mes doigts

   En voici un

   En voici trois

   Le petit rentre chez toi

   Le grand rentre chez toi

   Et toi mets ton nez là.

(For more finger rhymes, visit: www.comptinesetjeuxdedoigts.com/index.php). The children join in with the actions, then try to imitate the pronunciation and join in with both words and actions. The teacher draws their attention to a certain sound and the children identify words that rhyme with the initial word. Then the written form is displayed and the children spot the words that rhyme. They might segment the phonemes of *toi*, then the teacher could set them a reading and a writing challenge with simple words containing the phoneme *oi*.

3. In Y5, the children read descriptions of penfriends sent from the partner school and carry out a 'guess who' activity, identifying them from the pictures and pen portraits on a poster (details include favourite sports, other hobbies, clothes and so on).

4. In Y6, working in pairs, the children sort statements into groups. The classification includes forms of *aimer* and *avoir*, positives and negatives, but these categories were not given to the children. The teacher then asked the pairs to say how they had divided up the statement cards (that is, according to content or language forms) and why.

Auditing planning with the new National Curriculum

As we saw from the initial vignette quotation, the former Framework intended teachers to plan interesting, creative lessons. This must be the same with the new National Curriculum. If a teacher has a topic in mind and starts to plan the activities that seem to best fit the topic and the class (as a whole and as individuals), then he or she can match those activities to the National Curriculum Programmes of Study (and we suggest also using the former Framework to create more manageable, year group-appropriate objectives) and in this way audit the range of planning to ensure it has sufficient variety. Sometimes the objectives will themselves act as a stimulus for planning (see section below) and sometimes the 'organic' nature of the topic planning will produce a set of tasks that will only be matched up later.

Teachers do need to consider the types of tasks they set as these must be varied, engaging, literally thought-provoking and age-appropriate. They should also be enjoyable! Chapters 3 to 6 have contained examples of a range of activities that we have found are positively received and have contributed to successful learning. The example below uses some of these and also contains variants for the four year groups, three to six.

We need to remember, when using the National Curriculum, that we will be designing tasks to match the Programmes of Study on a very regular basis across the four years, so we should not become overly repetitive in terms of the classroom experience. It is still a worthwhile aim, however, to personalise these suggestions and, especially, to try to let the topic and the content drive the kind of work you plan, as that way the activities will have purpose and the learning will be better. We give a detailed example of such planning next and comment on it afterwards.

Planning example: healthy living using *La surprise de Handa*

A school chose the topic 'healthy living' for all its children and decided to integrate KS2 French into the topic as fully as possible. The main starter resource chosen for French for all years was the story *Handa's Surprise* in French – *La surprise de Handa/La sorprese de Handa* (Brown, 1994). Also produced and used were instructions for PE lessons, healthy meals at lunchtime and canteen menus in the target language. Some activities were designed to be used with the whole school, some were specific to year groups, as Table 7.1 shows. The learning objectives, as they appear in the scheme, are presented in the first column and the parallel. Framework learning outcomes are in the second column. The key column in terms of what the teacher and children are actually doing, and which was the first part of the plan to evolve in this case, is the third column. The resources needed for the activities appear in the fourth column in order that teachers wanting to use or adapt the scheme can have an easy checklist of what would be necessary.

In addition to the activities above, during a whole-school assembly, the children presented the work that they had completed and this included from KS1 classes a play, a version of *The Enormous Turnip – Le navet géant, Die Riesenrübe* and *El nabo gigante* (Lewis, 1999) – with the teacher reading and the children acting and joining in with the recurring sentence, *'Ils ont tiré, tiré, tiré, mais le navet n'a pas bougé'*. There was also whole-school singing, such as the song *Savez-vous planter les choux*.

Table 7.1 Planning scheme: healthy living using *La surprise de Handa*

Year 3

Learning objectives	Learning outcomes (relating to the National Curriculum Programme of Study)	Teaching activity/language	Resources
Listen and respond to simple stories Recognise and respond to sound patterns and words	Listen attentively to spoken language and show understanding by joining in and responding	Children hear story, hold up laminated pictures of fruit when their one is mentioned	Story, *La surprise de Handa*, laminated pictures of fruit and basket
Identify specific sounds, phonemes and words Understand that familiar things have different names in different countries Use gesture or mime to show the children understand Play games to help the children remember Use context of what they see/read to determine some of the meaning	Develop accurate pronunciation and intonation so that others understand when they are using familiar words and phrases	The teacher calls out different fruits that children place in the basket Focusing on pronunciation, the children play simple repetition game *Répétez si c'est vrai*	
Recognise some familiar words in written form	Read carefully and show understanding of words	Pictures of fruits and word cards are given to individual children who have to find their partners	Word cards with names of fruits
Listen and respond to simple rhymes Make links between some phoneme, rhymes and spellings and read aloud familiar words Identify specific sounds, phonemes and words Remember rhyming words	Appreciate stories, songs, poems and rhymes in the language; explore the patterns and sounds of language through songs and rhymes and link the spelling, sounds and meanings of words	To extend knowledge of fruit vocabulary and focus on rhyming sounds (*abricot, trop*), the children learn French comptine '*Pêche, pomme, poire, abricot*'	Comptine '*Pêche, pomme, poire, abricot*' (phoneme focus on silent consonant at end of word, such as *abricot, trop, avocat, vert, fruit*)
Locate country/countries where the language is spoken	Describe places and things orally; ask and answer questions	Display pictures and words of fruits mentioned in story and a map of the world. Ask children to place fruits on country of origin using guided questioning, such as, *la mangue vient de …*	Word cards with names of fruits to support writing

Year 3

Learning objectives	Teaching activity/language	Resources
Experiment with the writing of simple words	Children design their own fruit basket (*La surprise de …*), writing a list of the fruits included (*Dans mon panier j'ai une orange.*) Children are encouraged to use plurals	
Recognise how sounds are represented in written form		
Understand how far letters/letter strings are both similar to and different from English		
Describe things in writing; understand basic grammar (plurals)		
Develop accurate pronunciation and intonation so that others understand when they are reading aloud	Shared second reading of story. Teacher leaves out some of the words (*fruits, bonjour, surprise*) for the children to fill in missing words	

Year 4

Learning objectives	Learning outcomes (relating to the National Curriculum Programme of Study)	Teaching activity/language	Resources
Listen for specific words and phrases	Listen attentively to spoken language and show understanding by joining in and responding; appreciate stories, songs, poems and rhymes in the language	Children hear story and hold up laminated pictures of fruit when their one is mentioned	Story, *La surprise de Handa*, and laminated pictures of fruit
Follow a short familiar text, listening and reading at the same time			
Know about some aspects of everyday life and compare them to their own			
Use prior knowledge of text types in English and other languages			
Apply previous knowledge and language cues to help understanding and pronunciation			
Play games to help remember	Listen attentively to spoken language and show understanding by joining in and responding	They play *Salade de fruits* – sitting in a circle, the children are each given a name of a fruit. When their fruit is called out, they get up and change places	

(Continued)

Table 7.1 (Continued)

Year 4

Learning objectives	Learning outcomes	Teaching activity/language	Resources
Ask and answer questions on several topics	Engage in conversations, ask and answer questions; express opinions and respond to those of others	Fruit tasting: children taste a range of fruits mentioned in the story and are invited to express likes and dislikes – *Tu aimes des mandarins? Tu aimes la mangue?* Children offer different types of fruit to each other, asking whether they like them or not. *'Passe-moi … s'il te plaît.' 'Voilà!' 'Merci!'* or *Tu aimes …?' 'Oui, j'adore …/Non, je n'aime pas. '*	Real fruit and prompt cards to support role play scenarios
Read some familiar words and phrases aloud and pronounce them accurately			
Recognise negative statements			
Use question forms			
Practise saying new words aloud			
Write simple words and phrases using a model and some words from memory	Describe things in writing	They then fill in a grid, giving their opinion on each of the fruits tasted. Finally, they conduct a class survey to find out the most popular fruit and convert the information into a bar chart	Grid to note findings of fruit tasting
Apply phonic and whole-word knowledge to write simple words and phrases			
Use spelling strategies appropriately	Write phrases from memory and adapt these to create new sentences to express ideas clearly	Throughout the week, the children fill in their healthy eating record – *'Mangez 5!', 'Lundi, je mange une pomme, des carottes. Je bois un jus d'orange.'*	Healthy eating diary

Year 5

Learning objectives	Learning outcomes (relating to the National Curriculum Programme of Study)	Teaching activity/language	Resources
Prepare and practise a simple conversation reusing familiar vocabulary and structures in new contexts	Broaden the children's vocabulary and develop their ability to understand new words that are introduced into familiar written material	The children are given a range of visuals of food items. Classify them into groups – *les fruits, les légumes, la viande, les produits laitiers* and so on. Focus on fruits, asking the children to select the tropical fruits – *les fruits tropicaux.* Call out fruits, ask the children to hold up the correct one	Laminated pictures of food items
Understand and express simple opinions			
Recognise that languages borrow words from other languages			

Year 5

Reread frequently a variety of short texts Look at aspects of their everyday lives from the perspective of someone from another country	Read the story, ask the children to join in with names of fruit and colours – some will join in with repetitive phrases. The children make predictions as to where the story could be set. Locate some French-speaking countries in Africa. In pairs, the children list aspects of the story that are similar to/different from their own everyday life	Story, *La surprise de Handa*, and photocopies of text of story
Prepare and practise a simple conversation reusing familiar vocabulary and structures in new contexts Understand and express simple opinions Understand and use negative statements	Children classify different food into healthy/unhealthy, discussing in pairs – 'C'est bon pour la santé ou C'est mauvais pour la santé?' Teacher tries to elicit why – 'Pourquoi? C'est trop sucré?'	Picture/word cards of food items
Understand basic grammar appropriate to the language (sentence structure, word order, adjectival endings) Use a physical response Integrate language into previously learned language	Whole class play word class game (different actions for different word classes called out). Then, in groups, they make sentences using word cards to practise position of adjectives and reinforce adjectival agreements	
Make simple sentences and short texts Manipulate language by changing a single element in a sentence. Apply knowledge of language rules and conventions when building short sentences Recognise some basic aspects of agreement where relevant, such as gender, singular/plural, pronoun/verb, adjectives	Children write fruit poems, including adjectives from story – *délicieux (-se), juteux(-se), sucré(e), rond(e), crémeux(-se), rouge, jaune* Practise reading poems in pairs to perform in assembly	Word bank to support writing of fruit poems

(Continued)

Table 7.1 (Continued)

Year 6

Learning objectives	Learning outcomes (relating to the National Curriculum Programme of Study)	Teaching activity/language	Resources
Read and understand the main points and some detail from a short written passage Identify different text types and read short, authentic texts for enjoyment or information LLS Make sensible guesses based on cues	Read carefully and show understanding of words, phrases and simple writing; broaden their vocabulary and develop their ability to understand new words that are introduced into familiar written material	Show children a recipe of a fruit salad. Ask them to identify the text type Focus on fruits, asking the children to select the tropical fruits – *les fruits tropicaux*	Recipe of fruit salad on the interactive whiteboard
Read and understand the main points and some detail from a short written passage Apply knowledge of word order and sentence construction to support understanding Apply previous knowledge and language cues to help understanding and pronunciation	Develop accurate pronunciation and intonation so that others understand when they are reading aloud; appreciate stories, songs, poems and rhymes in the language; describe people, places, things and actions in writing	Children read the story in pairs, highlighting the names of fruits while reading. Shared reading of story, children encouraged to join in, continuing reading of words left out by teacher	Story, *La surprise de Handa*
Understand longer and more complex phrases or sentences Work out meanings by using a range of cues Analyse what they need to know in order to carry out a task	Listen attentively to spoken language and show understanding by responding	Teacher reads out recipe, gives jumbled up instructions of how to make a fruit salad to the children; working in groups of four, the children reconstitute the recipe, then collect the correct equipment and follow instructions to make a salad	Instructions for recipe cut up, equipment and ingredients for fruit salad
Write sentences on a range of topics using a mode Perform to an audience Present information about an aspect of culture Use knowledge of form, including plurals and notations of gender to improve access to a range of texts Apply knowledge of word order and sentence construction to support understanding Analyse what they need to know in order to carry out a task Recall, retain and use words, phrases and sentences Apply grammatical knowledge to make sentences	Present ideas and information orally to a range of audiences	Using the Internet, the children search for recipes from different French-speaking countries. Each group presents its recipe with some short information about the country focused on to the rest of the class	Access to the Internet and dictionaries

Progression in the whole-school topic

The scheme given above clearly shows that we need to build our progression into the types of categories we introduced earlier in the chapter, notably in areas such as independence, the complexity of the ways in which the language is linked to the content and, very importantly, in the level of language function demanded.

The new National Curriculum, unlike the former KS2 Framework, does not provide the level of detail to support year-on-year progression; it really only lists the skills that should be developed by the end of this Key Stage. In the scheme described here, the younger children are engaged by the story and then begin to use the language at a simple level, responding to what they hear, repeating words and phrases and focusing on sounds. In this way they gradually learn the vocabulary for the fruit items and then later begin to consider an intercultural perspective as a result of undertaking a task on where the fruits originate from.

By Y4, the children are being more active from the start – the *Salade de fruits* game demands more concentration than before, for example. They link to the general topic by tasting and then responding to the fruits and by sharing opinions with each other. The language of likes and dislikes, questioning and polite requests is all included here, bringing together material learned in other contexts and teaching any new items needed via the situated topic and purposeful activity of tasting and reacting.

By Y5, the children are using their acquired knowledge of fruit and other foods to carry out a classification task before hearing the story, then focusing on fruit, then subsequently tropical fruit, so they are primed for important details before they are read to them. By classifying visual images with labels, they are beginning to learn vocabulary without going through a teacher-led presentation session. Also, the task requires them to think as they classify and this concentration on the items should help their learning.

As we indicated earlier, children need the language to accompany the tasks the teacher uses regularly (in this case, the language of discussion while making classifications, such as, 'I disagree, because that is a …', 'Isn't that a …?', 'Yes that's right.' and so on). If they have used this before, the classification task becomes a more language-rich experience for them.

The Y5 children are also asked to identify possible locations for the story after the reading, bringing in an intercultural element that reflects existing knowledge or gives new ideas about where French (or Spanish) is spoken in the world.

By Y6, the class is working from a recipe for a dish that they will later actually create. The children are reading the story in pairs and they also hear it read by the teacher, but by then there is an expectation that they can join in and take over if he or she pauses or misses words.

Towards the end of the scheme for each year, the children are being active and productive in different ways, which also reflects the progression in the amount or complexity of both the material they use and the style of their production. In Y3, the emphasis is on controlled sentence writing, along with creative activity (drawing a fruit basket) and gap-fill oral production when the teacher reads the story again. Y4 manage a class survey using simple questions and also list their 'five a day' intake. Y5 move on to more creative writing by producing fruit poems and later perform these in assembly, while Y6 follow instructions to make a recipe and also search for other recipes with a connection to different French-speaking countries. Again, they present findings both in the class and in assembly.

This brief summary shows how important it is to consider the children's age, prior world knowledge, thinking and reasoning capability, independence and ability to plan and carry out oral presentations to different audiences, in addition to planning from a starting point of knowledge of language or competence in language skills. The scheme considers all of these elements, perhaps not overtly, but in the way it has identified progression across so many fields.

Primary teachers know well how individual year groups manage the demands made by different styles of work. They often stay with a year group and so become accustomed to planning to raise capabilities within their year and sphere of influence. An incoming new class teacher does not necessarily have that overview, but will need to gain it for a specific year group and reflect it in the ML planning he or she undertakes. An incoming language specialist who may be teaching a range of groups needs to balance the two strands of overall skills and capabilities, as well as knowledge of language and competence in language skills Language capabilities may not be progressive across the year groups if, for example, a whole Key Stage is starting a foreign language at the same time, but the other core abilities will be in place and do need to be reflected in the planning.

We have seen examples in Chapters 5 and 6 of how we might reach higher levels of language activity by putting in place careful scaffolding and the use of prior knowledge to help make new language clear. By approaching our planning in this way, we can avoid a situation where Y6 children are still learning language (even if a new topic) at the same level as Y3 children and are practising and manipulating language using the same activity types (in terms of games, dialogues and worksheet formats). The former Key Stage 2 Framework shows clear types of approaches, using different strands, and, to an extent, reflects ways of using language to learn. As we showed in Chapter 2, it is possible to make associations between the literacy strands and approaches to foreign language learning and use, as long as we keep the level of expectation manageable. However we plan, a clear progression focus will make the subject vibrant, stimulating and challenging – without losing any of the fun.

 ## Reflection point

Take an existing plan for a ML unit that relates to a school or class topic, audit it against the new National Curriculum Programmes of Study and, if you wish to, the former KS2 Framework, then review it against the sample scheme given in this chapter. Would you alter it if you teach it again? If so, how and why?

Progression across the Key Stage

We include next (Figure 7.1) an example of a school's progression ladder across KS2, with some material for KS1 also included as this school teaches a language throughout. This trial model, which was written for the New Curriculum and would be reviewed in July 2015, has used the new National Curriculum

Oracy	Literacy	Intercultural understanding
Year 6 Develop accurate pronunciation and intonation so that others understand when they are reading aloud or using familiar words and phrases. Present ideas and information orally to a range of audiences. Describe people, places, things and actions orally. Understand the main points and simple opinions in a spoken story, song or passage. Understand longer and more complex phrases or sentences.	**Year 6 Write phrases from memory and adapt these to create new sentences to express their ideas clearly. Describe people, places, things and actions in writing. Understand basic grammar, key features and patterns of language, how to apply these and how these differ from or are similar to English.** Read and understand the main points and some detail from a short text. Identify different text types and read short, authentic texts for enjoyment or information. Write sentences on a range of topics using a model.	**Year 6** Compare attitudes towards aspects of everyday life. Recognise and understand some of the differences between people. Present information about an aspect of culture.
Year 5 Express opinions and respond to those of others. Seek clarification and help. Speak in sentences, using familiar vocabulary, phrases and basic language structures. Prepare a short presentation on a familiar topic.	**Year 5 Broaden their vocabulary and develop their ability to understand new words that are introduced into familiar written material, including through using a dictionary. Understand basic grammar (conjugation of high-frequency words).** Reread frequently a variety of short texts. Make simple sentences and short texts. Write words, phrases and short sentences, using a reference.	**Year 5** Look at aspects of their everyday lives from the perspective of someone from another country. Recognise similarities and differences between places. Compare symbols, objects or products which represent their own culture with those of another country.
Year 4 Engage in conversations; ask and answer questions. Memorise and present a short spoken text. Listen for specific words and phrases. Listen for sounds, rhyme and rhythm.	**Year 4 Read carefully and show understanding of words, phrases and simple writing. Understand basic grammar (feminine/masculine).** Follow a short familiar text, listening and reading at the same time. Write simple words and phrases using a model and some words from memory.	**Year 4** Learn about festivals and celebrations in different cultures. Know about some aspects of everyday life and compare them to their own. Compare traditional stories.
Year 3 Listen attentively to spoken language and show understanding by joining in and responding. Explore the patterns and sounds of language through songs and rhymes and link the spelling, sound and meaning of words.	**Year 3 Appreciate stories, songs, poems and rhymes in the language.** Make links between some phonemes, rhymes and spellings and read aloud familiar words. Experiment with the writing of simple words.	**Year 3** Identify social conventions at home and in other cultures. Make indirect or direct contact with the country/countries where the language is spoken.
Year 2 Listen and make a physical response to simple rhymes, stories and songs.	**Year 2** Start to recognise some familiar words in written form. Start to make links between some phonemes, rhymes and spellings.	**Year 2** Learn about the different languages spoken by children in the school.
Year 1 Listen to and join in with simple rhymes, stories and songs.	**Year 1** Show interest in following a story where text is visible.	**Year 1** Locate country/countries where the language is spoken. To learn about ways of travelling to the country/countries.

Figure 7.1   New Curriculum progressive skills ladder for ML

Programmes of Study (shown in bold), but with items from the former KS2 Framework also included (in normal font). The columns have maintained the previous headings of oracy and literacy and the intercultural understanding header has also been retained as this is seen as good practice.

Chapter summary

In this chapter we have presented the key features and qualities of the new National Curriculum and have referenced this to the former KS2 Framework. We have tried to suggest ways in which these documents can be used to audit medium-term schemes for breadth and progression.

We have identified the nature of the progression contained within the former KS2 Framework by comparing objectives at different levels and analysing the range of skills it seems to suggest. We have suggested that this may still be necessary as the new National Curriculum does not contain exemplars of progression

We have presented a scheme of work that shows how the objectives could look in practice and how they can be used to audit a workplan with coherence in itself, but can be checked for breadth and progression by such cross-referencing.

Finally, we have shown an example of a Key Stage skills progression ladder that attempts to marry items from the former KS2 Framework with the new National Curriculum Programmes of Study to break down the general statements into smaller steps.

Key reading

The *Language Learning Journal*, 37 (2) and 38 (2) are each special issues on primary languages containing curriculum-related articles.

Visit the FLAME website of the Association for Language Learning at: www.flame-plus.net

Swarbrick, A. (2011) 'Languages: Building on firm foundations', *Curriculum Journal*, 22 (2): 227–41.

CHAPTER 8

HOW DO I KNOW IF THE CHILDREN ARE LEARNING? HOW CAN I HELP THEM TO PROGRESS SMOOTHLY TO KS3?

Chapter objectives

- To remind the reader of the important issues surrounding different forms and types of monitoring and assessment.
- To address how to establish 'what we know' without a test – and how to use plenary in a language class to consolidate, extend and assess.
- To address the means of assessment of 'language in use' – content, communication of content, pronunciation/intonation, creativity/ spontaneity, accuracy.
- To focus on the potential of peer- and self-evaluation and show how success criteria can be used to help children improve their competence and set targets.
- To explore models for managing the transition between KS2 and KS3.
- To suggest recording formats for the children to use and how these may be involved in giving children more ownership over the transition process.

Teachers' standards			
A teacher must:			
2			Promote good progress and outcomes by pupils
	a		be accountable for pupils' attainment, progress and outcomes
	b		be aware of pupils' capabilities and their prior knowledge, and plan teaching to build on these
	c		guide pupils to reflect on the progress they have made and their emerging needs
	d		demonstrate knowledge and understanding of how pupils learn and how this impacts on teaching
	e		encourage pupils to take a responsible and conscientious attitude to their own work and study
6			Make accurate and productive use of assessment
	a		know and understand how to assess the relevant subject and curriculum areas, including statutory assessment requirements
	b		make use of formative and summative assessment to secure pupils' progress
	c		use relevant data to monitor progress, set targets, and plan subsequent lessons
	d		give pupils regular feedback, both orally and through accurate marking, and encourage pupils to respond to the feedback

Source: DfE, 2013a

Introductory vignette

Y3 focus group discussing learning French:

Y3 Pupil 5: The colours is hard, *rouge* is red, *jaune* is yellow.

Y3 Pupil 4: *Noir* ...

Y3 Pupil 5: No *noir* is black.

Researcher: That's funny, because you said they were hard and then you told me three colours in French.

Y3 Pupil 5: (Proudly.) Yeah, but it's hard!

Comment

In many ways, learning a language is much more of a continuous process than learning other subjects. Despite the use of a topic-based curriculum, it is harder to box off knowledge into neat files than it can be in, say, science or history. Where this is done too rigidly in language learning, we find that content such as vocabulary does not always transfer between topics. As a result, children are often uncertain as to what they *do* actually know. This makes it all the more important that we both monitor their learning (for our own information and planning) and enable them to see their own progress. For this reason, this chapter looks at both the teacher's and the children's roles in assessment and, very importantly as we enter the time of compulsory language learning in KS2, in the transition process between primary and secondary settings.

The previous chapter dealt with the National Curriculum Programmes of Study and the former KS2 Framework as planning tools and showed how teachers might set up learning objectives for communication and language learning and the other elements that are involved in the wider curriculum taught in the chosen ML. This chapter reviews how you might want to undertake assessment activity, based on the objectives you set.

The chapter also, importantly, deals with transition issues that will need to be formalised within clusters of schools if we are to avoid the dangers of a 'back to the beginning' approach characteristic of some KS3 settings, either where schools have not communicated sufficiently well or the primary schools are teaching different languages or different amounts of language in different ways.

Initial reflection point

How do you measure your progress with language learning? Whether you class yourself as a beginner or have a high-level qualification, think back over a recent period of time and try to establish what you have learned and how you know this? If you find you cannot evaluate this easily, try to think of ways in which you could monitor and measure future learning.

Definitions of terms and rationale for changes

Assessment practice has changed enormously over the last 25 years. One of the perennial debates (each August) concerns whether the improving results at GCSE and A level reflect a 'watering down' of standards, a different examination focus or methodology or a strong improvement in teaching and learning. Some changes are easily identified, others can be guessed at, while others are more the projection of a political view held by a proponent than anything else.

The older O level and previous incarnations of A level examinations were usually negatively marked and the results produced by means of 'norm-referencing'. This means that papers had marks for each mistake made taken from a 'starting total' and, when the overall scores were produced, they were ordered into grades by means of a distribution curve. There were therefore approximately the same numbers of A, B and other grades each year. The justification for this was that, in large populations, there should not be much deviation in attainment across several years, so this was a fair system for producing a cohort's results. Details of scores were not made available so it was difficult to know how papers had been marked, but anecdotal reports suggest that in O level foreign language written papers, for example, the average mark for more open-ended writing tasks such as a picture story was 0! The culture seemed to be focused more on what people could *not* do rather than on what they *could* do.

The first big change, which happened formally with the introduction of the GCSE examinations in 1988, was to move to 'criterion-referenced marking'. This system rewards candidates for successes in defined tasks. So, in writing tasks, the new GCSE papers gave a brief for a communication (message, postcard, letter, story and so on) and listed areas of content that needed to be included. Marks were awarded on a content basis first and assessors simply had to decide if a sympathetic native speaker would understand the message without any trouble, would be able to piece it together, infer it or would not understand it. This was decided for each task on a 2–1–0 basis. Then a score was given for the range of language used to communicate the message and, finally, a mark for accuracy. In both cases there were descriptors for the examiners to use that defined how a piece of writing could score, say, between 10 and 12 marks or between 6 and 9 and so on. This meant that a reasonably accurate, reasonably appropriate message gained a majority of the marks available even if some of the very small niceties of grammatical accuracy were missing. This contrasted with the previous system in that, before, the smaller errors would still have been counted and therefore the marks would have been lower even if the message had been fairly clearly communicated. The other difference, of course, is that as many candidates gain the top grades as meet those criteria, so the 'norm' curve is no longer used to fix grades.

When the change happened, it was not a 'watering down' of standards but, rather, a redefinition of language assessment priorities. Instead of grammatical accuracy being the single most important element, communication of 'real' messages was now the focus, reflecting the changes in teaching objectives, syllabuses and materials (see Chapter 9 for a fuller discussion of these changes).

As early as 1984, Ames and Ames wrote about the preference for a task-mastery structure in which a learner's past performance was used to structure goals for future improvement not in a competitive, class-based scenario, but on an individual basis. A focus on what had been dubbed 'formative assessment' by writers in the 1960s (Scriven, 1967; Bloom, 1968) began to develop on both a theoretical basis and in classroom practice. This brought together two different groups:

- writers on motivation, such as Dweck (1986), who argued that 'summative assessment' demotivated learners
- assessment researchers.

Of the latter, Sadler (1989), for example, argued there was a need for authentic evaluative experience for the learners so that they could identify high-quality work and measure their own progress towards it. Cohen (1994) brought a language learning perspective to the issue – specifically, recommending formative activity alongside classroom tasks so that the teacher could better understand the skills and competencies of the children.

Following Black and Wiliam's work (1998), a major government initiative on assessment for learning was launched. The work of Clarke (1998, 2001, 2003, 2005) is often used as an example of how this approach is realised in primary classrooms. Clarke herself (2001: 2) presents the differences between *summative* and *formative* assessment in the following way:

> If we think of our children as plants, summative assessment of plants is the process of simply measuring them. The measurements might be interesting to compare and analyse, but, in themselves, they do not affect the growth of the plants. Formative assessment, on the other hand, is the garden equivalent of feeding and watering the plants – directly affecting their growth.

The argument for formative assessment is that it does not interrupt teaching and learning, but is an integral part of the process. So, it need *not* take longer, which some state is the case by way of objection to this method.

We mentioned in an earlier chapter the implications for motivation of a learner being told what she had to say and write in a language test, irrespective of whether or not it included her own real experience. Clearly such a scenario does not make learners feel that the testing they are undergoing has value either. There is sometimes in the secondary sector the rather dubious practice of formally testing each unit as it is finished and 'retro-structuring' the teaching according to the content of that test. So, the focus is very much on preparing for the assessment that is to come (sometimes by copying down the vocabulary and structures that should be learned) and so teaching principally the material that the teacher *knows* will feature in the test. This makes language learning a mere process of setting out a perfectly spaced line of very similar hurdles, practising jumping over each one several times and then running the race, finding a remarkably predictable outcome. The problem is that, for some children, it does not work and they only achieve a string of failures. For others, the hurdles are structured so the runner can simply take them in her or his stride with little effort and their regular placement and predictable appearance means that no particular thinking focus is needed to evaluate how best to jump each one. In neither case does the particular group of learners benefit. Worse than that, of course, unfortunately, regular lines of hurdles are rarely seen in target language-using countries. So, even those who reach the finishing line successfully unit after unit find themselves stranded when placed in *real* communicative situations.

Formulaic summative testing, then, is not the answer – especially not in the primary phase. Nevertheless, teachers do need to know how children are progressing. So, teachers need to know how to use classroom activities to find out about children's knowledge, understanding and skills. We should never forget that monitoring and assessment are as much intended to inform teachers about their own teaching and support their future planning as they are intended to inform children and their parents about achievement. Assessment is not about judging children, but it is about making their future learning opportunities as good as possible.

How might we find out what the children know without a test?

We can start to set out a general set of principles by looking at the findings of two research studies (Gattullo, 2000; Zangl, 2000) that looked specifically at how children aged between 8 and 12 might be assessed in their English lessons in Italy and Austria respectively.

Gattullo (2000: 279) highlighted the type of assessment she wanted to explore in the following terms:

> For the next phase in the research, a broad definition of 'classroom assessment for formative purposes' was adopted as a starting point. The following are identified as the main traits of this type of assessment:
>
> • it is an ongoing multi-phase process that is carried out on a daily basis through teacher–pupil interaction;
>
> • it provides feedback for immediate action; and
>
> • it aims at modifying teaching activities in order to improve learning processes and results.

After her exploratory study, Gattullo (2000: 284) noted that:

> The classroom data analysed to date suggests that some formative assessment actions are more common than others (i.e., questioning, correcting, judging), at the expense of those that could be considered more beneficial for learning (e.g., observing process, examining product, metacognitive questioning).

We will take up this point later in the chapter as we examine examples of assessment practice.

Zangl (2000: 251), similarly, set out her beliefs in her introduction, maintaining that:

> Oral testing in playful situations with the integration of visual and tactile stimuli can be used ... to elicit valuable information about the learners' foreign language development.

Her (2000: 257) conclusion contained three major considerations with regard to assessment objectives that teachers should try:

1. to assess the learner's proficiency within a multi-component framework, comprising not only domain-/structure-specific items but also the use of language within the social context of the classroom;
2. to capture both the learner's individual profile and the performance level of the class as a whole; and
3. to trace the learner along his or her developmental path where time and experience act as constructive factors.

The previous government's statement on primary languages assessment taken from the 'Languages review' (DfES, 2007a: 10) highlighted the need for some summative assessment at the end of KS2, but stressed this was still intended for *formative* purposes:

> There should be informal classroom assessment of every child's learning near the end of Key Stage 2 ... The assessment we recommend is formative in purpose, fit for the individual child, not aggregated, and should not be the basis for any league tables.

The former 'Languages Ladder' structure was intended to cross-reference to the *Common European Framework of Reference for Languages: Learning, teaching and assessment* (Council of Europe, 2001). This is a very detailed document that gives both the background for and detailed descriptors of language competence at all levels from basic use up to mastery. The two levels associated with basic use are (globally) as shown in Table 8.1 (2001: 24), although much more detailed individual descriptors associated with the four skills are also available.

Table 8.1 The levels of language competence associated with basic use, as given in the Common European Framework (CEF) of Reference for Languages: Learning, Teaching, Assessment (Council of Europe, 2001)

Basic user	A2	Can understand sentences and frequently used expressions related to areas of most immediate relevance (e.g. very basic personal and family information, shopping, local geography, employment). Can communicate in simple and routine tasks requiring a simple and direct exchange of information on familiar and routine matters. Can describe in simple terms aspects of his/her background, immediate environment and matters in areas of immediate need.
	A1	Can understand and use familiar everyday expressions and very basic phrases aimed at the satisfaction of needs of a concrete type. Can introduce him/herself and others and can ask and answer questions about personal details such as where he/she lives, people he/she knows and things he/she has. Can interact in a simple way provided the other person talks slowly and clearly and is prepared to help.

At the time of writing, there is little guidance available on the assessment of the non-core subjects of the new National Curriculum. It would be helpful to retain links to the CEF to place language learning in England in a recognisable context with standards abroad, but there is as yet no indication of whether or not this will be the case. With regard to assessment, however, and as we stated in the previous chapter concerning the Programmes of Study, while it may be something that our work with children should be referenced to, it should not be a starting point for planning. Any of these descriptor-type assessment tools may offer a useful way to review learning at periodic intervals, but should not be a frame that defines what or, even worse, *how* language is taught. Nevertheless, it is important that these instruments become familiar to teachers and are used when the school and the teacher feel it would be appropriate to take a snapshot of progress.

Initial thoughts on monitoring learning

Monitoring is a complex practice. When considering how to assess language more formally, we often break it down into separate skills and so find ways to test specifically listening, speaking, reading and writing. This is, of course, unnatural in real language use as the skills are inevitably interlinked. An obvious example of this is that a normal conversation demands both listening and speaking skills to be activated. Language learning, however, does often involve differential abilities in these skills so there is some logic behind single-skill testing.

When monitoring, we need to remember that children will normally understand more than they can produce. (If they do not, a teacher needs to review how he or she is exposing the children to the language.) Logically, a primary-age child, especially at the younger end of the age range, should be able to *listen* and understand to a greater degree than he or she can *read* and understand (although, of course, this will never apply to 100 per cent of any class). Similarly, the majority of children will be able to *understand* language better than they can *produce* language and, in the production process, will generally be able to *speak* more readily than they can *write*.

Receptive language

Let us consider first how we might monitor children's 'receptive language' development – in other words, how they cope with the language they encounter by hearing or reading the target language. This is not, however, the same process as is used in GCSE listening and reading tests, nor is it really assessing in the same way.

Remember that we are using in-class activity as an assessment source. We first need to consider non-verbal responses as a useful methodology. If we track back through Chapters 3 to 6, we will recall activities such as the Reception-age children making masks, the early starters making a collage and the more advanced learners following recipes. In all of these cases there was an outcome which showed that the children had comprehended the instructional language used, had followed those instructions and had created an art object or a dish. At one level and in one respect, then, they had demonstrated their ability to understand what might be quite complex instructional language without the need for a 'test' on that particular set of vocabulary.

When children regularly hear a stimulus foreign language utterance (no matter how quickly spoken or how grammatically complex it is) that prompts a real classroom action and is a familiar element of classroom life, it is easy to forget they are acting intuitively and language is a mere vehicle. Over a period of time, the languages teacher should build up a wide range of language that children hear, understand and act on. This will include, as we saw in Chapters 4 and 5, the language of:

- greeting
- checking (genuinely) on children's well-being
- organisation of the classroom
- management of behaviour
- routines, such as getting ready for other activities – assemblies, playtime, lunch, fruit distribution, getting changed for PE, getting ready to go home, (in faith schools) saying a prayer
- assembling the materials and parameters for work (equipment, date, topic)
- establishing prior knowledge and familiar language
- asking questions about routines.

In all of these areas, over a period of four years, the children should become completely at ease with the language. They generally have to respond non-verbally and spoken responses can be made at a variety of levels that all children will manage in time, as long as they are not 'tested' by being 'demanded'. When they do this, without fuss, in a natural way, they are operating in the language as a native speaker would. We cannot state too strongly that where this happens, it is a major achievement of primary language learning. It puts children at the beginning of KS3 at a clear advantage over 11-year-old beginners, not just in terms of what they know but also the fact that they can operate naturally, cope with a wider variety of language, hopefully spoken at near natural speed, and, most importantly, it does not seem like a chore or something difficult. In other words, they are equipped to keep operating in the language and learn more and more how to cope with authentic language that they might meet abroad. This is sometimes never achieved by learners starting at the age of 11, having two or three scattered hours per week.

Despite this being the case, if we tried to test this same language of instructions in a traditional way (perhaps by giving a vocabulary test), then we might find that some learners would not score very highly. Yet, if we regularly use such instructions and the children do what we have asked them to do, why should we 'test' them? At primary level we do not need to convert everything from receptive into active language and children will best remember, use and operate in the language if they see a clear purpose and context for doing so.

If we want to discover whether or not those phrases and structures have become an active part of their knowledge, then a more positive alternative to a test would be to play a game where a small group of children have responsibility for giving instructions for a day. This contextualises the demand you are making on them and is also potentially an enjoyable and humorous activity. Often children do not, in fact, produce these commands very well because usually they only need to understand them rather than say them, but it may be a good extension for more linguistically able, more confident children.

So far, we have considered the language accompanying routines and instructions and the language used to set up other activities, such as art or design and technology or PE, where language production may not be required at all. There are also, of course, receptive contexts where the language that has to be understood is intended to become active because it is the topic content. Whether or not the language is the content or the language is being used to teach another content (for example, something cultural about the target-language-speaking country or an element of another school subject), the teacher needs to know that what is being in some way presented to or encountered by the children is comprehensible.

We have seen the way in which we can build content via a series of smaller steps (simple decisions, responses chosen from a limited range of possibilities, the use of natural repetition by asking a question that has genuinely possible different answers to a range of children, the review of key words from time to time). These are all ways teachers can monitor as they teach, without needing to stop to assess, and, clearly, we need to use our 'normal' classroom assessment techniques to do this. These techniques might include:

- mini-whiteboards (used individually and by pairs)
- think–pair–share activities (individuals formulate thoughts and share with another child, then with another pair before they respond as a group)
- asking for agreement/disagreement with a response given by a child
- as well as using volunteers, the naming of children to answer, perhaps by using lolly sticks (for example, drawing from a class set with each one having a child's name written on it).

All of these techniques are just as valid in a language lesson as in any other. This means we are essentially using routine (but well-planned and carefully implemented) teacher questioning to monitor learning. This can be formalised into a review process, perhaps on the carpet, where the teacher has a clear agenda of wanting to find out what the class as a whole and perhaps certain individuals know and understand, but it can be more opportunistic and flexible.

Productive language

If we turn towards the monitoring of production, it is important first of all to recall that, even in formal assessment, the communication of content is prioritised and so teachers should always do everything they can to understand what a child is trying to say. This is a vital part of the motivational process referred to early in Chapter 5 and, whether or not we are 'testing', we should always give a child making an effort the maximum credit that we can. If a child feels he or she has failed to say the right thing, issues of self-esteem begin to come into play and anxiety levels in a parallel situation (in other words, any speaking turn the child might have thereafter) will become raised. Too many experiences like this will lead to the child withdrawing from participating and this will, in turn, lead to a lessening of focus and concentration. At this point, the whole downward spiral begins. Showing interest and encouraging children does not affect the conclusions we make from the monitoring process and the impact this has on our future planning. So, objective monitoring is a different issue from the motivation of the class and individuals in it.

When working out where children are in their language development, it can help if we try to distinguish between children using a simple stimulus–response strategy – that is, consciously recalling the vocabulary or structure for a response before making it – and what we might term 'operating in the language'. The simpler items will not be easy to interpret. For example, when a child hears *¡Hola!* and repeats *¡Hola!*, is it a programmed response or is he or she naturally using the language? Even a slightly more complex item, how-ever, such as, *¿Qué tal?*, can be revealing.

We should always look to avoid any language becoming merely a routine stripped of meaning and should remind ourselves of the particular detached tone that takes over a school full of children at the start of assemblies when they respond to a 'Good afternoon', with a chorused 'Good afternoon Mrs … Good afternoon everyone!' So, a response to *¿Qué tal?* of *¡Muy bien!* from an entire class smacks of, 'When we hear *¿Qué tal?*, we all say *¡Muy bien!*', rather than, 'She's asking how we are, now how do I say "OK"?' and is certainly not *'¡Mal!'* or even better, *'Tengo dolor de cabeza'*. The incident narrated earlier (see the box on page 50) of a child clutching her stomach, but still replying to her headteacher's question in French is a good example of that in action. If we do think that the responses are becoming mechanistic, we need to alter our use of language for the routines that are causing the problem.

Associated with assessment is the correction process. In a useful brief sum-mary of the different types of correction, Loewen (2007) makes the point that we might use correction simply in the form of a recast, which does not call attention to the mistake directly. We might be more explicit that it is an error, we might prompt for a correct form or we might overtly discuss the grammar of the mistake. Different researchers make claims for different approaches, but we should always remember that different learners respond differently to dif-ferent techniques so we should perhaps look carefully at the needs and responses of our children so we can choose the best method for *them*.

Generally, there is consensus that some kind of focus on form is needed if we want accuracy to be developed. This means that we can decide on a 'level of error', perhaps governed by successful or unsuccessful communica-tion. If the mistake is so great it jeopardises understanding, then correction is certainly desirable and could be explicit. Often at primary level it is pronun-ciation or choice of word rather than grammar that impedes communication, so a response consisting of the correct version and perhaps asking for a repetition is justified. By upper primary, these corrections are normally per-ceived as support and used accordingly. Younger children may not be able to correct in spite of all their teacher's efforts – if they are not ready, they will simply not do it. If a mistake is minor, often a recast with no indication that it is wrong is all that is needed. There is evidence that recasts do also have an effect on language competence, although it is usually at a slow rate, with less than half of recasts being noticed and acted on.

 Reflection point

Take a plan for a forthcoming language unit. How might you assess both during and towards the end of that unit? Will there be an outcome of some sort at the very end? Make some initial notes, then read on and add to them as you go.

When should we assess? Blurring the edges between 'learning activities' and 'plenaries'

All teachers tend to be very conscious now of the importance of plenaries at key stages of learning. The former National Literacy Strategy suggested the pattern of a three-part lesson and defined the plenary as a very vital part of a process that sought to maximise learning and continuous progression. After some use, and with the natural professional development that teachers always seem to create for themselves, the rigidity of the three-part lesson structure began to break down as teachers saw a need for several smaller 'checkpoints' within a lesson and so mini-plenaries began to emerge.

Current thinking seems to be that teachers should always seek to move on and develop progression within a lesson, but only when they are sure that the class is ready. In other words, we should always both plan and monitor with this two-pronged focus: learning should always develop and challenge should slowly grow, but learning should always be checked. Progression is vital, but not as some form of mechanistic automatised process. In the above section on children meeting new language and content, we showed that there is a continuum, with the teacher controlling the demand for more production carefully until confidence and familiarity begin to build.

One use of a mini-plenary is to retrace the steps of a PowerPoint presentation, selecting key vocabulary and concepts and checking them. This is where the classroom can sometimes become bilingual. A teacher asking a question in the foreign language may elicit a response in English because a child *wants* to explain something, but just does not have the language to do so. If the teacher picks up from the child's points, cross-references them visually to elements of the presentation and paraphrases the child's response into simple target language, then the use of the foreign language for learning has not been compromised and the children will have been exposed to further examples of key language in use.

Teachers do not, of course, spend the whole time with the children on the carpet questioning and monitoring learning. So how and when can we assess at other points? Children need to spend time working independently and together. They need to practise speaking the language in a non-threatening and purposeful environment, with a task that engages their interest and makes them think. When children are so occupied, it is easy for the teacher to monitor the talk and form a view on how well both the class as a whole and the individuals within it have internalised the content and language for the topic they are learning. It takes time to do this and no teacher can assess a whole class during each speaking activity, but a well-organised approach and an easy recording method makes it possible, manageable and not too stressful.

Imagine a common teaching topic – buying some basic food and drink in a café. This topic contains some active key vocabulary in the form of nouns (food and drink items), some functional language relating to politeness ('hello', 'please', 'thank you'), some structures ('Do you have … ?', 'I would like … ', 'Can I pay?') and some more receptive language ('What would you like?', 'That's [X amount]'). If the teacher sets up role plays, these may be differentiated with an easy task being followed by a more complex interaction. It is important to teach children to monitor their own and each other's learning and know when to move on to a more challenging activity (see the next section on peer- and self-assessment), but we also need to know that they can do this by monitoring what they are doing. A grid can be used for such monitoring – one that allows a teacher to eavesdrop and very easily and quickly note strengths and development areas. For the café topic, the grid might look like that shown in Table 8.2.

The standard grid would have the class list on the left-hand side and then blank boxes at the top (apart from the last two), so the relevant items could be inserted for different topics. A simple tick would mean the child was using the item properly. A question mark could be used to indicate a lack of confidence and a cross that the child appeared not to know the language needed to express this function. At this stage, accuracy can be interpreted from the tick/question mark records. If a teacher aimed to monitor a third of the class during any one activity (if more proved possible, so much the better), then he or she would gain a picture of the whole class in action fairly regularly, even if it was across a spread of activities. If monitoring just this third showed a pattern of any sort, it would still give a prompt for the teacher to take appropriate action and consolidate or extend language. The last two boxes allow for more precise notes to be made, where relevant.

Pronunciation can be impacted very successfully at primary level and whole-class discrimination and articulation games can be used to enhance this, focusing either on single or tricky words that the teacher's notes have highlighted are a common problem. The children now have a real understanding of the role of phonics in reading and this can be developed for the foreign language as well.

So, should the teacher intervene while monitoring or simply use the grid? As always, the answer is not a simple one. If the children are working well and there is a level of both engagement and fluency emerging in the dialogue, then intervention is probably not justified. If one partner is struggling

Table 8.2

Name	Drinks	Foods	Greetings	Politeness	Ich möchte	Haben Sie?	Zahlen bitte	Pronunciation issues	Other issues
Viktor									
Timea									
Callum									
Holly									

for words, then clearly it is appropriate to support and model. This might be the teacher taking over the role briefly to show how it could be done or it might be that the teacher suggests a couple of vocabulary items, but lets the pupil take it on immediately. Very poor pronunciation, especially if it might mean a native speaker would struggle to understand, should be corrected by means of a recast (the teacher saying the word or phrase) and possibly a request for both partners to repeat it. Smaller-scale errors, however, should be noted but not corrected there and then.

Should we test this sort of vocabulary in a 'conventional' format? What we can be sure of is that knowing a set of nouns or short phrases for a test does not automatically mean they can be used in real situations. It might even be that *not* knowing them for a test does not rule out them being retrieved in a real situation. Testing of vocabulary at primary level, especially in the first two years of learning, is probably best done as a whole-class interactive game, using an interactive whiteboard. In other words, it is better to practise language by means of a game than to test it by carrying out a test!

We have not so far addressed the assessment of grammar as a specific item because, again, we are not convinced that grammar needs to be separated from the use of language. A quick scan of the Knowledge about language strand in the former KS2 Framework shows that the major specific grammar issues addressed are plurals, gender agreements and word order. The new National Curriculum is couched in general terms, but possibly goes further because of this (see the text in bold below in the quote taken from DfE, 2013b):

- understand basic grammar **appropriate to the language being studied**, including (where relevant): feminine, masculine and neuter forms and **the conjugation of high-frequency verbs; key features and patterns of the language; how to apply these, for instance, to build sentences; and how these differ from or are similar to English**.

So, we may now be talking about learning some verb conjugations or cases, but we should be careful to not stray into either teaching or testing grammar per se. Children may always have noticed a range of verb endings and they may have encountered a past tense in a text. They can still be told about these things, but certainly do not need to learn them as a class and absolutely do not need to be tested on them!

Peer- and self-assessment – the role of success criteria

Before any meaningful peer- or self-assessment can take place, children must understand what they are assessing and how to do it. This means teachers must set success criteria and help the children to become aware of how to understand and use them. Because of this, success criteria might as well always be couched in child-friendly language from the start – there is little point in having two sets.

For the café activity, this might include:

- I know three drinks and three food items.
- I can say 'hello', 'please' and 'thank you'.
- I can ask for my food and drink politely.
- I can ask to pay.
- I can say the words properly.
- I can take part in the conversation without hesitating too much.

The first four criteria can be judged fairly easily by the pair working together. Assessing a dialogue activity in this way effectively combines self- and peer-evaluation as the judgement is made on both partners by both partners. The last two criteria are harder for them to evaluate but this tends to come with practice and can be drawn to the teacher's attention if there is disagreement between partners.

Clearly peer- and self-assessment are not substitutes for the teacher's monitoring, but, organised properly, have advantages in that they can sit alongside it as another evidence stream. Far more importantly, however, they help children to understand their own learning better and that enables them, ultimately, to make greater progress. Any targets teachers feel are needed are much more likely to have impact if they are negotiated and, for negotiation to be successful, children need to understand the starting point, a desirable next step and how to reach this.

There is an element of language learning here that might need to be worked through more in English. 'Learning to learn' (L2L) involves some complex ideas and complex words. As long as we signal to the class that we need to use English for a special reason, we can come out of target language mode and enter 'L2L time'. Whole-class work can be tailored towards individual or group targets, too, simply by the teacher reviewing the need for attention to be paid to certain aspects, with the lead-in being:, 'Those of you working on improving your pronunciation of the *ch* phoneme (in German) should pay special attention to this game now and should be putting your hands up to answer.'

Feedback on simple writing

Primary teachers know from literacy planning and the policies that apply across the curriculum that the correction of written work and the feedback that is given need to be explicit, constructive and positively phrased.

With an emerging focus on grammar, punctuation and spelling in the primary school English curriculum and in the new KS1 and KS2 tests (from

2016), we need to be a little careful about our expectations for writing in a foreign language. Previous exemplars of work featured by the QCA NC in Action site (no longer available) show via annotations that the expected level at the end of KS2 was signalled by inaccuracies connected with knowledge about language as well as a still developing ability to organise thoughts. It gave a clear message that we should not be too demanding in our expectations of emergent writing among primary language learners. The children, however, will become more focused on accuracy and some level of explicit correction can improve second language capability, as we saw in the section on the speaking task assessment.

Feedback is best centred on key language items in focus at that time and comments about how to improve are very important. Neither simply correcting nor simply praising effort will be successful in bringing about improvement, whereas a targeted comment and a suggestion for a way to improve, plus some kind of encouraging message, will, together, have a potentially positive impact.

Monitoring overall KS progress and managing the transition to KS3

Vignette

A primary languages teacher told us about her experiences of liaison with a partner secondary school:

The secondary primary liaison languages teacher came to observe me teaching at my school and saw me working with Y5. We were using a French story in the lesson, which the children quite liked as it involved a plot line where they were guessing what would come next. A few weeks later I went to see a Y7 French class at the secondary school. I was looking forward to it as I thought I might see some of the children I had taught for the two previous years. I was really sad to see a lesson based around single words and short phrases (colours) in a fast-paced but very teacher-centred games-based lesson – one of my very able boys looked so bored and I felt terrible, as I knew that he had learned most of that vocabulary in his first year of French in Y4. That afternoon I went back to my primary school and taught his sister in Y4 – we did something much more complex than he had been doing in the Y7 lesson.

As children start to learn languages in KS2, transition issues are raised and, year on year, become more acute. It is problematic enough when a group of children have learned a language for a year in Y6 and then join other Y7 students who have learned a different language or no language, but soon we will have the situation where children have learned a language for four years throughout KS2 and will present secondary colleagues with a wide range of knowledge, skills and understanding. Of course this is a normal scenario for other secondary teachers. It has only been with languages that the 'blank canvas' argument has ever been used. This 'convenient' view has always masked a reality, which was that the incoming students were rarely completely 'blank' in terms of their exposure to foreign languages and their cultural awareness. They were also far from equal in terms of aptitude and attitudes at that comparatively late starting age.

It is relevant to start with a brief discussion of some general transition issues. Languages transition needs to be seen in a context of the problems children may have on a social and personal as well as an academic level and in the context of other existing practice. In most secondary schools, there is now a very strong focus on the need to bring new children in each year with a measure of established familiarity with the buildings and facilities and routines of the 'big school'. Many secondaries have liaison teams who visit partner primaries and they hold open and induction days, involving students who transferred a year earlier to give a peer perspective to the newcomers. Some departments have well-organised subject liaison procedures and most attempt to make handover information as useful as possible.

In contrast to this more optimistic picture is the fact that secondaries often now take in children from a much greater range of primary schools than was the case some years ago and so the liaison is much more complex. Of course, the urban myths will always persist and each child preparing for transition will hear some variant on the 'horror stories' of secondary school life.

The notion of specialist teachers and specialist facilities is often a big attraction of the move, but it is easy to forget that children are used to just one or two teachers with whom they generally work out a productive relationship. Suddenly finding that they need to relate to more than ten teachers can be very daunting and may lead to a regrettable pattern of associating a subject with the teacher and not with the content and skills it covers. So, while, 'Which subject do you like best at the moment then Tom?' 'I like French best because Mr/Mrs ... is awesome!' may be a pleasing reaction when it is our own subject, it is a worrying one nevertheless. In fact, in many cases where KS2 languages are taught by an outreach or PPA cover teacher or even by another member of the school staff, this person is perhaps in a strong position to talk about transition in a generic way. Because he or she already represents a process (the need to relate to a less familiar teacher figure) that children will have to face many times over in a very short period at the beginning of a school year, he or she will be able to talk more convincingly about how to manage that difficult stage.

Many children are also anxious about losing the power to determine how they are placed in both classes and learning spaces within classes, forcing them to relate to a whole host of new peers with no friendship circle to fall back on. Essentially, they want to manage this big change by undertaking it with friends. Demetriou et al. (2000) found evidence that children have quite a sophisticated understanding of who they should *work* with as opposed to who they like to *socialise* with and concluded secondary schools should perhaps trust students' views of this a little more. The practice of seating students boy, girl, boy, girl was especially disliked at this stage.

Parallel to this, in a study of attainment rather than attitudes, Gibbons and Telhaj (2006) found that the general prior peer group attainment had little effect on the attainment of individual students, so, again, perhaps familiar pairings continuing through to Y7 would not have any detrimental effect on attainment.

Against this list of negative aspects we have now made, we should also note that Lucey and Reay (2000) write about the dual nature of the transition experience, which they characterise using Giddens' (1991) phrase 'anxious readiness'. They assert that much in the transition literature deals with the negatives of the move from primary to secondary schools, but, in their experience, most children have a mixture of emotions. They explain this in their conclusion (Lucey and Reay, 2000: 203):

> We would argue that the prospect of going to 'big school' presents children with a dilemma central to the experience of 'growing up'; that in order to gain freedom and autonomy from adult regulation one must be willing to relinquish some measure of the protection which that regulation affords. ... Despite the very great fears which children at times expressed in relation to the move from primary to secondary school, and challenges which the new environment will present to them, there was much evidence to suggest that most are able to call on hopeful feelings that on some level, at least some of the time, that move will be a benign one, populated by people who will be willing and able to support them through the changes.

In the transition report by Galton et al. (1999), the focus is on general attainment across the curriculum and the tendency for levels to fall at crucial change points, such as Y3, Y7 and Y8. They noted that, at the time of writing, the social and personal issues were being addressed effectively in many cases, but continuity in the curriculum remained a problem. One of their conclusions – the tendency for work to be repetitive and unchallenging after a transition – is a particular concern for us as ML teachers. As we saw in the introductory vignette, there are anecdotal stories of Y7 students starting again and, indeed, this was highlighted as a central reason for the failure of the 1960s Primary French initiative (Burstall et al., 1974; Hood, 1994). The systems for transfer of information and the establishment of mutual understanding of teaching styles, resources and assessment patterns are largely still in the future.

Galton et al. (1999) also noted that able boys were particularly vulnerable at Y7 to a dip in attainment across the curriculum and, given the gender issue that applies to language learning by older students, this would be a matter of real concern to us if it were true also for languages. In the very good CILT report on transition (O'Hagan, 2007, available at www.cilt.org.uk/secondary/transition.aspx), the interplay between Galton et al.'s general findings and ML-specific issues is addressed in some detail.

Overall, the transition to KS3 clearly represents a very major change for all 11-year-olds and we should bear in mind this more global context when we focus on language learning and teaching issues. Transition will now be spoken about much more frequently because it will become an urgent agenda.

Exploring existing transition processes

An Internet search entering the phrase 'primary languages transition' will yield a variety of results associated with local authorities or individual schools. Sometimes these contain quite detailed material and in other cases we find a simple grid to record experience or standards attained. The European Union has long offered formats for language learners to express their level of attainment at both adult and child levels and the final part of this chapter will look at an example of this structure.

One example of a documented and evaluated transition process is available at Links into Languages (at: www.linksintolanguages.ac.uk/resources/2549). This was evolved by a group of schools in Berkshire and the website makes available a range of documents, including a brief evaluation report, a scheme of work, resources and a small number of exemplars of pupil work, all in French. Searches for similar material from the Birmingham LA and West Sussex LA will also offer further examples.

Scotland has addressed this issue in greater depth and coherence as primary languages have for a long time been firmly embedded in its school system. Two websites – Education Scotland (at: www.educationscotland.gov.uk/video/p/primarysecondaryelearning.asp) and Scotland's National Centre for Languages (SCILT) (at: www.scilt.org.uk/Portals/24/Library/research/slwg/Transition.pdf) – show aspects of the provision in Scotland. The first, interestingly, involves a school abroad as well as the two partner schools in Scotland, while the second is a PowerPoint presentation from a conference that offers links to a range of good practice examples of transition projects in different areas.

The topic is also popular with researchers. As well as the report by Hunt et al. (2008) that reviewed the work of the LA Pathfinders (a series of eight case studies) and looked at what were then the future implications for schools, there are currently two projects ongoing until 2015, funded by the Nuffield Foundation (www.nuffieldfoundation.org/primary-modern-languages-impact-teaching-approaches) and the British Academy (www.education.leeds.ac.uk/research/projects/the-challenge-of-transition). It is to be hoped that, with funded research programmes also involving academics and schools abroad in the second case, real lessons will be established for future programmes to guide local authorities, teaching school alliances and academy chains towards making the complex partnerships between primary and secondary settings pupil-centred and progressive. The presentation from Scotland noted above (Breslin, 2011: slide 5) contains the words, 'You say transition, I say progression.'

The importance of transition should be signalled as early as the teacher training phase. Clearly, if new teachers enter the classroom with a deep understanding of these issues, good practice can be maintained where it already exists and established where it is not yet in place. At Liverpool Hope University, the ML specialists on the primary and secondary PGCE courses have over the past five years joined together for some tasks. Their work on transition, reflected in an OFSTED report (available at: www.ofsted.gov.uk/ resources/good-practice-resource-languages-for-all-initial-teacher-education-liverpool-hope-university), has included, as well as university-based discussion, some collaborative cross-phase work between secondary and primary PGCE students, such as that by Rowe (2008a), who suggests:

- a Y7 audit as part of subject training plan and feedback to department
- the changing of the timing of primary placement for secondary trainees
- a week of 'shared placement'
- the collaborative design of 'bridging units' and 'taster days'
- some joint mentor training.

A programme containing such elements sets a standard for Initial Teacher Education (ITE) courses by ensuring real and focused contact between the teachers operating on either side of the 11+ gateway.

In a task used by these student teachers (Rowe, 2008b), some statements about transition were reviewed (see Figure 8.1). The intention is that they are ranked and a sample selected for more detailed discussion in terms of the logistics, responsibility, accountability and potential benefits. These statements can also be used as a checklist of good practice in transition, as we will show shortly.

Every one of these statements is a purposeful activity and we can see that they fall into several different categories (see Figure 8.2), which offer a useful guide to the sheer range of approaches we should be considering. Of course, not all of these are possible for everyone, but the use of at least some activities from each of the categories represents a very real step forwards towards good practice.

In Figure 8.2, we have offered six categories of activities, ranked in what we feel is a logical order of steps, that together involve all three 'constituents': the LA, the secondary schools and the primary schools. It is immediately apparent that the onus falls on the secondary schools to ensure that transition is effective. The specific secondary column includes a series of actions that ask the school to look carefully at the incoming students and put in place a range of measures to ensure progression for all.

Collaborative teaching in Y6 and Y7 between primary and secondary colleagues
Observation of ML lessons by secondary colleagues
Exchange of documentation between phases, such as schemes of work
Transfer of ML assessment records from primary to secondary
Adaptation of Y7 schemes of work to take into account prior learning of children
Development of 'bridging units' within a cluster of primaries and feeder secondary schools
Development of strategies for revisiting language learned in primary in new contexts at secondary
Taster lessons for Y6 in secondary prior to transfer
Enhanced strategies for differentiation in Y7 ML lessons
Cross-phase ML working groups and meetings
Observation of Y7 lessons by primary colleagues
A named ML coordinator in every primary school who can liaise with feeder secondary schools
'Fast-track' groups in Y7 for those with ML experience
A 'change of language' policy in Y7
A common LA scheme of work for ML

Figure 8.1 Transition statements (Rowe, 2008b). Our grateful thanks to Jan Rowe for sharing this resource with us

The adaptation of schemes of work is key to the whole task and should be informed by taster lessons, the observations by secondary colleagues and any joint teaching activities carried out in both schools. Only then (if needed) should revisiting the agenda be considered, so that no unnecessary revision takes place. The need for differentiation or fast-track groups will follow logically if the previous steps have been carried out well.

A change of language is a way of side-stepping the issue in terms of the content that is known by children, but, still, their existing skills must be evaluated and the right level of engagement with a new language implemented. Also, of course, the reasons for a change of language at 11 years must be clear and accepted by the family of schools if resentment and frustration are to be avoided.

The real challenge then is to make sure that the children involved in transition have a role, a voice and some ownership over the process. The activities given above will work even better if a pupil column of action can be evolved.

The duty of the primary phase is to teach children as well as possible and follow any agreed course that has been negotiated with (and not imposed by!) the partners.

A primary ML coordinator is a very clear and obvious need and should not be contentious. In fact, when we look closely at Figure 8.2 we see that there is a substantial (in terms of the time commitment involved) shared role between KS2 and KS3. The activities are deliberately sequenced to build mutual understanding and some collaboration before any joint activity in the form of bridging units is launched.

It is vital through all of this process that the secondary school staff understand how primary children learn and, therefore, how primary teachers teach. Throughout this book we have commented that we should not simply adopt secondary methodology in fashioning how we teach languages at primary level. This understanding needs to be at the core of transition activity, too, or problems will be experienced at transition and later.

How can we address the strand that is missing from Figure 8.2 – the role of the children themselves – in this process? There is some established practice in the form of the Junior European Language Portfolio and the Languages Passport (both available to download at: www.primarylanguages.org.uk/resources/assessment_and_recording/european_language_portfolio.aspx).

Primary school	Secondary school	Classroom liaison	Document liaison
A named ML coordinator in every primary school who can liaise with feeder secondary schools	Taster lessons for Y6 in secondary prior to transfer	Observation of ML lessons by secondary colleagues	Exchange of documentation between phases, such as schemes of work
	Adaptation of Y7 schemes of work to take into account prior learning of children	Observation of Y7 lessons by primary colleagues	Transfer of ML assessment records from primary to secondary
	Development of strategies for revisiting language learned in primary in new contexts at secondary	Collaborative teaching in Y6 and Y7 between primary and secondary colleagues	
	Enhanced strategies for differentiation in Y7 ML lessons	Development of 'bridging units' within a cluster of primaries and feeder secondary schools	
Liaison through meetings		'Fast-track' groups in Y7 for those with ML experience	**LA**
Cross-phase ML working groups and meetings	A 'change of language' policy in Y7		A common LA scheme of work for PL

Figure 8.2   Transition statements by category (adapted from Rowe, 2008b)

Of the two, the Junior European Language Portfolio has been in existence longer and is intended to be a formative document, based on 'I can' statements. The major pattern here is to colour in speech bubbles that express competencies related to each of the four skills, as and when each child is ready to do so.

The Languages Passport (see example below) is badged by the Council of Europe and contains a pro forma to record progress on the Languages Ladder scheme up to A2 (the first stage of intermediate level) – and note intercultural experiences. It is intended to be used as a transfer document between schools and, in that sense, is a summative attainment record at the point of transfer.

Speaking and talking to someone

Tick when you can do these things. ✓

Breakthrough		
A1 COUNCIL OF EUROPE CONSEIL DE L'EUROPE		
I can use simple phrases and sentences and I can also talk with someone in a simple way, asking and answering questions.		
Grade 1	I can say/repeat a few words and short simple phrases *e.g. what the weather is like; greeting someone; naming classroom objects …*	
Grade 2	I can answer simple questions and give basic information *e.g. about the weather; where I live; whether I have brothers or sisters, or a pet …*	
Grade 3	I can ask and answer simple questions and talk about my interests *e.g. taking part in an interview about my area and interests; a survey about pets or favourite foods; talking with a friend about what we like to do and wear …*	

	Preliminary	
	COUNCIL OF EUROPE CONSEIL DE L'EUROPE	
A2	*I can give a short prepared talk e.g. describe a picture or people, my school, my home, and take part in a simple conversation on familiar topics.*	
Grade 4	I can take part in a simple conversation and I can express my opinions *e.g. discussing a picture with a partner, describing colours, shapes and saying whether I like it or not; asking for and giving directions; discussing houses, pets, food …*	
Grade 5	I can give a short prepared talk, on a topic of my choice, including expressing my opinions *e.g. talking on a familiar subject; describing a picture or part of a story; making a presentation to the class …*	

Source: © CfBT Education Trust

The vital importance of mixing peer- and self-evaluation and especially of success criteria, as demonstrated earlier in the chapter, is paramount here. If the Languages Passport is going to be a meaningful document that can also contribute to a better start in Y7, it needs to reflect true competence accurately. It also needs to be something that the children can talk about with confidence. This cannot be emphasised too much as the children can be their own ambassadors for change, as long as they have the written evidence and can support it with their use of language.

This brings together the two major strands of the chapter: the need for a range of monitoring and assessment strategies used by the teacher and the issues surrounding transition. If the Junior European Language Portfolio or the Languages Passport is used, there needs to be a portfolio of work and exemplars of the level of language the children are regularly meeting in Y6 supplied with it. This is a vital part of the information needed for communicating effectively with KS3 teachers. Equally, secondary colleagues need to look at this evidence carefully to start up the KS3 curriculum at an appropriate point. The inherent danger is, if they find that the transfer data is unreliable, secondary colleagues will cease to trust the judgement of primary colleagues. If that happens, the only losers will be the children.

> 〰️ **Reflection point**
>
> How is transition organised in your current context? Do the measures currently taken fit into the table? Are there other activities that have not been mentioned? How do the children currently see transition and what do they use to help them manage it?

Chapter summary

This chapter has looked at a range of aspects relating to assessment, including the:

- overarching rationale for approaches in general
- issues around specific types of language use in the classroom and what sorts of assessment are demanded
- issues of correction and feedback
- finding guidance
- issues of transition, especially the supply of reliable and purposeful information to colleagues in KS3.

It has attempted to locate ML assessment in the current overall assessment context and has suggested that the principles should be those adopted for other areas of the curriculum. It has also especially drawn attention to the value of children understanding the assessment process and being empowered to self- and peer-assess themselves.

Key reading

The standard text on assessment for learning is by P. Black and D. Wiliam (1998) *Inside the Black Box: Raising standards through classroom assessment*. London: GL Assessment.

A very full guide to the issues, but not aimed at the primary age range, is by F. Genesee and J.A. Upshur (1996) *Classroom Evaluation in Second Language Learning*. Cambridge: Cambridge University Press.

The special issue of the journal (2000) *Language Testing*, 17, April, has a series of useful articles, including two we quoted from in this chapter.

A forthcoming unpublished thesis by Katherine Richardson on pupils' perceptions of and experience of primary languages transition will be available online in 2015 from the e-theses collection of the University of Warwick.

CHAPTER 9

WHAT DOES RESEARCH TELL US ABOUT THE INTEGRATION OF LANGUAGES INTO THE CURRICULUM?

Chapter objectives

- To outline the major elements of communicative language teaching and task-based language teaching and to relate these to a primary context.
- To offer a definition of content and language integrated learning (CLIL) and show how research has evaluated it.
- To offer a framework for CLIL curriculum design, drawing on Coyle's (2006) 4Cs curriculum and categories of language and learning and on the Cummins matrix (1984).

Teachers' standards		
A teacher must:		
3		Demonstrate good subject and curriculum knowledge
	a	have a secure knowledge of the relevant subject(s) and curriculum areas, foster and maintain pupils' interest in the subject, and address misunderstandings
	b	demonstrate a critical understanding of developments in the subject and curriculum areas, and promote the value of scholarship

(Continued)

(Continued)

4		Plan and teach well-structured lessons
	e	contribute to the design and provision of an engaging curriculum within the relevant subject area(s)

Source: DfE, 2013a

Introductory vignette

It's not very interesting and not very motivational because it's not personalised to us and we learn words, but we don't learn how to use them together.

(Student at the beginning of Y9 speaking about her experience of language learning from being a Y7 beginner, 2008)

Comment

We have heard testimony from several secondary-age learners in this book because, as we quoted in Chapter 1 from '14–19: Opportunity and excellence' (DfES, 2003), when 'students struggle with a subject in which they have little interest or aptitude', it is important to try to analyse why this has happened and what should be done to avoid repeating such apparent 'mistakes' in the primary phase.

This chapter tries, in a more theoretical way, to describe some of the influences on what we might now call the 'traditional' foreign language methodology, which is present in our secondary schools in a range of manifestations.

 ### Initial reflection point

How do you best learn a language yourself? How did you learn at school? Do you learn any differently now? Try to think about the roles in this learning process – what did your teachers do at school and what does the 'tutor' (person or machine you learn with) do now? What was and is your role in this learning process and did you feel comfortable with that role? What are the main barriers for you when you try to learn?

Response

The roles of teacher and learner are an important aspect of analysing learning. In a classroom situation, most of us (school students or adults) accept whatever structure we are given and work with it, yet that structure has usu-ally been chosen by the teacher or institution and works to suit their preferences.

While classrooms cannot be personalised to suit all the different learning preferences of the children within it, it is important to plan to cater for at least a small range of different approaches. Above all, we should certainly, as teachers, select a main approach that will set up a motivational and par-ticipatory basis for the majority of learners. This should be structured to allow them to engage with meaningful content, see the purpose of the class-room activities and gain as much as possible that is useable and transferable from the process.

Communicative language teaching

ML teachers in England have used the term 'communicative' to describe their practice for over 30 years and, after so long a period, in many ways this approach to teaching can almost be regarded now as 'traditional'.

The change to this style occurred during the 1970s, when curriculum shapers, syllabus designers, examiners, publishers and teachers started to turn away from what had previously been felt to be a radical innovation – the audio-lingual approach, typified by resources such as the Nuffield language courses (*En Avant!, Vorwärts!, Adalante!*). This methodology itself grew out of the 'direct method', which introduced major use of the target language in teaching for the first time and placed oral competence above grammatical capability. In audio-lingual approaches, despite the use of tape recordings and film clips to enliven lessons, the shape of units was very fixed, the role of repetition and the order of using the skills was strictly prescribed. Drills were used to internalise both vocabulary and grammar and the units were still often grammar-led rather than centred on a topic.

The moves away from this method began with a focus on the syllabus content. There was a shift towards survival topics, inspired by the work on the 'threshold level' (van Ek, 1975; van Ek and Trim, 1991), which was explored briefly in Chapter 2, and there was a demand for authenticity of materials and tasks and a lessening of the focus on grammar. This led to the new GCSE syllabuses of 1988, which built on Mode 3 CSE work developed over the preceding five years. The new emphasis was on the communication of real or pseudo-real messages and so the term 'communicative' was picked up from mainly English as a foreign language (EFL) writers of the time and quickly applied to language learning generally. The intention was certainly to personalise and develop a real use of language.

An introduction to Krashen's hypotheses and terminology

Krashen's (1985) theory of second language acquisition consists of five main hypotheses:

- *acquisition learning* that we acquire language in a natural process of exposure to the target language and learn grammar formally in classrooms
- *monitor* that what we have 'learned' acts as an editor of what we have 'acquired' as we speak
- *natural order* that we tend to acquire and learn grammatical constructs in a set order
- *input* that we need contextualised messages carrying clear meaning in order to acquire naturally
- *affective filter* that personal feelings, such as confidence or anxiety, as well as motivational level, directly affect the extent to which we manage to learn language and communicate successfully.

Krashen's key work in the 1980s, as well as work since then, introduced terms such as those in the box above. An important term for classrooms and the use of the target language was 'comprehensible input' (Krashen, 1988), which describes the meaningful messages in context, used by teachers themselves or in the texts they choose. When learners are able to understand these messages, they 'intake' language and add it to their store. This is a relatively extreme view, but is vindicated by immersion contexts – that is, if the conditions are right (and they are not easy to set up) children can acquire language simply from being exposed to it.

The principle of i+1 (Krashen, 1988) stated that the language of the message should be just beyond current capability so that the learner has to work and think in order to process and intake. This is rooted in sound learning theory principles and Krashen's major message, though sometimes challenged, has tended to be amended and added to rather than overturned. It is the basis for structured 100 per cent target language use in classrooms now and certainly the notion that we should push the children to hear or read a little more than they already know is an important principle behind both learning and progression.

Krashen's (1988) distinction between acquisition and learning in the monitor model is perhaps more problematic, however. He sees learning as a process that is affected by error correction and form focus, but acquisition is a more natural process than this, which error correction cannot affect. What has been learned acts as a monitor of what is said during the output/productive process, but competence in a language is driven by the material that has been acquired.

In the vast literature on acquisition in communicative contexts and what exactly is and is not acquired in this way, many researchers agree that there is a clear need for a focus on form as well as a focus on meaning if accurate language use is an aim of a learning programme. Swain and Lapkin's (1995) output hypothesis claimed that learners notice gaps in their competence as they produce language and that feedback at this point has an important role in learning. We noted the different effects of varieties of approach to error correction in Chapter 8, citing Loewen (2007), and saw that giving feedback to learners about the accuracy of their utterances is necessary if they are to improve over time.

Wesche and Skehan (2002) refer to strong and weak varieties of communicative language teaching and show that meaning-focused instruction (such as content-based courses) is the basis for stronger models. In this they agree with Krashen, but they also comment (2002: 216) that the stronger models 'have ... increasingly sought ways to incorporate a focus on form and language awareness into classroom practice' and go on to discuss the need for micro-strategies for specific purposes within a general teaching approach.

Taking into account these views about language learning using an essentially communicative model, if we now review practice since the 1980s, how communicative have we really been? The quote in the introductory vignette suggests that even in 2008 this was not always being achieved. The standard work, Littlewood's *Communicative Language Teaching: An introduction* (1981), highlighted the difference between precommunicative (practice) activities and communicative (production) activities. (We will focus on the so-called 3Ps of presentation, practice and production shortly.) Littlewood also stressed the difference between a focus on meaning and a focus on form – that is, syntax and grammar – and explored in some detail communicative functions, such as how we use language to enquire, apologise, complain and so on. In this way, he attempted to show how the teaching and learning could progress from a necessary practising and fixing stage to something like real communication that truly prepares learners for language use in a target language setting.

In his concluding chapter, Littlewood (1981: 89) defined the communicative activities as being where '[t]he learner is ... selecting suitable language forms from his total repertoire, and producing them fluently. The criterion for success is whether the meaning is conveyed effectively'. In contrast, precommunicative activities (1981: 85):

> include the majority of the learning activities currently to be found in textbooks ... These aim above all to provide learners with a fluent command of the linguistic system, without actually requiring them to use this system for communicative purposes. Accordingly, the learners' main purpose is to produce language which is acceptable (i.e. sufficiently accurate or appropriate) rather than to communicate meanings effectively.

We have chosen these quotations from Littlewood deliberately because many of the teaching and learning tasks that have been commonly used in language learning at any stage over the last 30 years have been decidedly precommunicative in their nature. The culmination of a precommunicative phase – that children can then move on to more authentic message-bearing communication – has often been absent, even though it appears, on the surface, to be part of the design. This is echoed by Legutke and Thomas (1991) who make a distinction between language learning tasks, precommunicative and communicative tasks and, between all of these things and an overall 'project', which should be the organising whole.

Communicative tasks are intended to create discourse from genuine communicative needs and interaction and go beyond the simple stage where learners merely begin to express their own opinions and meanings (which is still characterised as precommunicative in Legutke and Thomas' system).

One way to exemplify this is to examine a teaching and learning structure known as the 3Ps – presentation, practice, production, mentioned above – which is still recommended by some teacher educators and consultants. In this format, the teacher first presents the material to be learned – often a topic-related vocabulary set, a structure or perhaps a grammar point exemplified by using a range of topic-related examples. Normally the teacher has chosen this material using a syllabus or course textbook or perhaps knowledge of what the learners may find useful and interesting. The teacher models the language, the learners imitate and give the language back in a cycle that generally involves simple repetition, then a choice of alternatives offered by the teacher, then production of a word or phrase in response to a visual stimulus. Teachers are told that the best way to do this is to use the target language the entire time and use physical and visual prompt techniques to elicit the language.

After this first phase, learners are given tight practice tasks, based on substitution tables, guided role plays, matching items to what is read or heard or gap fill activities.

Finally, more open-ended tasks are given where learners have the opportunity to use language more fluently and independently – production activities.

In reality, much of the audio-lingual methodology seems to have survived in the presentation and practice phases of this approach and drilling is still, in effect, a vital part of these early stages. In our work on the PGCE secondary course in the 1990s, the team at the University of Nottingham moved away from the 3Ps structure because we felt it emphasised teacher control too much and practice dominated production. Presentations and free role plays that *should* have been production tasks too often seemed to revert to students reading out texts with a very unnatural accent and intonation, so it appeared that lip service was being paid to the independent phase, perhaps because of the earlier control by the teacher, the timeframe and lack of thinking involved in the practice stage.

Our response to this, as we tried to link an alternative approach to the reality of language learning in schools, was to recharacterise the cycle as

3Ms – meeting language, manipulating language and making language my own. This stressed at the beginning that learners should encounter language in a range of ways, including via free reading and listening. The difference here was that, more often, they were being asked to work out meanings from context clues rather than being presented with meanings by a teacher. The range of vocabulary and structures they met was also less controlled and defined, especially if they were more able students.

We characterised the manipulation phase as one that should involve some thinking embedded in the tasks, not just the use of a context for essentially a language drill. From a language only perspective, the desirable nature of practice can be summarised as (Lightbown, 2003: 6):

> When practice is defined as experience in using language for meaningful purposes, including opportunities for thoughtful retrieval of language features that ... have not become automatic, then practice is likely to be more predictive of long-term success.

We challenged our students to ensure that the production task was scaffolded rather than scripted. In this way, the learners had to know the language well before they moved to that stage or at least have strategies to 'keep talking' when they had forgotten an item. This was easier if they had become accustomed from the outset to using memorised language spontaneously – if need be with a prompt, but not to using a fully drafted piece of writing from which to 'speak'.

It seemed to us then, as it still does, that one of the biggest pitfalls of the 3Ps model is teachers tend to 'measure out' what they think they can reasonably expect to get back in the production stage and then limit the input during presentation to precisely that. There is no language-rich classroom in which to meet and slowly acquire a range of language and, when in a target-language-speaking context, the normal language flow is too difficult for students to manage. In KS3, there is some resistance to the language-rich classroom from the consumers – they are by then much more concerned about not understanding every word and much more self-conscious if they feel they do not understand what is being said.

Contrast this with the primary age group, who, as we have shown, accept much more naturally that they will interpret language as it comes, as long as the teacher is 'invisibly' conscious of managing what comes with a sensitive eye to the individual class context. As we have seen, much of what has already been explored in this book is aimed at developing that language-rich classroom and using what are really communicative approaches at all points in the learning cycle.

Our conclusion from this review is that we have an opportunity to create much more communicative learning environments in our primary classrooms, but an imitation of secondary course textbook approaches will probably not achieve this as well as we might wish.

Reflection point

You want the children to experience getting their fruit in the target language. You could preteach the fruit vocabulary and practise in pairs asking for items with cards containing pictures or you could simply offer choices of fruit with the frame: *'Möchtest du einen Apfel oder eine Banane?'*, eliciting the answer, *'Eine Banane bitte'* or perhaps *'Ich möchte eine Banane.'* What is the difference between the processes that happen in the child's mind during these two variants?

Response

The first method emphasises the language focus as a task and makes a game of using the cards. It remains a little abstract as no real items are used and no real purpose is activated. There is more intense practice because each item might be used several times between pairs, but less able children might find the functional language of offering and accepting more difficult. The use of the cards works very much on a simple stimulus–response pattern, which may internalise language but may also become mechanistic and accomplished without thinking. So there are both gains and pitfalls with this approach.

In the second method, there is a real choice to be made (that is, which fruit does the child really want?) and a genuine politeness function (of accepting, using 'please' or 'thank you') that the teacher or teaching assistant could legitimately insist on for non-linguistic reasons. Although each child only says the item once, this occurs in a personalised dialogue with an adult and he or she is aware of the language as the teacher asks different members of the class, too. There is a great deal of opportunity for repetition, as this is a daily activity. The need to communicate a real message makes the point that language is a vehicle for authentic situations and this may give a better overall subconscious rationale for using the language than other activities.

The importance of task has emerged in this section as we have been looking at communicative teaching, both in terms of end activities in a language learning cycle structure and in the reflection point above. We now explore aspects of task-based learning as another important variation of communicative language teaching.

Task-based learning

In the world of teachers of English to speakers of other languages (TESOL), there has been a move over the last 30 years from a broadly defined communicative form of language teaching to a range of more specific approaches. One of these is task-based learning, which has been consistently explored and developed by a range of writers, such as Willis (1996), Nunan (1989, 2004), Skehan (1998, 2003), Ellis (2003), Willis and Willis (2007) and Samuda and Bygate (2008).

This range also reflects an array of different approaches to the methodology and, in fact, at one point, Samuda and Bygate (2008: 195) offer six different interpretations of the term 'task-based'. Willis (1996) relates her view of task-based learning to the 3Ps structure with a pretask, during and post-task series, where the learners' language focus follows actual task performance, such as a whole role play, so that learners can see what they are aiming for. Thus, the use of the 3Ps is part of a more independent structure.

Skehan (1998) also sees tasks as a means rather than an end. He visualises a three-stage process in which material is encountered, fitted into the system and then added to total knowledge. Learners may be striving for any or all of the objectives of fluency, accuracy and complexity, depending on their needs, and this may affect how they use the material given to complete the task. Thus, he views tasks in this language learning cycle as a positive way of offering a concrete context to bring these elements of the process together and give an overall purpose to these activities.

Samuda and Bygate (2008) present an overview of several different approaches and, as part of this, they include examples where task-based learning can be an end as well as a means. They note, for example, that, 'Much first language learning occurs through holistic activities, and it seems likely that holistic activities can also play a significant role in second language learning, teaching and testing' (2008: 7). This view is closer to an approach that sees the task as an important factor in causing the learning rather than simply providing a way of implementing another theory. This was echoed in an interview with two girls at a Midlands language college at the start of their Y11. They had secured Grade A GCSE passes in French a year early, at the end of Y10. They were asked which period of their four years of French had been the most successful and enjoyable and they replied that their two years of learning geography in French in Y7 and Y8 had been the best. On being asked why, they replied that the outcomes they produced for each of those geography topics (that is, the products of the overriding tasks set) constituted the work they were still most proud of more than two years later.

Linked to this is Breen's (1987) reference to the different phases of tasks. He makes the important point that task-as-work plan may differ from task-in-process. The underlying message of this is that teachers should design tasks to be stepped and progressive and, in this sense, maintain some directive control over learner activity, but tasks should also be open-ended enough to allow the learners with particular abilities and needs to fulfil them in their own way and learn from them what they can.

Projects in any language always result in a range of different end products – some more detailed, some more general, some more accurately presented, some more visually exciting – but what children should always feel is that they had an opportunity to learn new information and to show their knowledge in a way they feel proud of.

In language learning there is often additional pride, as the outcome has been produced in another language. Clearly task-based learning, when structured in this way, also meets most of the criteria for communicative teaching and learning.

This short summary of just a small set of facets of task-based learning is designed, therefore, to give a more concrete focus to what communicative language teaching could be and how to get there. We have spoken often throughout this book about the need for purposeful activities involving purposeful and natural use of language – real messages, language for enjoyment, such as stories and songs, competitive and collaborative games, texts that teach something new or incorporate humorous use of language. We have argued that repetition should occur but, as far as possible, in the form of sequences of questioning with an exploratory purpose and not just overt practice sessions. We have also recommended authentic materials and highlighted continuously the need for these to reflect the real cultures of the target countries. In this way, we have certainly advocated a form of true communicative teaching and, some might maintain, we have been presenting a version of task-based learning.

What is CLIL and do we know if it can benefit learners?

Content and language integrated learning (CLIL) has been both alluded to and directly referenced throughout this book. To reiterate, we are not holding up CLIL as the single way for primary ML to develop. This is not our 'preferred method'. Indeed, it is not an overt method of language teaching at all. As we will see, CLIL is a way of organising a curriculum that leads to the *learning* of second or foreign languages, and is very close to EAL in the way it is theorised. As we mentioned in Chapter 2, it shows in a teacher's doorstep intentions what he or she is bringing to that class as a learning objective for that lesson. We hope that the next two sections will also shed some light on ways in which we might interpret communicative and task-based language teaching.

According to the CLIL Cascade Network website (at: www.ccn-clil.eu/ index.php?name=File&nodeIDX=5060):

> CLIL is a dual-focused teaching and learning approach in which the L1 and an additional language or two are used for promoting both content mastery and language acquisition to pre-defined levels.

We maintain, however that the main focus in a CLIL approach is on the content to be taught, not primarily on the language. The key writer in this interpretation of CLIL is Do Coyle, with the best brief summary of the approach to be found in Coyle (2006) and developed further in Coyle et al. (2009).

By 'content' we mean either a subject, such as geography or science, or a cross-curricular topic, such as 'Water' or 'Our local environment' or 'World War II'. CLIL aims to teach content *via* the language by using methodologies associated with the content subjects rather than ML teaching methodology. We can demonstrate from research findings that the teaching of such content material in an *immersion* process is successful in terms of both the subject content and the language.

In his overview of international research findings in school-based immersion programmes, Johnstone (2000: 2) writes:

> Of the various main forms of immersion, research indicates that generally pupils develop a much higher level of proficiency in their IL [immersion language] than occurs when this language is simply taught as a school subject. They are not disadvantaged in their attainments in their L1 or in school subjects, e.g. mathematics, science, social studies.

There are many examples that have contributed to this overview and underpin its general findings. We can choose to look on a national scale and in a *second* rather than *foreign* language environment by examining the Canadian experience (for example, Day and Shapson, 1996; Johnson and Swain, 1997; Cenoz and Genesee, 1998). Similarly, the USA bilingual education field identifies a broad range of research support for what is termed content-based instruction (Grabe and Stoller, 1997). Alternatively, we can focus on a major regional foreign language experiment such as that in the Canton of Zurich (Stotz et al., 2005), where primary-age children are successfully learning via English. We can also draw from examples of individual schools that immerse in French as a foreign language, such as Walker Road Primary in Aberdeen (Johnstone, 2002; Johnstone and McKinstry, 2008). Escola Vila Olímpica in Barcelona uses three working languages – Catalan, Spanish and English – and tries to not differentiate these as mother tongue, second or foreign languages but, rather, uses each as a vehicle for learning parts of the curriculum.

All these research reports agree that language learning is enhanced and content subjects associated with CLIL do not suffer as a result of using another language. Clearly, the different reports vary in their focuses and produce different results, but there is a level of consistency about the findings from the different contexts that makes the case a serious one.

The Walker Road primary project

The most recent survey and the one single full evaluation that is UK-specific is the Walker Road – early primary partial immersion (EPPI) – research (Johnstone and McKinstry, 2008). We include here four sections in full from the researchers' conclusions (2008: 13–14) because the case they make is so clear.

Attainments of EPPI pupils in English, Environmental Studies and Mathematics

84. The evidence of EPPI at primary school shows clearly that pupils have not been disadvantaged in English, Environmental Studies or Mathematics by receiving some of their education through the medium of French. Indeed, in English EPPI pupils demonstrated markedly greater fluency, range and confidence than their non-EPPI counterparts from the same year-group.

Progress of EPPI pupils in French

85. EPPI pupils have reached a level of proficiency in French which goes far beyond what can reasonably be expected of MLPS [modern languages in the primary school]. This covers all four skills of listening, speaking, reading and writing. They have shown that they can use French in order to access with profit other areas of their curriculum. Their ability to cope with a fast flow of French input from their native-speaker teachers is particularly impressive.

Perceptions of EPPI by pupils, parents and native-speaker teachers

86. EPPI pupils hold positive perceptions of EPPI. In particular they clearly view it as an enjoyable experience and they would like to see it extended to other Scottish primary schools.

Factors linked to the success of EPPI

90. In the opinion of the evaluators, EPPI at Walker Road Primary School has been an outstanding success. It has brought something different and better into Scottish primary school education. In the era of Curriculum for Excellence it is preparing pupils very well for true international citizenship, not only through their outstanding proficiency in another major language but also in their confidence and international outlook.

Does CLIL work without immersion?

These different contexts (Canadian immersion, Swiss immersion, partial immersion in Catalunya and in Scotland) share the fact that learners have had access to a partial or full immersion setting. As a result of this they have succeeded in mastering content taught in a foreign language and have made linguistic progress, often in advance of that made by students on more conventional language learning programmes. Many CLIL contexts are not partial or full immersion contexts, however. In Germany, the tradition is to wait until language competence is well established. In Spain, there is a tendency to innovate earlier and in smaller units of time. In France, the secondary *sections européens* are slowly being supplemented by new projects in the primary age range.

In the UK, any CLIL experiment has usually started in secondary schools, beginning with a very limited timescale, but some of these trials have been successful. At Tile Hill Wood School and Language College, for example, the teachers appeared to achieve noticeable progress in achievement in French and geography and in attitudes towards language learning on an allocation of two hours per week of geography in French supported by a further two hours of more conventional French teaching and a further one hour of geography teaching in English (Woodfield and Neofitou, 2006, also referred to in Coyle et al., 2009).

The teachers involved acknowledged that their practice was influenced by the joint planning and resourcing of this programme – the teacher of French became more aware of the need for a deeper content in the language lessons and the teacher of geography became more aware of the role of language in learning in her geography teaching in English.

At Hockerill Anglo-European Language College the German model was followed and CLIL was introduced after intensive language preparation. Again, the model proved very successful.

Clearly, although immersion will always produce more, a limited time allocation can still produce something.

How common are these approaches?

These approaches are still rare, certainly in primary schools. In two important earlier reports produced for the Qualifications and Curriculum Authority (QCA), there were no instances of large-scale integration of this approach into the curriculum. Powell et al., who produced these reports (QCA: 2001: 64), found that, 'There were only a few overt examples of links with other subjects in the teaching observed. Links with Literacy were frequently mentioned but rather ill defined.'

Martin (2000: 35) discussed the terms 'embedding' and 'integration', but noted:

> Both embedding and integration should not be confused with either total or partial immersion, and *do not imply* that the substance of the curricular areas should be taught through the medium of the foreign language.

Muir (1999) examines extensively the potential for embedding language into the curriculum, but always speaks of it as reinforcement of content, also commenting that this is not subject teaching via the medium. He also quotes from Johnstone (1994: 8), who had warned about the possibility of a fragmented approach (that is, across several content subject areas) that could not easily be drawn together into a language system which could be used by the learners.

This view is more important now that topic planning is again becoming common in primary schools. We tried to show earlier in this book that there is a fully justified language curriculum around survival topics, as well as the embedded and integrated work we have also promoted, and teachers do need to deal with language aspects such as grammar, spelling, syntax when appropriate to do so. We hope in this way that we have addressed Johnstone's (1994) reservations about topic planning.

Martin (2000: 35) commented about the issues for teachers, citing Driscoll (1999): 'Even though generalist teachers have the opportunities to integrate the foreign language, they often have neither the personal linguistic resources nor materials to exploit these fully. The integrative approach is difficult to keep track of and to test.' Conversely, she cites Kubanek-German (1996) and notes, 'in Germany, where the cross-curricular dimension is highlighted, there is unanimous agreement that foreign language work should be embedded in the pedagogical work of the primary school' (Martin, 2000: 34). This is under-pinned by Wode (1999) and, although in Blondin et al. (1998), curriculum integration does not emerge as a strong theme in previous research or in recommended action, there is now clear European Commission support (Marsh, 2002).

At the time of writing, primary CLIL developments can be seen on the FLAME (Association for Language Learning) website (at: www.all-languages. org.uk/community/flame), where there are links to schools (mainly second-ary at present, but a primary video clip is also available at: www.ucet. ac.uk/4749). In terms of commercially published resources, only *A La Française* (Tobutt and Roche, 2007) is overtly CLIL-orientated, but other material can be downloaded.

How does CLIL work? Is there potential for confusion between languages?

With balanced bilingualism – that is, from birth (see summary in Baker, 2006), there is no real evidence of children or young adults confusing languages, even if they occasionally mix them. The code-switching (moving between languages even within a sentence) that occurs with bilinguals can often be one-way, into the more frequently spoken language, and a change of location can strip out such code-switching very quickly.

Similarly, we have no evidence that there is any language confusion caused by CLIL. Some people find it odd that children might know about a topic better in French, German or Spanish than in English (in terms of spe-cialist vocabulary, for example), but there is nothing inherently wrong with this and, if they need to talk about it in English, they can very quickly look for translations of the words they need. This is also a feature of linguistic competence, which, in the UK, is seen as rare, but elsewhere is much more accepted as the norm.

The functioning of the bilingual process (and therefore, by analogy, with well-developed CLIL schemes where there is a reasonable time allocation for the work) may be explained by the concept of the common underlying proficiency (Cummins, 1991), which suggests that cognitive functioning and information processing skills may be developed and channelled via two languages as well as via one language. Thus, the thoughts that accompany talking, reading, writing and listening come from the same central processor. Knowledge gained by using one language will be available to the other language. In one representation (Cummins, 1984), this is described as an iceberg that has two peaks showing above the surface of the sea, but they are joined below the water.

Baker (2006) is at pains to be even-handed in his review of evidence on bilinguals, but still concludes that there are clear cognitive gains at different intelligence levels from a bilingual experience. These may or may not be directly linked to having two languages and may also include cultural elements as major influences, but we can be sure that there is little negativity associated with 'natural' bilingualism.

There is a need, of course, for teachers to monitor the success of a programme as it develops and to do this rigorously. It often requires some professional development to be offered and it clearly works best when teachers plan and even teach collaboratively. A CLIL approach, then, can bring benefits, but does demand a flexible attitude (Brown, 1994: 220):

> Research on second language acquisition at various ages indicates the ultimate strength of learning that is pointed toward practical non-language goals. Content-based teaching presents some challenges to language teachers. Allowing the subject matter to control the selection and sequencing of language items means that you have to view your teaching from an entirely different perspective.

We will next look at how that doorstep intention we referred to earlier is theorised within a recognised CLIL framework and how it can then be applied to real curricula and schemes of work.

Designing a CLIL curriculum and planning CLIL lessons: the theoretical perspective

In work located in research, teaching, teacher education and continuing professional development at the University of Nottingham over the last 15 years, a CLIL framework has evolved that can be most easily accessed by means of two main publications: Coyle (2006) and Coyle et al. (2009). This is a summary of the principles involved seen through a planning process that is intended to make theory overt and practice-directed.

Imagine you are embarking on an art topic in lower KS2 along the lines of the former QCA scheme 'Unit 3a Portraying relationships'. You will want to decide, as you populate your medium-term plan with your art teaching hat on, which elements of content from the unit plan you would select (and what you might add), how this would build on prior knowledge and what activities you would choose to engage as well as challenge learners.

With your language teacher hat on, you would also be looking for opportunities for the children to hear and speak the target language and read and write to an appropriate extent. You will identify certain linguistic items that they will have the opportunity to learn in the course of this work and which items they already need to have in place in order to achieve this. You will be actively seeking ways to include intercultural elements.

The 4Cs approach

Coyle's 4Cs structure (1999, 2006) not only formalises this planning into four separate but interlinked areas – content, cognition, communication and culture – but also offers a framework for how the four areas interact. We will first look at this from a theoretical standpoint.

The pyramid diagram in Figure 9.1, adapted from Coyle (2006), shows the four key components of a CLIL curriculum. These can also be present in individual lesson plans, depending on the subject, topic and learners.

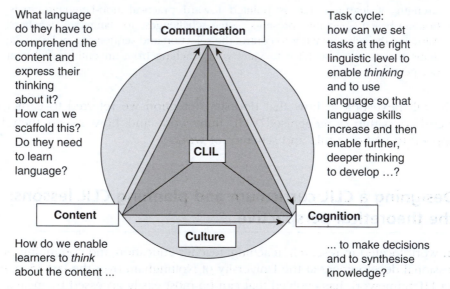

What language do they have to comprehend the content and express their thinking about it? How can we scaffold this? Do they need to learn language?

Communication

Task cycle: how can we set tasks at the right linguistic level to enable *thinking* and to use language so that language skills increase and then enable further, deeper thinking to develop …?

CLIL

Content

Culture

Cognition

How do we enable learners to *think* about the content ...

... to make decisions and to synthesise knowledge?

Figure 9.1 CLIL pyramid (adapted from Coyle, 2006)

Starting at the bottom of this diagram, we find a dynamic highlighted between content and cognition. The questions posed around the pyramid deliberately ground the planning into a series of processes. First, the teacher decides how the content he or she is including in the plan can be made into tasks that both explain the material and ask the learners to process and manipulate it. This is the initial planning step by every good teacher in every context, of course. Learning occurs via a whole range of interactions, both in the brain and externally with a teacher or other learners.

So, we work out how to get our children *thinking* about the concepts or experiences they are encountering, making decisions (the simplest way of describing a problem-solving process, by means of which input is filtered through a task to become output) and synthesising via an assimilation or accommodation process (Piaget, 1955) into new total knowledge. By fore-grounding this part of the planning, we ensure that the content remains the main objective and the science, art or PE gets taught.

In our mother tongue, the element of language in this process is often forgotten, although good primary teachers have a sense of 'language pitch' that allows them to consider it intuitively. Two processes are involved: receptive processing of information or concepts and the spoken or written expression of understanding resulting from participation in a task. In a CLIL context, language scaffolding becomes paramount, but we should remember that, in scaffolding the *language*, we are actually scaffolding the *thinking* – there is no point in offering language structures for the sake of it. To put it another way, we are first considering which vocabulary and structures will best allow children to make sense of the stimulus we have offered.

Next, we are considering which vocabulary and structures will allow children to move towards a response. Finally, we decide how to use the language that we have decided is at an appropriate level to facilitate that response. For example, a particular question sometimes suggests a particular answer format and so allows the thinking to be expressed with language as a *facilitator* rather than a *barrier*.

We can find many arguments on both sides of the contention that you can or cannot have thought without language, but we can be sure that if someone is presented with two tables of parallel data (for example, facts about two countries), they will instinctively make comparisons and be ready (language permitting) to express conclusions from those comparisons. In other words, the thinking can be relatively language-free, but the *expression* of that thinking is not, unless we include pictorial representation as a means of communicating ideas.

Here we are getting to grips with the two other sides of the pyramid base – the dynamics of content/language and language/cognition. The questions therefore ask us to consider how language can facilitate our intentions stemming from a content–cognition interaction. Can we find the form of language to use to achieve our objective? Will we stray into using language that will cloud comprehension, thinking and expression? Do learners need to learn some language in order to do this or can we structure the task so that they learn the language they need while doing it? Will we find the route through words, symbols, diagrams and images to input our content and then allow the learners to express the thinking we have engendered via a parallel set of 'outcome facilitator devices'?

The 4Cs in practice

We hope that we can make our description of the pyramid more concrete by focusing now on the following example.

Imagine we are planning the art unit and we want to look specifically at portraits showing more than one person, so we can begin to discuss relationships and how they might be shown in an image. A Google image search for family portraits in the target language (for example, *portraits famille*) will bring up a range of mostly modern images that could be used to start a discussion (as shown below). We could also use a published source where available (Salgado's (2003) *The Children* collection, for example) or even our own family and friends' portraits, if we do not mind exposing part of our real lives to the children! We might want to link this further with another curriculum area and could therefore choose a small set of portraits from the past to compare with the set we have assembled from the present. The National Portrait Gallery's website is one source where you can be sure that you will get some details about the artist and the sitter and when the work was created. From there you can do a search, for example, relating to a certain group from a historical period – 'sitters from the Pre-Raphaelite group', for example, brings up a large selection of Victorian portraits, from which five or six could easily be chosen.

If we take either set of portraits and brainstorm views of them in English, we could almost certainly quickly establish a number of ways to look at the pictures. This might include relationships (family, friends, colleagues), positions (sitting, standing, lying), attitudes to the camera or artist or others involved (posed, natural, facing camera/artist, engaged with someone else), dress, 'props' included and why – but we do not need to do this in English!

With a target language focus, a teacher preparing the unit can immediately divide the language into three categories: language that is already known by the class, new language we want to highlight because it is central and language we might want to have in reserve if children themselves raise it. By displaying the images in a PowerPoint presentation, we can show them to the class on a large scale, evoking interest and allowing the children to see the details. We can also control any foreign language words they actually see and when.

It is at this point that we discover whether or not we are using a CLIL approach. If we are, we will want the children to access language while they think and perform another task. Our questioning while showing the images might be along the lines discussed in Chapter 6. We would start by asking simple decision questions: 'Are they sitting or standing? Do they look happy or serious or sad? Are they quiet or speaking? Are they looking at the camera/artist, at each other, at nothing?' Many of these questions can be asked legitimately of more than one person because there can be different answers, at least to some, so we have an example of natural repetition rather than parroting. As we ask questions, we can use mime, supplementary images or notes to clarify what the choice is. As we gather in the responses, the children start to use words that may be half familiar or unknown and we can easily find ways of echoing in a natural manner so the exposure to this language continues to be very high.

Some portraits readily lend themselves to deeper questioning. The subjects may be looking quizzically at something that is not visible, for example, in which case you can ask if they look interested, bored, frightened or puzzled and then follow by asking what they are looking at. The question *why* might also be raised as children are asked to explain a mood. In these deeper questions, it helps to have possible simple answers ready, but not offer them too quickly. Let the children think first and then start to suggest, again by means of choices so that they still have to process, make a decision and then respond.

When sufficient discussion has taken place, the language can be gathered on to the whiteboard around an image, so it is still contextualised, and the children can be asked to start to think about describing one of the pictures to each other in very simple terms. You may want to do this as a competitive guessing game (which picture am I describing?) or a positive or negative preference to swap with a partner (my favourite or my least favourite) or a simple description of a portrait imagined by one partner to generate a simple drawing by the other partner or a small group.

We have achieved here the two sides of the pyramid, which have communication and language at their centre. We have prioritised language that is needed and have given the learners access to it while still allowing them to ask for other items they decide within the process that they want to use to express their thoughts. The language is consistently angled towards allowing them to think and express what they really want to say.

The language that we decide is key to the topic is described by Coyle (2006) as the language *of* learning. The language we need for that discussion – in this example, it is the positional language for description and the language of agreement or disagreement and of opinions – is identified as the language *for* learning. Any language that appears while the learning is in process is the language *by* learning. If these distinctions are made at the planning stage, it helps us to conceptualise both what we expect from the children and what we will give to them.

Figure 9.2 The Cummins matrix (adapted from Cummins, 1984, by Coyle, 2006)

Progression in questioning

The Cummins matrix (Cummins, 1984), shown in Figure 9.2, is intended to help with conceptualising the levels of questioning we use during a CLIL process, as described above. It explores the relationship between low and high cognitive demands and concrete/contextual as opposed to abstract social/educational contexts for learning.

Cummins devised the categories of languages' demand and nature called basic interpersonal communicative skills (BICS) and cognitive academic language proficiency (CALP), showing that learners could reach apparent oral fluency in interactional contexts comparatively quickly, but would take much longer to reach academic proficiency in the second language. He wanted teachers to focus on the different contexts in which learners of any age might find themselves and see what demands might be made on them in those contexts. Cummins uses a different layout and numbering system from Coyle's (2006) version of the matrix given in Figure 9.2 (he explains his thinking on the matrix very fully in an article available on his personal website at: *http://iteachilearn.org/cummins*).

Coyle's adaptation of the matrix, including the extra elements of low and high language level, was made to theorise a need in CLIL planning for the thinking to be seen as independent of the language levels and indicate the need for a focus on concrete/contextualised input and task materials. The questions in our portraits topic would fall mainly into our quadrants 1 and 2 because, realistically, with primary-age learners using another language, the more abstract context signalled by quadrant 3 is unlikely to be reached. When we ask questions that demand less thinking, such as those where we effectively offer the children a multiple choice framework for their responses, we are using quadrant 1, but still asking for some thinking and not just imitation or repetition. As we start to ask the question 'Why?', however, or ask for reasons or elaborations, we move into quadrant 2. The important point is that the language and content are still both fully contextualised. In addition, the language level has been structured to be accessible, with any new material very clearly guessable from the context.

In a way we are using Krashen's (1988) idea of comprehensible input – the current level of language known plus a small amount of new material (described by Krashen as being utilised for input in a context that will be meaningful and purposeful and therefore comprehensible). He felt that language learners experiencing this process would be more likely to acquire the language naturally.

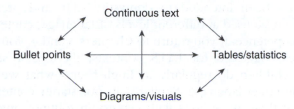

Figure 9.3 Text support and modification

Types and difficulty of text

Figure 9.3 considers the different types of text a language teacher might use during a unit, especially one that has a content base. 'Diagrams/visuals' can also include artefacts and other realia. In terms of comprehension, the diagram shows the more difficult text types at the top and the more accessible at the bottom. This is generally likely to be true, although, of course, some objects or pictures can be culturally more obscure.

As primary-age learners gain in age, experience and language knowledge and competence, however, they can be offered more complex text types to manage. The downward arrows show how a teacher may like to evaluate a text and seek something easier if it seems too difficult or modify it into an easier version if that is possible. A continuous text can often be turned quite quickly into simple bullet points or even a table, for example.

The upward-facing arrows are more likely to be used to extend more able children when they are creating a piece of work in written or spoken language. A diagram or a photo (or even a table) might be the source for a few very simple sentences. A small set of visuals might generate a summary table. So, a body of descriptive text around a portrait might be far too complex to use with primary learners, but, modified into a series of short, bulleted sentences and mixed in with others that describe other portraits, it becomes a resource which can be used to help gather thoughts and learn language via a simple matching to target process. Similarly, in another topic, a table of statistics about health factors in different countries can be used to stimulate true/false judgements on sentences that make comparisons. When this approach was used in a primary classroom, the children learned the comparative form in French by working on the task (Jones, 2004). The statistics table acted as a language-free stimulus to thinking, which then facilitated language learning.

Summary – why should a CLIL approach be part of our methodology?

This section has been intended to demystify CLIL and present it as an approach that can be used at different levels of language, content complexity and teacher competence. If you return to Chapters 3 and 4, you will find that, in the activities suggested for EYFS contexts, there is a strong parallel between what children do regularly in English and what we suggest they might do in the target language. Similarly, in our starter contexts of Y1 and Y3, we saw that there were links with classroom routines, into very simple work with art and mathematics and even more conventional language topics had an element of learning beyond just language.

CLIL is not an approach you progress towards when you have enough language (as either teacher or children), but one that can grow from the beginning. It can organise your entire teaching approach, but does not have to. Children respond well when it forms part of their language learning programme because it brings fresh topics into the classroom, links with things they are learning elsewhere in the week and takes the pressure off performing with the language and puts it on to using the language more naturally.

Clearly there is an issue in all of this about finding sufficient numbers of teaching personnel to deliver KS2 ML learning. This needs further funding and government research, but the path chosen by those who are in place now, teaching children, is crucial.

We have seen a decline in motivation in learners aged 14, resulting in a dramatic fall in uptake in KS4 as compulsory foreign language study was abolished. We cannot afford to engender the same decline in motivation at the age of 11. Where language learning is being located in KS1 or even in Foundation Stage, teachers are reporting that it appears to be entirely natural to a great number of children. This is where language is most often embedded by means of songs, stories and is activities based, around classroom role-play areas for example.

The topics chosen for inclusion in lessons are nearly always based on the current scheme of work and the ML input offers another perspective on that learning. The language children hear is rich and authentic, always forming complete sentences and chunks of meaning, not pared down to a few isolated words that are measured out and measured back in again by means of consolidation tasks. This is the approach that can inform the beginning of KS2 and can make links across to other learning that is happening at the same time. The language curriculum is therefore the existing curriculum because language is about what people sense to be all around them.

With some linking in place from the start, so that this is quickly established as a normal aspect of language learning, the extent to which another subject area can be covered can grow steadily. In the way that the CILT CLIP project proved that Y7 language-learning beginners can adapt quickly to integrated work in, for example, geography, clearly children in Y5 or Y6 after two to three years of language learning will be able to manage curricular topics in the foreign language. In following a science, history or geography unit entirely in the foreign language and not, as we saw earlier, simply taking quite trivial aspects of the cognition offered by a unit, they will have a richer experience that will also offer curriculum efficiency in the foundation subjects to an overcrowded timetable. From there, they will be able to embark on KS3 learning as natural language 'users' rather than only as word-level learners tied to a diet of survival topics. Their view of the ML will be able to move beyond descriptors such as 'fun' and into those associated with other subjects, such as 'challenging', 'satisfying' and 'motivating'. This is a real opportunity for primary teachers to make language learning different and, most importantly, sustainably successful for a majority rather than a minority of learners.

Chapter summary

This chapter has attempted to rationalise what has been discussed earlier in the book. We have shown that communicative and task-based learning have real relevance for primary ML, but to an even greater extent if these approaches are interpreted in the way that stresses real and authentic use of language. We have explored CLIL as a way of integrating ML into the wider curriculum and the wider curriculum into ML.

Key reading

Although difficult to obtain, for a short and concise overview of a recognised CLIL methodology, see D. Coyle (2006) *Monograph 6: Developing CLIL: Towards a theory of practice*. Barcelona: Associació de Professors d'Anglès de Catalunya (APAC).

For both a theoretical and more practical overview, see D. Coyle, D. Marsh and P. Hood (2009) *Content and Language Integrated Learning*. Cambridge: Cambridge University Press.

For insights into language teaching and learning methodology in general, we recommend you to read J.C. Richards and T.S. Rodgers (2001) *Approaches and Methods in Language Teaching*. Cambridge: Cambridge University Press.

A highly respected book on language learning, now in its third edition, is P. Lightbown and N. Spada (2006) *How Languages Are Learned*. Oxford: Oxford University Press. This work summarises the impact on the classroom of second language acquisition theories.

REFERENCES

Alexander, R. (ed.) (2009) *Children, their World, their Education: final report and recommendations of the Cambridge Primary Review*. (The Cambridge Primary Review.) Abingdon: Routledge.

Allford, D. (2000) 'Pictorial images, lexical phrases and culture', *Language Learning Journal*, 22 (1): 45–51.

Ames, C. and Ames, R. (1984) 'Systems of student and teacher motivation: Toward a qualitative definition', *Journal of Educational Psychology*, 76 (4): 535–56.

Arnold, J. (2007) 'Self concept and the affective domain in language learning', in F. Rubio (ed.), *Self-esteem and Foreign Language Learning*. Cambridge: Cambridge Scholars Publishing.

Baker, C. (2006) *Foundations of Bilingual Education and Bilingualism*. Clevedon, North Somerset: Multilingual Matters.

Barnett, M. (1991) *More Than Meets the Eye – Foreign Language Reading: Theory and practice*. Washington, DC: Center for Applied Linguistics.

Bauer, J. (2003) *Opas Engel*. Hamburg: Carlsen.

Bell N. (2005) 'Exploring L2 language play as an aid to SLL: A case study of humour in NS-NNS Interaction', *Applied Linguistics*, 26: 192–218.

Birdsong, D. (ed.) (1999) *Second Language Acquisition and the Critical Period Hypothesis*. Mahwah, NJ: Erlbaum.

Black, P. and Wiliam, D. (1998) *Inside the Black Box: Raising standards through classroom assessment*. London: GL Assessment. Available online at: http://weaeducation.typepad.co.uk/files/blackbox-1.pdf

Blanpain, J.-P. (2001) *Mon cochon*. Arles: Actes-Sud.

Blondin, C., Candelier, M., Edelenbos, P., Johnstone, R., Kubanek-German, A. and Taeschner, T. (1998) *Foreign Language in Primary and Pre-School Education*. London: CILT.

Bloom, B.S. (1968) 'Learning for mastery', *Evaluation comment*, 1 (2): 1–12.

Breen, M.P. (1987) 'Learner contributions to task design', in C.N. Candlin and D.F. Murphy (eds), *Language Learning Tasks*. Englewood Cliffs, NJ: Prentice Hall.

Breslin, S. (2011) 'Languages: bridging primary and secondary'. Available online at: www.scilt.org.uk/Portals/24/Library/research/slwg/Transition.pdf

Broadhead, P., Howard, J. and Wood, E.A (eds) (2010) *Play and Learning in the Early Years: From research to practice*. London: Sage.

Brown, H.D. (1994) *Teaching by Principles*. Englewood Cliffs, NJ: Prentice Hall.

Brown, R. (1992) A Dark, Dark Tale. London: Red Fox.

Brown, R. (2001) *Une histoire sombre, très sombre*. Paris: Gallimard Jeunesse.

Browne, E. (1994) *Handa's Surprise*. London: Mantra.

Burstall, C., Jamieson, M., Cohen, S. and Hargreaves, M. (1974) *Primary French in the Balance*. Slough: NFELR.

Byram, M.S. (1997) *Teaching and Assessing Intercultural Communicative Competence*. Clevedon, North Somerset: Multilingual Matters.

Byram, M. and Zarate, C. (1994) *Definitions, objectifs et évaluation de la competence socio-culturelle*. Strasbourg: Council of Europe.

Cable, C., Driscoll, P., Mitchell, R., Sing, S., Cremin, T., Earl, J., Eyres, I., Holmes, B., Martin, C. and Heins, B. (2012) 'Language learning at Key Stage 2: Findings from a longitudinal study', *Education 3–13*, 40 (4): 363–78 (primary languages special issue).

Cameron, L. (2001) *Teaching Languages to Young Learners*. Cambridge: Cambridge University Press.

Carle, E. (1979) *Do You Want to Be My Friend?* London: Puffin.

Carle, E. (1995) *The Very Hungry Caterpillar*. London: Puffin.

Carle, E. (2006) *Panda Bear, Panda Bear, What Do You See?* London: Holt.

Cenoz, J. and Genesee, F. (eds) (1998) *Beyond Bilingualism: Multilinguism and multilingual education*. Clevedon, North Somerset: Multilingual Matters.

Cheater, C. (2006) *The Catherine Cheater Scheme of Work*. Wakefield: Teaching and Learning Publications.

Clarke, S. (1998) *Targeting Assessment in the Primary School: Strategies for planning, assessment, pupil feedback and target setting*. London: Hodder & Stoughton.

Clarke, S. (2001) *Unlocking Formative Assessment: Practical strategies for enhancing pupils' learning in the primary classroom*. London: Hodder & Stoughton.

Clarke, S. (2003) *Enriching Feedback: Oral and written feedback from teachers and children*. London: Hodder & Stoughton.

Clarke, S. (2005) *Formative Assessment in Action: Weaving the elements together*. London: Hodder Education.

Coffield, F., Moseley, D., Hall, E. and Ecclestone, K. (2004) 'Should we be using learning styles? What research has to say to practice'. London: Learning and

Skills Research Centre. Available online at: www.itslifejimbutnotasweknowit. org.uk/files/LSRC_LearningStyles.pdf

Cohen, A. (1994) *Assessing Language Ability in the Classroom* (2nd edition). Boston, MA: Newbury House/Heinle & Heinle.

Commission of the European Communities (2003) 'Promoting language learning and linguistic diversity: An action plan 2004–2006'. (Brussels 24.07.2003 COM (2003) 449 final.) Brussels: Commission of the European Communities. Available online at: http://eur-lex.europa.eu/LexUriServ/LexUriServ. do?uri=COM:2003:0449:FIN:en:PDF

Cook, G. (1997) 'Language play, language learning', *ELT Journal*, 51 (3): 224–31.

Council of Europe (2001) *The Common European Framework of Reference for Languages: Learning, teaching and assessment*. Cambridge: Cambridge University Press.

Coyle, D. (1999) 'Theory and planning for effective classrooms: Supporting students in content and language integrated learning contexts: Planning for effective classrooms', in J. Masih (ed.), *Learning through a Foreign Language: Models, methods and outcomes*. London: Centre for Information on Language Teaching and Research (CILT). pp. 46–62.

Coyle, D. (2006) *Monograph 6: Developing CLIL: Towards a theory of practice*. Barcelona: Associació de Professors d'Anglès de Catalunya (APAC).

Coyle, D., Marsh, D. and Hood, P. (2009) *Content and Language Integrated Learning*. Cambridge: Cambridge University Press.

Crandall, J.A. (1999) 'Cooperative language learning and affective factors', in J. Arnold (ed.) *Affective Factors in Language Learning*. Cambridge: Cambridge University Press.

Cummins, J. (1984) *Bilingualism and Special Education*. Clevedon: Multilingual Matters.

Cummins, J. (1991) 'Language development and academic learning', in L. Malavé and G. Duquette (eds), *Language, Culture and Cognition*. Clevedon, North Somerset: Multilingual Matters. pp. 161–75.

Cury, F., Elliot, A., Da Fonseca, D. and Moller, A.C. (2006) 'The social cognitive model of achievement motivation and the 2 x 2 achievement goal framework', *Journal of Personality and Social Psychology*. 90: 666–79.

David, T. (2003) *What Do We Know about Teaching Young Children?* Southwell, Nottinghamshire: BERA. Available online at: www.bera.ac.uk/wp-content/ uploads/2014/01/eyyrsp1.pdf

Davies, M. (2000) 'Learning ... the beat goes on', *Childhood Education*, 76 (3): 148–53.

Day, E. and Shapson, S. (1996) 'A national survey: French immersion teachers' preparation and their professional development needs', *The Canadian Modern Language Review*, 52 (2): 248–70.

de Andres, V. (1999) 'Self-esteem in the classroom or the metamorphosis of butterflies', in J. Arnold (ed.), *Affect in Language Learning*. Cambridge: Cambridge University Press. pp. 87–102.

Demetriou, H., Goalen, P. and Rudduck, J. (2000) 'Academic performance, transfer, transition and friendship: Listening to the student voice', *International Journal of Educational Research*, 33: 425–41.

DES (1990) 'Starting with quality: The report of the Committee of Inquiry into the quality of educational experience offered to 3- and 4-year-olds'. (The Rumbold Report.) London: HMSO.

DfE (2012) 'Statutory Framework for the Early Years Foundation Stage'. Runcorn, Cheshire: DfE. Available online at: www.education.gov.uk/publications/ standard/AllPublications/Page1/DFE-00023-2012

DfE (2013a) 'Teachers' standards: Guidance for school leaders, school staff and governing bodies'. (DFE-00066–2011.) Runcorn, Cheshire: DfE. Available online at: www.gov.uk/government/uploads/system/uploads/attachment_ data/file/301107/Teachers__Standards.pdf

DfE (2013b) 'Languages programmes of study: Key Stage 2'. (DFE-00174–2013.) Runcorn, Cheshire: DfE. Available online at: www.gov.uk/government/ uploads/system/uploads/attachment_data/file/239042/PRIMARY_national_ curriculum_-_Languages.pdf

DfE (2014) 'Statutory Framework for the Early Years Foundation Stage'. Runcorn, Cheshire: DfE. Available online at: www.gov.uk/government/uploads/system/ uploads/attachment_data/file/299391/DFE-00337-2014.pdf

DfES (2002) 'Languages for all, languages for life'. Nottingham: DfES. Available online at: http://webarchive.nationalarchives.gov.uk/20130401151715/www. education.gov.uk/publications/eOrderingDownload/DfESLanguagesStrategy. pdf

DfES (2003) '14–19: Opportunity and excellence'. (0744/2002.) Nottingham: DfES. Available online at: http://dera.ioe.ac.uk/4705/1/DfES-0744-2002Main.pdf

DfES (2005) 'The Key Stage 2 Framework for languages' (Parts 1 and 2). Nottingham: DfES. Available online at: http://webarchive.nationalarchives. gov.uk/20110511211850/http:/nationalstrategies.standards.dcsf.gov.uk/ node/85274

DfES (2006) 'Grouping pupils for success'. (03945–2006 DWO-EN.) Nottingham: DfES. Available online at: http://webarchive.nationalarchives.gov. uk/20110809101133/nsonline.org.uk/node/84974

DfES (2007a) 'Languages review'. (The Dearing Review.) (00212–2007DOM-EN.) Nottingham: DfES. Available online at: http://webarchive.nationalarchives. gov.uk/20130401151715/www.teachernet.gov.uk/_doc/11124/ LanguageReview.pdf

DfES (2007b) 'Letters and sounds: Principles and practice of high quality phonics'. (00281–2007 BKT-EN.) Nottingham: DfES. Available online at: www.gov.uk/ government/uploads/system/uploads/attachment_data/file/190599/Letters_ and_Sounds_-_DFES-00281-2007.pdf

Dillenbourg, P. (1999) 'What do you mean by collaborative learning?', in P. Dillenbourg (ed.), Collaborative Learning: Cognitive and computational approaches. Oxford: Elsevier. pp. 1–19.

Dörnyei, Z. (2006) 'Individual differences in second language acquisition', *AILA Review*, 19: 42–68.

Dörnyei, Z. and Ushioda, E. (2011) *Teaching and Researching Motivation.* Harlow: Pearson.

Driscoll, P. (1999) 'Modern foreign languages in the primary school: A fresh start', in P. Driscoll and D. Frost, *The Teaching of Modern Foreign Languages in the Primary School.* Abingdon: Routledge.

Driscoll, P. and Frost, D. (1999) *The Teaching of Modern Foreign Languages in the Primary School.* Abingdon: Routledge.

Dweck, C.S. (1986) 'Motivational processes affecting learning', *American Psychologist,* 41: 1040–48.

Dweck, C.S. (2000) *Self Theories: Their role in motivation, personality and development.* Philadelphia, PA: Psychology Press.

Dweck, C.S. (2007) *Mindset: The new psychology of success.* New York: Ballantine.

Dweck, C.S. (2013) *Mindset: How you can fulfil your potential.* London: Constable & Robinson.

Early Education (2012) 'Development matters in the Early Years Foundation Stage (EYFS)'. London: Early Education. Available online at: www.early-education. org.uk/sites/default/files/Development%20Matters%20FINAL%20PRINT%20 AMENDED.pdf

Edgington, M. (2004) *The Foundation Stage Teacher in Action.* London: Paul Chapman.

Ellis, R. (2003) *Task-based Language Learning and Teaching.* Oxford: Oxford University Press.

Ellis, G. and Brewster, J. with Girard, D. (2002) *The Primary English Teacher's Guide.* London: Longman.

Elvin, P., Maagerø, E. and Simonsen, B. (2007) 'How do the dinosaurs speak in England? English in kindergarten', *European Early Childhood Education Research Journal,* 15 (1): 71–86.

Emberley, E. (1993) *Go Away, Big Green Monster!* London: Little, Brown & Co.

Fisher, J. (2013) *Starting from the Child: Teaching and learning from 4–8.* Maidenhead: Open University Press.

Fisher, R. (2002) *Inside the Literacy Hour: Learning from Classroom Experience.* London: Routledge.

Galton, M., Gray, J. and Rudduck, J. (1999) 'The impact of school transitions and transfers on pupil progress and attainment'. (Research Report 131.) Norwich: HMSO.

Gardner, R.C. (1985) *Social Psychology and Second Language Learning: The role of attitudes and motivation.* London: Edward Arnold.

Gattullo, F. (2000) 'Formative assessment in ELT primary (elementary) classrooms: An Italian case study', *Language Testing,* 17: 278–88.

Genesee, F. and Upshur, J.A. (1996) *Classroom Evaluation in Second Language Learning.* Cambridge: Cambridge University Press.

Gibbons, S. and Telhaj, S. (2006) *Peer Effects and Pupil Attainment: Evidence from secondary school transition.* London: Centre for the Economics of Education, London School of Economics.

Giddens, A. (1991) *Modernity and Self-Identity: Self and society in the late modern age.* Cambridge: Polity Press.

Grabe, W. and Stoller, F.L. (1997) 'Content-based instruction: Research foundations', in M.A. Snow and D.M. Brinton (eds), *The Content-based Classroom: Perspectives on integrating language and content*. New York: Longman. pp. 5–21.

Grabe, W. and Stoller, F. (2002) *Teaching and Researching Reading: Applied linguistics in action*. New York: Longman.

Grant, H. and Dweck, C.S. (2003) 'Clarifying achievement goals and their impact', *Journal of Personality and Social Psychology*, 85: 541–53.

Guilloteaux, M.J. and Dörnyei, Z. (2008) 'Motivating language learners: A classroom-oriented investigation of the effects of motivational strategies on student motivation', *TESOL Quarterly*, 42 (1): 55–77.

Hadfield, J. and Dörnyei, Z. (2013) *Motivating Learning*. Harlow: Pearson.

Hood, P. (unpublished) 'Children's voices: I like French and I always sing it when I walk home'. Keynote speech at Primary Languages Show, 16 March 2007.

Hood, P. (1994) 'Primary foreign languages – the integration model: Some parameters for research', *Curriculum Journal*, 5 (2): 235–47.

Hood, P. (2000) 'Reading the discourse of reading: A window on the meaning construction processes of their year as third year learners of French'. Unpublished doctoral thesis, University of Nottingham, Nottingham.

Hood, P. (2006) 'Can early foreign language learning contribute to the shared emotional and motivational landscape of a primary school?', *Pastoral Care in Education*, 24 (4): 4–12.

Horwitz, E.K. (2001) 'Language anxiety and achievement', *Annual Review of Applied Linguistics*, 21: 112–26.

Hunt, M.J., Barnes, A., Powell, B. and Martin, C. (2008) 'Moving on: The challenges for foreign language learning on transition from primary to secondary school', *Teaching and Teacher Education*, 24 (4): 915–26.

Ireson, J. and Hallam, S. (1999) 'Raising standards: Is ability grouping the answer?', *Oxford Review of Education*, 25 (3): 343–58.

Johnson, R.K. and Swain, M. (1997) *Immersion Education: International perspectives*. Cambridge: Cambridge University Press.

Johnstone, R.M. (1994) *The Impact of Current Developments to Support the Gaelic Language: Review of research*. Stirling: Scottish CILT.

Johnstone, R.M. (2000) *Immersion in a Second Language at School: Evidence from international research*. Stirling: Scottish CILT.

Johnstone, R.M. (2002) 'Context-sensitive assessment of children learning modern languages at primary school', *Language Testing*, 17: 123–43.

Johnstone, R.M. and McKinstry, R. (2008) 'Evaluation of EPPI: Early Primary Partial Immersion in French at Walker Road Primary School, Aberdeen: Final Report'. Stirling: Scottish CILT. Available online at: www.strath.ac.uk/media/faculties/hass/scilt/research/eppi_book.pdf

Jones, B., Halliwell, S. and Holmes, B. (2002) *You Speak, They Speak*. London: CILT.

Jones, N. (2004) Unpublished data, former Elliott School and Language College, Putney.

Koda, K. (2005) *Insights into Second Language Reading*. Cambridge: Cambridge University Press.

Krashen, S. (1985) *Language Acquisition and Language Education*. Haywood, CA: Alemany Press.

Krashen, S. (1988) *Second Language Acquisition and Second Language Learning*. Upper Saddle River, NJ: Prentice Hall.

Krashen, S.D. and Terrell, T.D. (1983) *The Natural Approach: Language acquisition in the classroom*. London: Prentice Hall.

Kress, G. and van Leeuwen, T. (2006) *Reading Images: The grammar of visual design*. Abingdon: Routledge.

Kubanek-German, A. (1996) 'Research into primary foreign-language learning in Germany: A trend towards qualitative studies', in P. Edelenbos and R. Johnston (eds), *Researching Languages at Primary School: Some European perspectives*. London: CILT. pp. 3–15.

Le Notre, P. (1999) *Mon Âne* (DVD). Wakefield: Teaching and Learning Publications.

Legutke, M. and Thomas, H. (1991) *Process and Experience in the Language Classroom*. London: Longman.

Lenneberg, E. (1967) *Biological Foundations of Language*. New York: Wiley.

Lepine, J.A., Lepine, M.A. and Jackson, C.L. (2004) 'Challenge and hindrance stress: Relationships with exhaustion, motivation to learn, and learning performance', *Journal of Applied Psychology*, 89 (5): 883–91.

Lewis, J. (1999) *The Enormous Turnip*. London: Ladybird Books.

Lightbown, P. (2003) 'SLA research in the classroom', *Language Learning Journal*, 28: 4–13.

Lightbown, P. and Spada, N. (2006) *How Languages are Learned*. Oxford: Oxford University Press.

Littlewood, W.A. (1981) *Communicative Language Teaching: An introduction*. Cambridge: Cambridge University Press.

Loewen, S. (2007) 'Error correction in the second language classroom', CLEAR News, 11 (2): 1–5. Available online at: http://clear.msu.edu/clear/newsletter/fall2007.pdf

Lucey, H. and Reay, D. (2000) 'Identities in transition: Anxiety and excitement in the move to secondary school', *Oxford Review of Education*, 26 (2): 191–205.

Lyster, R. (1998) 'Negotiation of form, recasts, and explicit correction in relation to error types and learner repair in immersion classrooms', *Language Learning*, 48 (2): 183–218.

Marsh, D. (2002) *CLIL/EMILE: The European dimension: Actions, trends and foresight potential*. Brussels: European Commission.

Martin, C. (2000) 'An analysis of national and international research on the provision of modern foreign languages in primary schools: Report prepared for the Qualifications and Curriculum Authority'. London: QCA. Available online at: http://rodillianprimarymfl.wikispaces.com/file/view/Research+on+MFL+Provision+in+Primary.pdf

Mayer, M. (1991) *There's an Alligator under My Bed*. London: Penguin.

Mayer, M. (1992) *There's a Nightmare in My Closet*. London: Picture Puffin.

Menken, K. (2006) 'Teaching to the test: How standardized testing promoted by No Child Left Behind impacts language policy, curriculum, and instruction for English language learners', *Bilingual Research Journal*, 30 (2): 521–46.

Mercer, N. (1995) *The Guided Construction of Knowledge*. Clevedon, North Somerset: Multilingual Matters.

Moyles, J. (2010) *The Excellence of Play*. Maidenhead: Open University Press.

Muijs, D., Barnes, A., Hunt, M., Powell, B., Martin, C. and Arweck, E. (2005) 'Evaluation of the Key Stage 2 language learning Pathfinders'. (Research Report RR692.) Nottingham: DfES. Available online at: http://webarchive.nationalarchives. gov.uk/20130401151715/www.education.gov.uk/publications/eOrdering Download/RR692.pdf

Muir, J. (1999) 'Classroom connections', in P. Driscoll and D. Frost (eds), *The Teaching of Modern Foreign Languages in the Primary School*. Abingdon: Routledge.

Nuffield Foundation (2000) 'Languages: The next generation'. London: Nuffield Foundation. Available online at: www.nuffieldfoundation.org/sites/default/ files/languages_finalreport.pdf

Nunan, D. (1989) *Designing Tasks for the Communicative Classroom*. Cambridge: Cambridge University Press.

Nunan, D. (2004) *Task-based Language Teaching*. Cambridge: Cambridge University Press.

Nutbrown, C. (2011) *Threads of Thinking: Schemas and young children's learning*. London: Sage.

O'Hagan, C. (2007) 'The CILT7–14 Project'. Reading: CILT. Available online at: www.cilt.org.uk/secondary/transition.aspx

Ortega, A.M. (2007) 'Anxiety and self-esteem', in F. Rubio (ed.), *Self-Esteem and Foreign Language Learning*. Cambridge: Cambridge Scholars Publishing.

Oxford, R.L. (1997) 'Cooperative learning, collaborative learning, and interaction: Three communicative strands in the language classroom', *Modern Language Journal*, 81 (4): 443–56.

Oxford, R.L. (1999) 'Anxiety and the language learner: New insights', in J. Arnold (ed.), *Affect in Language Learning*. Cambridge: Cambridge University Press.

Parliament, House of Lords (1990) 'European Schools and Language Learning: ECC Report'. HL Deb 13 July 1990, vol521 cc554–95.

Piaget, J. (1955) *The Construction of Reality in the Child* (trans. Margaret Cook). London: Routledge.

Pollard, A. and Triggs, P. (2000) *What Pupils Say: Changing policy and practice in primary education*. London: Continuum.

QCA (2001) 'QCA project to study the feasibility of introducing the teaching of a modern foreign language in to the statutory curriculum at Key Stage 2'. London: QCA.

QCA (2007) 'A scheme of work for KS2 French'. (QCA/07/3087.) London: QCA.

Reasoner, R. (1982) *Building Self-esteem in Secondary Schools*. Palo Alto, CA: Consulting Psychologists Press.

Richards, J.C. and Rodgers, T.S. (2001) *Approaches and Methods in Language Teaching*. Cambridge: Cambridge University Press.

Riding, R. and Rayner, S. (1998) *Cognitive Styles and Learning Strategies*. London: David Fulton.

Riley, J. (ed.) (2007) *Learning in the Early Years*. London: Sage.

Robinson, P. (ed.) (2002) *Individual Differences and Instructed Language Learning*. Amsterdam: John Benjamins.

Romeo, P. (2006) *Lilou a peur du noir*. Paris: Hachette Jeunesse.

Rose, J. (2006) 'Independent review of the teaching of early reading: Final report'. (The Rose Review.) (0201–2006DOC-EN.) Nottingham: DfES. Available online at: http://webarchive.nationalarchives.gov.uk/20130401151715/www.education. gov.uk/publications/eOrderingDownload/0201-2006pdf-EN-01.pdf

Rose, J. (2009) 'Independent review of the primary curriculum: Final report'. (00499–2009DOM-EN.) Nottingham: DfES. Available online at: www. educationengland.org.uk/documents/pdfs/2009-IRPC-final-report.pdf

Rosen, M. (1993) *We're Going on a Bear Hunt*. London: Walker Books.

Rowe, J. (2008a) 'Transition KS2–KS3'. Conference presentation, 12 September 2008, Loughborough.

Rowe, J. (2008b) 'Statements on Transition KS2–KS3'. Unpublished materials.

Rumney, G. (1990) *Pilote*. Dover: KETV.

Sadler, D.R. (1989) 'Formative assessment and the design of instructional systems', *Instructional Science*, 18: 119–44.

Salgado, S. (2003) *The Children*. New York: Aperture.

Samuda, V. and Bygate, M. (2008) *Tasks in Second Language Learning*. Basingstoke: Palgrave Macmillan.

Scriven, M. (1967) 'The methodology of evaluation', in R.W. Tyler, R.M. Gagne and M. Scriven (eds), *Perspectives of Curriculum Evaluation*. Chicago: Rand McNally. pp. 39–83.

Sharp, K. (2001) *Modern Languages in the Primary School*. Abingdon: Routledge.

Singleton, D. (2003) 'Le facteur de l'âge dans l'acquisition d'une L2: Remarques préliminaires', *Acquisition et Interaction en Langue Étrangère*, 18: 1–15.

Singleton, D. (2005) 'The critical period hypothesis: A coat of many colours', *International Review of Applied Linguistics in Language Teaching*, 43 (4): 269–85

Skehan, P. (1998) *A Cognitive Approach to Language Learning*. Oxford: Oxford Applied Linguistics.

Skehan, P. (2002) 'Theorising and updating aptitude', in P. Robinson (ed.), *Individual Differences and Instructed Language Learning*. Amsterdam: John Benjamins. pp. 69–93.

Skehan, P. (2003) 'Task-based instruction', *Language Learning*, 36: 1–14.

Smith, A. and Call, N. (1999) *The ALPS Approach: Accelerated Learning in Primary Schools*. London: Network Educational Press.

Sternberg, R.J. (1997) *Thinking Styles*. New York: Cambridge University Press.

Stewart, J.H. (2005) 'Foreign language study in elementary schools: Benefits and implications for achievement in reading and math', *Early Childhood Journal*, 33 (1): 11–16.

Stotz, D., Bossart, M. and Fischli, P. (2005) 'Bilingual secondary students and foreign language learning: Positionings and investments'. Zürich: University of Zürich. Available online at: www.phzh.ch/Documents/phzh.ch/Ueber_uns/Veranstaltungen/Forschungstag/d_stotz.pdf

Swain, M. and Lapkin, S. (1995) 'Problems in output and the cognitive processes they generate: A step towards second language learning', *Applied Linguistics*, 16 (3): 371–91.

Swann, M., Peacock, A., Hart, S. and Drummond, M.J. (2012) *Creating Learning Without Limits*. Maidenhead: Open University Press.

Swarbrick, A. (2011) 'Languages: Building on firm foundations', *Curriculum Journal*, 22 (2): 227–41.

Tarone, E. (2000) 'Getting serious about language play: Language play, interlanguage variation and second language acquisition', in B. Swierzbin, F. Morris, M. Anderson, C. Klee and E. Tarone (eds), *Social and Cognitive Factors in SLA: Proceedings of the 1999 Second Language Research Forum*. Somerville, MA: Cascadilla Press.

Tobutt, K. and Roche, C. (2007) *A La Française: A cross-curricular approach to teaching French*. Dublin: Authentik.

Tinsley, T. and Comfort, T. (2012) 'Lessons from abroad'. Reading: CfBT Education Trust.

Tremblay, P.F., Gardner, R.C. and Heipel, G. (2000) 'A model of the relationships among measures of affect, aptitude, and performance in introductory statistics', *Canadian Journal of Behavioural Science*, 32 (1): 40–8.

van Ek, J.A. (1975) *The Threshold Level for Modern Language Learning in Schools*. Strasbourg: Council of Europe.

van Ek, J.A. and Trim, J. (1991) *Waystage 1990*. Cambridge: Cambridge University Press.

Volante, L. (2004) 'Teaching to the test: What every educator and policy-maker should know', *Canadian Journal of Educational Administration and Policy*, 35 (unpaginated). Available online at: www.umanitoba.ca/publications/cjeap

Vygotsky, L.S. (1978) *Mind in Society: The development of higher psychological processes*. Cambridge, MA: Harvard University Press.

Weare, K. (2004) *Developing the Emotionally Literate School*. London: Paul Chapman.

Wells, G. (1999) *Dialogic Inquiry: Towards a sociocultural practice and theory of education*. Cambridge: Cambridge University Press.

Wesche, M.B. and Skehan, P. (2002) 'Communicative, task-based, and content-based language instruction', in R.B. Kaplan (ed.), *The Oxford Handbook of Applied Linguistics*. Oxford: Oxford University Press.

West Sussex Grid for Learning (2006) *Le Départ: Children in wartime*. Chichester: West Sussex Local Authority.

West Sussex Grid for Learning (2008) *Storms and Shipwrecks*. Chichester: West Sussex Local Authority.

Willis, J. (1996) *Challenge and Change in Language Teaching*. London: Macmillan.

Willis, D. and Willis, J. (2007) *Doing Task-based Teaching*. Oxford: Oxford University Press.

Wode, H. (1999) 'Incidental vocabulary acquisition in the foreign language classroom', *Studies in Second Language Acquisition*, 21: 243–58.

Wood, E.A. (2013) *Play, Learning and the Early Childhood Curriculum*. London: Sage.

Woodfield, J. and Neofitou, A. (2006) 'Evaluating a CLIL Project'. Unpublished data.

Zangl, R. (2000) 'Monitoring language skills in Austrian primary (elementary) schools: A case study', *Language Testing*, 17: 250–60.

INDEX